SAMBO SAHIB

ELIZABETH HAY

Sambo Sahib

THE STORY OF
LITTLE BLACK SAMBO
AND HELEN BANNERMAN

'I am in a bad cut this week, and my pictures are all by-ordnar bad,
however I can't help it, I must e'en send you what I *can* do, not what I
should like to do.'

HELEN BANNERMAN, 1910

PAUL HARRIS PUBLISHING

EDINBURGH

First published 1981 in Great Britain by
PAUL HARRIS PUBLISHING
40 York Place
Edinburgh

The publisher acknowledges the financial assistance of the Scottish Arts Council in the publication of this volume.

ISBN 0 904505 91 X

Photoset printed and bound in Great Britain by
REDWOOD BURN LIMITED
Trowbridge & Esher

Sambo:	Applied in America and Asia to persons of various degrees of mixed negro and Indian or European blood.	*Oxford English Dictionary*
	Offspring of a negro and a mulatto.	*A Concise Etymological Dictionary of the English Language*, by the Rev. Walter W. Skeat
	A nickname for a negro.	*Oxford English Dictionary*
	As nickname for a negro perhaps from Foulah *Sambo*: uncle, but a West African tribe called the Samboses is repeatedly mentioned in the narrative of the Hawkins voyage of 1564 and *Sambo* would be a natural back formation from this.	*A Concise Etymological of Modern English*, ed Ernest Weekley.
	(slang). An offensive word for a negro, often used as a term of address.	*Collins English Dictionary*
Sahib:	(in India). A form of address or title placed after a man's name or designation, used as a mark of respect.	*Collins English Dictionary*

CONTENTS

LIST OF ILLUSTRATIONS

LIST OF ILLUSTRATIONS

ACKNOWLEDGEMENTS

This biography – like most others – could not have been written without access to the subject's private papers and letters. For this access I am indebted to the Bannerman family. In particular, I am grateful to Mr Robert Bannerman for his co-operation and information, and, before their deaths in 1972, to Mrs Janet Kibble and Dr Day Bannerman, and, before her death in 1976, to Mrs Cecilia Bannerman. I would like to thank Mrs Anne Fisher and Mr Paddy Bannerman for their help and advice, and Professor Tom Kibble and Mr Robert Martin for the loan of photographs.

I am grateful to Phyllis Yuill, who supplied invaluable information and advice on the publishing history of *The Story of Little Black Sambo* in the U.S.A., and supplied me with many pictures from her collection of American editions and Justin Schiller, who is an authority on the first edition. I have very much appreciated the information given by Selma Lanes and Edythe Lutzker, who is preparing a biography of Haffkine.

I am also indebted to Mr Ian Parsons, formerly Chairman of Chatto and Windus for access to the firm's papers relating to Helen Bannerman, and to the India Office Library, and the National Library of Scotland; and, through correspondence, to the University of Illinois Library at Urbana-Champagne, and the University Library, Jerusalem.

E.H.

Chapter One

Origins

It is not realised by everyone just how old a book *The Story of Little Black Sambo* is; there is a certain timeless quality about the pictures. It first appeared in 1899, two years before Beatrix Potter's first book *Peter Rabbit*, which was privately printed in 1901. *Little Black Sambo* embodied nearly all the principles on which present-day books for young children are based and was revolutionary in its day. It was one of the first books small enough for a young child to hold comfortably. The pictures were direct and vivid, and were printed in primary colours. The story – a simple tale of a little black boy escaping from tigers which has the deeper symbolism of a child with a brave spirit going out to face the world alone – is action-packed and yet repetitive. It also lacked what had been considered essential in a children's book up till that moment: a moral purpose or improving tone.

With such advantages, it was from the start a runaway best-seller. In its first year it went through four editions and sold 21,000 copies. Within the next three years it had been through four further editions.[1] It was published in 1900 in the U.S.A. Its success there was such that publishers rushed to bring out their own versions and it was soon available in a variety of formats with pictures by a number of different artists. It was translated into most European languages, and also into Hebrew and Arabic.[2]

The book is still sold in substantial numbers today, though there has been a drop in sales in recent years, particularly in America. In Britain some 300,000 copies were sold between 1962 and 1971, and 160,000 between 1971 and 1979. In the U.S.A. the edition with pictures by Helen Bannerman, published by J.B. Lippincott Company, sold 15,000 to 18,000 copies a year until a few years ago and now sells between 10,000 and 12,000 copies a year. Then there are all the other American editions – over fifty of them since 1900. One of these, the Platt and Munk edition, put out a revised version of the book in 1972 and 1974 and quickly ran through two prints of 15,000.[3]

Granted that the book was oustanding when it first appeared, why does it still sell today, over eighty years after it first appeared? Maurice Sendak, illustrator and author of the modern children's classic *Where*

1

the Wild Things Are thinks *Little Black Sambo* is one of the great all time picture books for its perfect synchronisation of words with simple pictures. But that alone is not enough. There is also the pleasure a child takes in seeing him or herself as the hero setting out alone into a fascinating and dangerous world, and the satisfying climax where the tigers chase each other so hard that they turn into melted butter – a climax that one psychoanalist has pointed out has parallels in sexual fulfilment.[4]

It is a book that has been accepted so fully into the consciousness of generations of people, particularly in the U.S.A., that it has affected their images and thought processes. It is this power that has made the book matter, and matter to an extent far beyond the author's original intentions. As some liked the image of a primitive world which it offered, some came to hate it. Those who hate it do so with an intensity which amazes its admirers.

The critics of *The Story of Little Black Sambo* make many charges against the book, and these are discussed in detail in the last chapter. The most serious charges, however, are that the name 'Sambo' has come to symbolise the depersonalisation of black people which was an aspect of slavery, and that the pictures, particularly in some of the unauthorised versions, offer demeaning stereotypes of black people in plantation or jungle settings. As the controversy has raged, with some librarians banning the book from their shelves and others shouting 'Censorship!', protagonists on both sides have lacked any but the barest biographical details about the author.

Much of the information which has been available is wrong. The first source was the preface in the first edition of 1899. It said:

There is very little to say about the story of *Little Black Sambo*. Once upon a time there was an English lady in India, where black children abound and tigers are everyday affairs, who had two little girls. To amuse these little girls she used now and then to invent stories, for which, being extremely talented, she also drew and coloured the pictures. Among these stories, *Little Black Sambo*, which was made up on a long railway journey, was the favourite; and it has been put into a DUMPY BOOK, and the pictures copied as exactly as possible, in the hope that you will like it as much as the two little girls did.

Helen Bannerman must have been very amused to hear herself described as English. She was a Scot, from Edinburgh, and, in the way of expatriates, a very Scottish Scot. But there is a more serious flaw in this publisher's preface: it implies that the story is set in India, which, as will be shown in chapter two, it certainly was not.

ORIGINS

There was also some biographical material published in the *Horn Book Magazine* in 1936 and 1937. In 1936 Horace W. Stokes, a new York publisher from the firm which published her version of the book in the U.S.A., visited her in Edinburgh to try to persuade her to write a sequel to *Little Black Sambo*. He recounts how he succeeded in this and also gives a new and colourful account of the origin of *Little Black Sambo*:[6]

Almost forty years ago a young Scotch matron with a highly original sense of humour was taking a railway journey in India with her two little girls. It was hot and the children were tired and restless. "Tell us a story, Mother," one of them demanded. "And make it funny!", the other child ordered.

Mrs Helen Bannerman looked out of the window.

"I will tell you," said Mrs Bannerman "'The Story of Little Black Sambo.'"

The article in *Horn Book Magazine* in 1937 by Helen Dean Fish[5] was an account of a visit to Helen in Edinburgh. The article has no comment from Helen on Mr Stokes' imaginative account of the origin of the book, but does give Helen's view of the preface to the first edition: 'Well, that wasn't exactly true but something Mr E.V. Lucas gave out when the book was published.' The article then fails to go on and give what was the true version.

Fans of the book had to wait till 1942 for their next piece of biographical information. This appeared in the Publisher's Foreword to *The Jumbo Sambo* brought out in this year by Frederick A. Stokes Company, and was even more misleading. It is worth quoting so that the misconceptions it implanted in the minds of generations of children's book experts can be corrected straight away:

In 1899 Helen Bannerman, a young English mother, wife of a British Army Surgeon stationed in India, was returning to her husband's post after leaving her two little daughters 'at home' in Edinburgh to be educated. Homesick for her little girls, on the long journey taking her away from them, she composed a story for their amusement and coloured the little drawings she made to go with each sentence. It was the now classic *Story of Little Black Sambo*.

Mrs Bannerman mailed the story home to her children and it became a family treasure, so loved by the little girls and their friends that the author-artist ventured to have it offered to a publisher.

It was "discovered" by E.V. Lucas, published in London by Grant Richards and the next year in America by Frederick A. Stokes Company, still publishers of the authorised American edition.

Helen's husband, however, was not a British Army Surgeon. He was in the Indian Medical Service, and, apart from his early years which were spent on regimental duties, worked mostly in public health and medical research. More misleading still is the claim that the book was written in India while the author's children were left in Scotland. On this presumed fact a psychoanalist based a whole paper, explaining the book in terms of a traumatic separation.[4]

The truth is that Helen Bannerman wrote her book in India and her daughters were at that time in India too. The story – explained in this biography by those very daughters – is that they were left in the cool- ness of the hill resort of Kodaikanal while their mother rejoined their father, for a brief spell, in Madras. There certainly was a separation involved; but not a separation of continents.

Why did Helen give interviews so rarely and allow inaccurate in- formation about herself to remain in circulation? She could easily have written an account of how she had come to write the book and there would have been great interest in it. By the time she died in 1946 the information had still not been corrected. The first accurate bio- graphical information appeared in a BBC radio broadcast in April 1971[7] which I produced and in which her three surviving children took part. Then in 1976, Phyllis Yuill published a brief authentic bio- graphical outline, referring to the material in the broadcast, in *Little Black Sambo: A Closer Look*.[2] According to Horace Stokes,[6] letters were written to her but remained unanswered.' Why?

The answer emerges through this book. It lies partly in her situ- ation and partly in her character. As will be explained, she lost control of the copyright so had no financial interest in the sale of copies of Little Black Sambo, and no control over what happened to the book, particularly in the U.S.A. She was also modest and shy – but at the same time a person of originality and determination. Her life story is full of paradox. She was a devout Christian, what would today be called an Evangelical. She was a strict Sabbatarian who refused to travel by tram in Edinburgh on a Sunday. Yet she found herself living the life of a Memsahib in India in the high noon of the British empire and was. after her death, accused of being a racist. She was musical, ar- tistic, a linguist and widely read; her husband would spread news- papers on the dining room table and skin different species of rats. It is in disentangling these diverse elements in her life that the fascination of her personality lies. To begin to understand it we have to go back to its beginnings.

Edinburgh, with its castle soaring above it, its medieval High

Street and elegant Georgian New Town, is widely thought of as one of the world's loveliest cities. For those who live there, it also has its own peculiar flavour. It is at the same time both intellectually vigorous and a touch narrow-minded. This is probably because it is dominated by a tightly-knit professional class. It is essentially a city of doctors, lawyers, teachers and ministers. In this it is unchanged from the days of Lord Cockburn and Sir Walter Scott, and from the time when Helen Brodie Cowan Watson was born there in 1862.

She was later to say of Edinburgh that she always felt that everyone in the city was related to her. This had a surprising degree of truth. Her mother was one of the twenty-one children of a certain Alexander Cowan.[8] He married twice and lived for many years in the historic Moray House in the High Street, now the Moray House Teachers' Training College. He financed his substantial establishment through two paper mills, Valleyfield Mill at Penicuik and one at Eskbank which has long since disappeared.

Through her mother Helen was part of the prosperous establishment of the day, and in particular those parts which had connections with printing and publishing. Her uncle James Cowan, for example, worked in his father's paper business and was a close friend of R.M. Ballantyne,[9] author of *Coral Island* and other adventure stories. Edinburgh's publishing world was small and closely knit. R.M. Ballantyne worked for a while for Alexander Cowan, who advanced him an interest-free loan to buy a junior partnership in the firm of Thomas Constable and Son. This was the publishing firm which had been associated with the financial collapse of Sir Walter Scott in 1826. The printing firm which had also been dragged down in that debacle had been that of James Ballantyne, uncle of R.M. Ballantyne. After the collapse, R.M. Ballantyne's father, who was also in the business, had been forced to leave his comfortable house in Ann Street and take refuge for a while with the Cowan family in the High Street.

Through her mother Helen could trace roots back into early Scottish history, to St Columba, credited with bringing Christianity to Scotland in the sixth century. As Helen was to explain to her daughter Janet in a letter in 1903,[10] when Janet was nine: 'It is through Grandmother you are related to St Columba. Her mother's mother's mother was an Irish lady named McCormack, and these McCormacks counted themselves descendents of old Neil of the Nine Hostages, who was St Columba's grandfather. And you are related through grandfather to a number of good men too, like Robert Ross, who was imprisoned on the Bass Rock, and who was obliged to wander so that his ten children were born in ten different places.'

This connection with the early Church in Scotland, and with the Covenanters who fought for their Presbyterian religion in the seventeenth century, was of great importance to Helen. It was reinforced by the influence of her father, a minister in the Free Church of Scotland. The Reverend Robert Boog Watson[11] was, however, the opposite of a narrow Calvinist. His great interest was science, particularly geology and the study of sea shells. He was not content to stay in a parish in Scotland, and took a post as Chaplain to the Forces. He served with the 93rd Highlanders in the Crimea till he was invalided out in 1855, then, after a year in Dover, set off to India with the Highland Brigade. His two eldest children – twin boys – were born in Bombay in 1858 and, after gaining an Indian Mutiny medal, he was invalided back to Britain the following year. With two vulnerable infants, this journey was a hazardous undertaking. With their own cow on board, the family sailed in a windjammer to Suez – the Canal was not to open for another ten years – and then travelled overland. After Mr Boog Watson ended his connection with the Army he returned to settle in Edinburgh. There, another son was born in 1860, followed by Helen two years later.

Helen's birth took place in number 35 Royal Terrace, Edinburgh, on 25 February 1862. The three elegant terraces of Royal Terrace, Carlton Terrace and Regent Terrace, which look out in the shape of a hairpin towards Leith and then round to Holyrood Palace, were built by the engineer grandfather of Robert Louis Stevenson. Commodious and comfortable, Royal Terrace was then known as whisky row after the merchants who lived there and looked down to Leith to see their ships coming in.[12]

Edinburgh, however, was not to be the only influence on Helen's early life. When she was two her father took a post as minister to the Scots Church in Madeira. There he was able to pursue his interests in conchology, in climbing and in other aspects of outdoor life and science. Madeira had the great advantage for him that it was not overburdened with Free Church parishioners.

Helen's earliest recollection[13] dated from the journey to Madeira in 1864 when she was two. As the island came in sight, the shout went up "There it is! There's Madeira!" All the passengers rushed to the side to look and she crept between their legs to look as well. All she could see was the shadow of the ship moving over the sand at the bottom of the sea. How, she wondered, could the people in Madeira possibly live under water?

Madeira – a great rocky mass rising out of the Atlantic off the North-West coast of Africa – was settled mainly by the Portugese, though there was also a small international community. Moist in the winter, the soil is so fertile that almost every plant can grow there. Bananas and sugar cane grow at sea level and pines and heathers higher up. The slopes are so steep that there were then no wheeled vehicles but a type of tough wooden sledge for heavy transport. The island is now served by international jet flights, but then it must have been a paradise to grow up in – particularly as Helen avoided school. By now she had another sister, Isabella, born just before they left Edinburgh, and two more sisters were born in Madeira.

The children were all taught together by their father. This meant that Helen received a strong grounding in the sciences. In this she was well ahead of other girls of her day; they were lucky if they learnt enough botany to arrange their collections of pressed flowers. She also learnt fluent Portugese, French, Italian and German. She developed such an aptitude for Latin that in later years her children were to complain that she was forever correcting their spelling by taking them back to the Latin root. Languages were to be such an interest of Helen's and her brothers and sisters that they would have days when they would talk nothing but French, or German or Italian or Portugese or Latin. Helen also showed exceptional talent for what were then the essential feminine accomplishments – art and music. Her unusual education left her with an insatiable appetite for books; in later years she was to confess that she could no more pass a bookshop than an alcholic a pub.[13]

It should not be thought, however, that Helen's family were solemn – or even serious. The conversation at their table mattered more than the food; but that conversation was likely to be full of puns, jokes and repartee. The family was highly individualistic. Helen's mother, for example, had ridden down Edinburgh's High Street on a pig, and Helen's uncles had once held up the coach taking the wages to their father's mills and made off with the money.[13] (They returned it later). They were a family of great exhuberance and irreverence – qualities which were soon evident in Helen.

In 1874, when Helen was twelve, the family returned to Edinburgh and went to live in the south of the city at 20 Merchiston Terrace. Helen, for the first time, went to school, to Miss Oliphant's Establishment, and she turned out to be the fortunate kind of person for whom passing exams was easy. By now she was writing stories and poems and drawing cartoons. One notebook filled with these survives.[14] It is seven inches by four inches, has the name Nellie Watson on the inside cover and is written in neat copperplate. Some of the entries are dreadful jokes such as: 'What delicacies express a mad dog's feeling? Answer: Water ices and ice creams and then comfits.'

One story dated 1876 when she was fourteen, indicates that she already had a fixation about tigers:

There was once an individual who, knowing that cats and tigers both belong to the same family, wished his cat to become as like a tiger as possible. He therefore fed it on Indian roots and watched for the appearance of stripes, but the cat only died, it never changed colours at all.

Clearly she had a lot to learn about building up to a climax, but she at least recognised the merit of brevity.

Even at fourteen, Helen had that macabre streak which was to delight bloodthirsty children in her later books. In her juvenile notebook she wrote a tale about the disputed ownership of a leg amputated at Edinburgh Royal Infirmary. Did it belong to the amputator or the amputatee? Both apparently wanted it. The doctor won in the end, but had to pay £10 for it.

Another story is very much that of a child who had travelled, who knew more of the world than just Edinburgh:

There was once upon a time a sea captain who used to take people on different voyages. He used to feed them always on salt junk, but he kept all the good pieces of meat for himself and only gave them the hard old bits. He was very proud of his table, which he declared was real mahogony, while they all said it was only veneered. One day, when the junk was more than usually tough, one of the passengers cut a lump out of the table, as if taking it for the junk, and tried to eat it, and then everybody saw that it was only veneered, so after that the captain had to give them tenderer junk and to hold his tongue about the table.

Her liking for improbable plots had already developed.

Most interesting, however, are her early cartoons. Her drawings show that she was probably influenced by the *Punch* cartoons of the day, and that already she enjoyed exaggerating peoples' salient features and pointing up the funny side of a situation.

Jokes, stories and cartoons were not her only interests, however. She was already friendly with a friend of her brother Alec – Will Bannerman. Will and Alec were at school together at Edinburgh Academy, and the friendship between Will and Helen became so marked that it led to a ticking off for Will from his father after games of hide and seek at a party: 'You mustn't go off with one girl all the time, you know.'

Will's background was similar to that of Helen in a number of ways. His family had connections with the literary world. His mother was related to the novelist Fanny Burney, and was a co-lateral of the economist Adam Smith – her father, Lord Reston, was Adam Smith's heir. The Bannerman, family was, like the Boog Watson family, also deeply involved with the Free Church of Scotland. Will's father was a minister, and so were his grandfather, great grandfather and great-great-grandfather. Family records show that each generation of Bannermans from the Reformation had included at least one who served the Church. (This even carries on to the present day; one of Helen's daughters became a missionary and one of her grandsons is an Anglican priest in Australia.)

The time spanned by Will's father was a troubled one for the Church of Scotland. It included the greatest controversy in Scotland in the nineteenth century – the Disruption of 1843, in which almost half the ministers walked out to set up their own Free Church.[15] The dispute was over the position of the Church of Scotland as the established Church. One group, led by the eloquent Dr Thomas Chalmers, wanted to see lay patronage abolished, so that ministers would be appointed not by patrons but democratically by the congregation. When changes along those lines could not be brought about he and some two hundred fathers and brethren followed the Moderator, Dr Welsh, out of St Andrew's Church in Edinburgh's George Street, in a procession to Tanfield Hall, Canonmills. The scene in the hall, where, over the next three days the signing of the Act of Separation and Deed of Demission took place, has been captured in the large-scale *Disruption Painting* by David Octavius Hill, based on calotypes (early photographs in soft browns and sepias) by Robert Adamson.[16] When the picture was complete, it contained four hundred and seventy likenesses. Among those who signed, though he is not – so far as is known – in the picture, was Will's father, the Rev. James Bannerman.

James Bannerman was a leading religious figure in his day. He was appointed the Free Church's first Professor of Divinity, and taught in their New College (now the University's Faculty of Divinity), a grim perpendicular building, with a statue of John Knox in its forecourt, finger outstretched, looking down from the Mound on Edinburgh and all its sins.

The Free Church had no endowments or buildings: it depended on the gifts of those of its parishioners who followed their Ministers out of the Church of Scotland. The scale of the walkout can be seen from figures showing that out of 1,203 Ministers in the Church of Scotland, 451 left for the Free Church.[15] To do this, Ministers abandoned their churches, manses, incomes and prospects. As one Bannerman document[17] puts it: 'they chose privation rather than submission to direction by the state in the affairs of the Church'.

It was into this Free Church background that Will was born on 6 July 1858.[18] The eighth child and third son, he was brought up in number 7 Clarendon Crescent, a curving stone terrace near Edinburgh's West End. His parents also had a country house, Abernyte in

Perthshire. Some idea of his childhood, and particularly the influences upon him, can be gathered from an article[19] he was to write many years later in Bombay. The bleak Scottish Sabbath which drove so many of his contempories mad with boredom was for him at Abernyte filled with happiness:

> After family prayers and breakfast there were various little jobs for the bairns to do; the feeding of the pet rabbits – surely a "work of necessity and mercy" – which implied a run to the garden to gather the necessary cabbage blades, was full of delight. Then the gathering of buttonholes for the boys and girls, with a special bunch for the beloved mother, was always a joy. Then, just before starting for church, the learning of the Psalm to be said after dinner, and the rush to the nursery to be dressed for church by the faithful servant who spent fifty years of her life in the family, and who has only recently herself crossed the River she used to read to us about out of the *Pilgrim's Progress*.
>
> Before starting for the walk to church, each member stows in his or her pockets the biscuits and sweeties necessary to sustain the youngsters through the double service, which was the rule in those days.
>
> That walk to church would require the pen of Barrie to do it justice. The streams of folk moving steadily along the quiet roads, the division of the groups into two; the Auld Kirk or 'Staiblishment division being looked at somewhat askance by us youngsters as being yet in the bonds of iniquity. We were not in those days so far removed from the Disruption as we are now, and youth is proverbially intolerant. How quiet and orderly are the groups as they move along, sober greetings being interchanged as friends meet who are, during the week, separated by not a few miles of distance ... The church I allude to was a small and poor one, not able to afford even the luxury of a beadle, so the 'Books' used to be taken up to the pulpit by one of the elders, who on his return would hold open the green baize door of the vestry while the white-haired minister passed through.
>
> I can remember the feeling of peace in the place, the balmy air laden with the scent of flowers wafted in through the open windows, the shimmer of the leaves through the lozenge-shaped panes, and the glimpse of the well-beloved grey crag, where we climbed and played during the week.
>
> The early Sunday dinner was always a great feature of the day, for the youngsters were allowed to have dinner at the big table with the parents and elders of the family. At dessert the Psalms learned during the week were repeated by each in turn, followed by a harm-

less potion of eau sucrée much prized by the bairns.

Then the family scattered, for the reading of such books as *The Traditions of the Covenanters*, or *The Scots Worthies*. On fine days we used to resort to favourite seats in the woods behind the house, and when autumn came, to the 'hay-sow', where we made ourselves snug among the hay, with rugs to keep us warm.

Then followed supper and bed for the bairns, where securely tucked up they would hear the strains of 'French' or 'Martyrdom,' or some other favourite 'grave sweet melody' ascending from below, as family prayers closed the day for the elders.

When Will left school he went to the University of Edinburgh and studied medicine. His course covered an interesting time of transition in the history of Edinburgh medical studies – the changeover from the old Edinburgh Infirmary buildings to the new. The old buildings in Infirmary Street and High School Yards had become overcrowded and were subject to that scourge of unhealthy hospitals, pyaemia or blood poisoning. As was explained in a letter[20] from James Syme, then Professor of Clinical Surgery: 'When the confined, smokey condition of the present site' (this was near the ancient High Street and the Cowgate) 'is contrasted with the airy, cheerful and salubrious site now within reach, it is difficult to imagine what possible objection there can be to removal'. The new buildings, constructed on the site of George Watson's Hospital, between Lauriston Place and the Meadows, were opened in 1879. The Baronial style of architecture makes it look old-fashioned today, but the new Royal Infirmary was then in the forefront of medicine in Europe.

While Will was enjoying studying medicine, and his friendship with Helen was flourishing, Helen's family suddenly faced financial difficulties. Her father had been fifty-one when he had returned from Madeira. He was a Fellow of the Royal Society of Edinburgh, President of the Conchological Society of Great Britain, and an acknowledged expert on molluscs. He had settled down to a life of comfort, pursuing his scientific interests. He had been asked to classify and describe the molluscs collected by H.M.S. *Challenger* on her voyage round the southern hemisphere exploring the ocean. That expedition took place in 1873–76, some fifty years after Darwins' voyage on H.M.S. *Beagle*, and was part of the great surge in scientific exploration by the Victorians. Classifying all the samples brought back was a considerable task; there were about one thousand three hundred objects. At the beginning of the project, however, Mr Boog Watson found himself with unexpected problems. As he explained: 'When asked, in 1876, to take charge of the whole mollusca of the Expedition, I was master of my own time and I could consult both collections and books as the need arose. In 1878, however, circumstances occurred which brought back on me the residence in a country district at a distance from museums and scientific works. I at once returned the whole collection and all my bulky yet chaotic work to the *Challenger's* office, seeing no possibility of completing my task. It was only at my friend's most urgent request that I consented to prosecute it as I could.'[21]

What had happened was that he and his wife – and it was his wife with her income from the Cowan paper mills who was the wealthy one – had lost all their money in the collapse of the City of Glasgow Bank. This was, for Scotland, the biggest financial crisis of the day. The Bank collapsed in 1875; because of the principle of unlimited liability depositors were liable for the Bank's debts. In the years succeeding the crash, depositors lost not only the money they had left with the Bank, they were called on to hand over more to meet the Bank's liabilities, which ran into many millions. It was a salutory lesson for the people of Scotland and it quickly led to the abandonment of the principle of unlimited liability.

Individuals such as Helen's father were ruined. In 1878 he was fifty five. He decided to go back into the ministry, and applied for the post of Minister of the Free Church at Cardross. He would have preferred a post in Edinburgh, where his seven children were at school, but he had to take what he could get. Appointments were made then – as they are now in the Church of Scotland – by inviting the candidates to preach a sermon one Sunday and to meet the congregation. The congregation would then choose the candidate they thought the most appropriate. In Helen's notebook[14] is a poem which relates to her father's appointment in 1879 when she was fifteen.

> Mr Crerar and Mr Shearer
> Have both of them preached at Cardross
> But Father is dearer than Crerar or Shearer
> And now he is fixed at Cardross.

Though Cardross is to the West of Glasgow, on the north of the Clyde, the family kept their connection with Edinburgh, for education and for access to scientific libraries. Their financial difficulties, however, were such that there was talk at that time of Helen becoming a governess. In the end, however, with help from relatives, the Boog Watson family saw their way through their financial troubles, and the children carried on at school and in some cases at University. Helen's eldest brother Charles did an engineering apprenticeship and his twin, Alec, studied medicine. The next son Robert went into Alexander Cowan's paper business and then went to Australia to look after the Cowan interests there.

By the time Helen was nineteen, Will had graduated. He was twenty three and a doctor but still a long way from being in a financial position to get married. There was however, an 'understanding' between them. Will took a junior hospital appointment, but it paid very little. General practice needed capital to get established and the only way, it seemed to Will, for him to earn enough for him to get married within a reasonable length of time was to take a salaried post such as that offered in the Indian Medical Service. Entry was by competitive examination and without telling Helen, he sat the exam in 1883. He passed and went straight to Helen to ask her to marry him. The news of his appointment came as a surprise to Helen. She had not been consulted and she thought on first hearing it that her hopes of marriage must be at an end.[13] To her relief, however, Will arranged a formal engagement. They would be married on his return from his first tour of duty in five years time.

In Will's absence, Helen worked for an external university degree in languages and literature from the University of St Andrews. At that time women could not enroll as full members of the University or sit the degree exams, but some of the Scottish Universities had just begun to let women sit external examinations held in various centres. Successful candidates at St Andrews were awarded the title L.L.A. As R.G. Cant explains in his *The University of St Andrews:*[22] 'A certain mystery surrounds the connotation of the initials L.L.A.. The original title was L.A. (Literate in Arts). The second L was added in 1881 to avoid confusion with the L.A. instituted in Glasgow in 1880 but no official alteration was ever made in the formal title. In ordinary usage, the initials were taken to mean Lady Literate in Arts.' Helen sat her first exam for this title in 1885. This was for English (Honours), followed by French (Honours) the following year. Two years later she sat exams in Botany (Honours) and German (Ordinary), and gained her L.L.A. in 1887. She then studied in Hanover and in Torre Pellice in North Italy and took further exams in German (Honours) and Comparative Philology (Honours). Some indication of her academic standard is given in the marks for those last two exams – 94% and 79%. Ironically, it was only two years after she gained her L.L.A. that the Universities (Scotland) Act was passed which enabled the Universities to admit women and to award them degrees.[23]

Helen's father, meanwhile, finally brought his work on molluscs to a conclusion and published a massive volume – some two feet by one and a half feet – with over fifty detailed plates and 756 large pages of text in 1886 as Volume XV of the *Report on the Scaphopoda and Gasteropoda Collected by H.M.S. Challenger during 1873–6.*[21]

Will was posted with a regiment to India's North-West Frontier, to conditions similar to those described by Winston Churchill in *The Story of the Malakand Field Force*, published in 1898.[24] The incompetence of the higher reaches of the Army – a favourite Churchillian theme – meant that Will was sent into the mountains in summer clothing to deal with a cholera epidemic.[25] As the days lengthened into months he found the winter at 4,000 feet under canvas a little chilly. He must have shivered even more when he operated, surrounded by armed men, on the son of the leader of a hostile group of hill soldiers.[18] The boy stopped breathing; Will gave no indication that this was unexpected, applied artificial respiration, and carried on. In that situation it was not only the patient who was close to death. Had the child died, there could have been no *Story of Little Black Sambo*; though had Helen never married, her interest in writing was such that, rather than children's books she might well have turned to poetry or fiction for adults.

Will also came very close to death in his next posting. This was to Burma, and his niece Craigie gave no account of his time there, in her own breathtakingly dramatic style.[25] She described his role in the 1886–89 campaign:

> They were fighting in dense, swampy, fever-ridden jungle, and the unseen enemy lurked on every hand. The soldiers were shot down at a range of ten to twenty yards without a chance of retaliation on their unseen foes. The injuries inflicted at such close range were almost always fatal, and after a night spent attending to his wounded, the morning would reveal nothing but mutilated corpses. With the strain of the campaign Will went down eventually with malignant malaria and was sent to the coast, half conscious and strapped to the back of an elephant – the only transport animal able to wade through the jungle swamps. No one expected to see him alive again. But he was taken to the house of a Scotch M.O. and after remaining unconscious for ten days, he pulled through.

If the malaria knocked him unconscious, his treatment possibly damaged him even more. Details survive in a certificate[26] headed Mandalay, 24 October 1888. He was given 'quinine and arsenic and antipyrin when required and diaphoretic mixture for sweating'. To reduce his temperature he was packed in a wet sheet for an hour at a time. He went quite deaf for a while, and permanently bald, except for a fringe round the back of his head. He was sent on home leave to recuperate, and, still far from well, he arrived in Edinburgh in the New Year of 1889. After his experiences and his illness, Helen can hardly have recognised him; but plans for the wedding went ahead.

14

ORIGINS

A portrait of Helen, painted at the time of her wedding, when she was twenty-seven, shows a young woman with her hair piled on top of her head and an air of quick intelligence. Helen had blue eyes and fair hair, Will had brown eyes and what was left of his hair was black. She was small and neat-figured, he was tall and in later years heavy.

The marriage was conducted by Helen's father and one of her sisters – Isabella – was married at the same time, also to a doctor. Helen's parents had by that time moved to 11 Strathearn Place, in the south of Edinburgh, and the ceremony was held there. It took place in perfect weather on 26 June 1889, and the reception, complete with what was then a novelty, ice cream, was held in the garden. Will and Helen spent their honeymoon on a walking tour of the Highlands. Then, after Will had been awarded an M.D. by the University of Edinburgh for a thesis on the illness from which he had just recovered – malaria – they sailed in the autumn for India.

Chapter Two

Separations and 'Sambo'

When Helen arrived in Madras with Will on 26 November 1889, what kind of a society did she find? India was ruled by a Viceroy as part of the British Empire. Despite poverty and deprivation on a scale almost unbelievable to someone from Europe, the surface appearance was of peace and stability. The uncontroversial Lord Lansdowne was Viceroy; all was quiet on India's vulnerable North-West frontier; the Mutiny was a fading memory from thirty years before.

Despite its horrors and the atrocities on both sides, the Mutiny had led to various reforms. The rule of the East India Company had been swept away and power had been transferred to the Secretary of State for India in London and to the Viceroy. The army had been reorganised and a number of changes in education had been carried through. At the same time, India was rapidly becoming industrialised. A network of railways linked the major centres of the country and that was being added to. India's cities were expanding and her industries were growing fast. Her educated middle classes were now beginning to make their voice heard, as they argued for increased opportunity and a greater say in the government of their country. By the time Helen arrived, the first meeting of the Indian National Congress, in 1885, had already been held.

Helen and Will, however, were not involved in the government of the country. To begin with, Will's role was as medical officer to a regiment.[27] It was a very limited assignment; caring for healthy young man in peacetime meant dealing mostly with blisters, sunstroke and dysentery, enlivened by the odd epidemic. Will's first orders on reaching Madras were to travel to Berhampur, some four hundred miles up the coast in Orissa. From there he set off to march with his regiment some two hundred and sixty-five miles inland to Sambalpore. By the time he arrived in Sambalpore on 20 January 1890 he must have known more about blistered feet than he had ever wanted to.

Helen followed at a slower pace,[25] accompanied by servants, and staying at Government rest houses, known as dak bungalows, on the way. She travelled through some remote country on this trip, some of it of a kind where a person could in fact go 'out for a walk in the jungle'.

16

One night she heard a roaring noise outside her forest rest house and thought she was surrounded by fierce wild animals. She called out to her servants, but none of them was there. In the morning, however, she had to laugh at her fears, when the tigers of her imagination turned out to be buffaloes.

After a year in Sambalpore, followed by six months in Berhampur, Will was moved to the post of District Surgeon at Mangalore on the Western side of India.[27] He also left his army duties and was from this time onwards on the civil side of the Indian Medical Service. The I.M.S. offered medical care to the Indian Army and also to Government servants in India. Officers in the I.M.S. usually spent their early years on duty with a regiment and then moved to civilian work. They were still part of a service with military rank, however. Through this means, the I.M.S. kept a group of salaried doctors who could be sent to the most inhospitable parts to work in difficult conditions.

The work on the civil side was very varied; it usually included supervising a jail and sometimes a lunatic asylum. The Civil Surgeon would also be responsible for a hospital; under him would be a Civil Assistant Surgeon who would usually be, as Dirom Grey Crawford put it in his *History of the Indian Medical Service*[28] published in 1914: 'a graduate of one of the Indian Universities, a highly trained and educated officer, speaking English fluently and generally quite competent to take charge of the hospital.'

In some civil posts there was opportunity for private practice, though officers of the I.M.S. were expected to attend, free of charge, 'all civil officers at the headquarters of the district, European or native, whose pay is over 250 rupees a month.' Attendance on their wives and families was private practice, the usual arrangement being for a civil officer to pay one week's pay a year for medical attendance on his family. In addition to posts such as Civil Surgeon, or District Surgeon, which Will held in Mangalore, there were also a number of posts in public health. Those, with the unglamorous title of Sanitary Commissioner, offered no private practice but were concerned with matters affecting the health of the whole community such as clean water supplies and the disposal of sewage. Being a Sanitary Commissioner was, in comparison with other posts in the I.M.S., neither particularly prestigious nor particularly lucrative. It was, however, a way of serving the people of India, and it is significant that this was the field into which Will was to move.

After a year and a half in Mangalore, Will was transferred to the post of Deputy Sanitary Commissioner in Madras. It must have seemed a great metropolis after some of the remote places they had been in. It was then the third city of India and the administrative centre for Madras Presidency. They settled down in a pleasant residential area,

Harrington Road in the suburb of Chetput.

Will was exceptionally well suited to the varied life of a doctor in the I.M.S. He was one of those people who knew instinctively how everything worked. He was a natural organiser, with an infallible sense of direction, and even the unlikely accomplishment of being able to sew. People would send him a dead swan or a dead bear and ask him to find out what it had died of; he would be delighted to produce a mango stone from the gut. He was the kind of person who would spot a tree going mouldy in the monsoon, and would go out and apply a mixture of kerosene, soap and water. The tree would recover. He was far more, though, than just a technologist: he was interested in literature and history and all aspects of the study of nature. As the years went by he was much in demand to give talks on Walter Scott, Scottish songs and poisonous snakes.

And Helen? Unlike many other British women of her day, she was not put off by insects or snakes or rats; rather, as her later letters show, she took a naturalist's interest in everything around her. She also pursued her interests in painting and music and reading. What she does not seem to have cared deeply about was the routine management of the house, which was usually rather untidy.[29]

Helen and Will had only been in Madras a month when their first child was born. This was Janet, and she arrived on 13 October 1893. She was a much-wanted baby, arriving after an earlier miscarriage.[13] By this time Helen was thirty-one and had been married for four years. She told Janet many years later that she – at that time – would not have minded if she had not had any children, but that she was very glad when Janet was born because Will so much wanted children.

When Janet was eight weeks old Will's sister Mary – known as Ata (a Hindustani word meaning 'sister of the husband') – arrived on a year-long visit. She was some fourteen years older than her brother and had never married. Her trip to India was a great event for Ata. She kept a diary, only three inches by three and a half, in cheap paper with a flowery cardboard cover.[30] In it she recorded some addresses, some recipes, some dressmaking measurements, a list of books and an entry for each day. Using very few words she conveys the excitement of her arrival:

'Got into harbour at 6 a.m., dressed and went on deck. Saw Will just arriving in boat – looking so well and so like himself in spite of helmet and white suit. Got quickly ashore and got into his gharrie. Lassie' – this was Will's horse – 'goes beautifully. Drove up here four miles. Baby and Ayah in verandah – a dear wee babe, like old Mrs Watson, her grandmother. Helen soon appeared looking very well though a little thin. After breakfast rested. Tea at five out in the compound. Then Will drove off to Church, where we strolled about'.

After Ata had been in Madras for a week the baby was christened. She records that she and Will drove to Church – presumably in their carriage – and that Helen and Ayah and the baby followed in the dog cart. Helen, she noted, looked 'so sweet in her new white dress and hat'.

After Ata had been with them for a year, it was time for Will's home leave, and they all set off for Edinburgh together. They sailed from Bombay on the P.&O. Liner SS *Ganges* on 5 December 1884. Home leaves were usually granted after five years, and would last for a year. They were often used to acquire further qualifications for which extensions were usually available. Will used his furlough to take a B.Sc. in Public Health, doing some of the work for this in Liverpool.

By the time they were due to return to India in March 1896 Helen was none too fit. She was expecting another baby in four months time. It was thought it would be wise to leave the two-year old Janet in Edinburgh with Ata, whom she knew well, until the new baby arrived. With some misgivings, Helen set sail without Janet. She expressed these misgivings in a lullaby she wrote for her daughter at this time, and sang to her. To the modern ear it sounds over-sentimental; but it has to be set against the background of the time, with a far higher infant mortality, and understood as a poetic rationalisation of a situation which Helen disliked.

Far away, far away, over the sea,
Slumber my pretty one, precious to me.
Though no mother's arms enfold thee,
Though no mother's lips have kissed thee,
Slumber soft my little bird,
Far away, far away, over the sea.

Far away, far away, over the deep,
Slumber my baby, my little one sleep,
May a kind eye watch thy slumber,
May a soft hand smooth thy bed,
May a fond lip breathe a blessing
O'er thy little sleeping head,
Far away, far away, over the sea.

Far away, far away, there in the West,
Slumber and dream thou art safe on my breast.
Dream a little dream of mother
Yet not all too sweet and clear,

And forget it in the morning
Lest thy waking should be drear
Far away, far away, over the sea.[13]

The separation turned out to be for six months. Helen's second daughter was born on 4 July 1896, and Janet, travelling with a nurse, rejoined her mother in Madras shortly after. Janet told me that she remembered – and she was not quite three at the time – her mother putting the baby into her arms and telling her that this was her sister Day and that she must love and care for her always.

Across on the other side of India, however, threatening developments were taking place – developments which were to disrupt the peace of Helen and Will for many years to come, and bring horror and tragedy to India. Soon after the monsoon of 1896, a series of deaths from an unknown fever took place in the Mandvi district of Bombay. The first cases occurred among the porters at the grain stores, then among grain merchants, some of whom had just had dealings with Canton. As the weeks passed the deaths rose quickly to thousands, and on 24 September 1896 the story broke in the Bombay Gazette: it was bubonic plague.

This plague, known to the middle ages as the 'Black Death', was a merciless killer. Descriptions of it have come down from earliest times, and horror stories about it abound in Boccaccio, Defoe and Pepys. In the great pandemic which swept across Europe in the years following 1347, populations in some areas were almost wiped out; in others they were halved, or cut by a third.

Bombay had been free of plague for many years. It was regarded as a disease of interest to historians rather than to practical medical men. As Will was to write twelve years later:[31] 'It was therefore with surprise, and some incredulity, that the announcement of the presence of bubonic plague in Bombay was received in October 1896. As the epidemic spread through the city one realised the truth of the many tales of terror handed down from the past. The railway stations were besieged by thousands . . . streets were deserted, whole families found dead with no record to tell who they were . . . mothers lying cold with helpless babies beside them whom no-one dared pick up to take care of, for fear of this dreadful disease . . . Business came to a standstill, the inhabitants fled to the country.'

Mark Popovsky in *The Story of Dr Haffkine*,[32] published in Moscow in 1967, claims that at this point the, 'colonial authorities, fearful of damage to foreign trade . . . continued the conspiracy of silence in regard to the spreading epidemic'. Yet news of it had already appeared in the press, and within a fortnight of bacteriological proof that it was plague, the Government summoned Waldemar Haffkine,

1. Portrait of Helen Bannerman, painted at the time of her marriage in 1889 when she was twenty-seven.

2. Will seated at the front of his family in Edinburgh in the late 1860s. Not long after this photo was taken, when Will was ten, his mother died. He was then brought up by his sister Mary, or Ata (second from the right), the same sister who many years later was to look after his four children in Edinburgh.

3. Helen with Rob in Edinburgh in 1902.

4. Waldemar Haffkine
in his laboratory at
Parel, Bombay, at the
turn of the century,
after he had developed
the first plague vaccine.

5. Surgeon-General
William Burney
Bannerman, M.D.,
D.Sc., C.S.I.

Parel, Bombay
Friday 7 Ap. 1905
my own darling Janet
We have some sorrowful

6. Helen and Will lived in Bombay through the plague epidemic which began in 1896, with people all around them dying of the disease. In this illustrated letter which she sent to her daughters in Edinburgh, Helen described the grief of their coachman whose only surviving son had just died of plague (see page 66).

7. Life in India was never dull. Helen, in a letter to her daughters, described how her younger son Rob saved the life of one of the family's servants by his screams when she fell down a well (see page 78).

8. Helen's children avoided school when they were young. Growing up in the shadow of the plague laboratory, there was a time when they could identify a plague liver even though they could not read or write. They, and a servant, Poonoosawmy, who wanted to become literate, were taught their letters by Helen (see page 84).

Parel, Bombay
Saturday 7 July 1906
My own darling Janet
By last mail Day wrote
asking what a popai was,
it is rather appropriate that

9. Helen's children, running free in the grounds of Old Government House, Parel (used for the Plague Laboratory where their father worked) were often saved from accidents by the Laboratory and household staff.

Parel, Bombay
Friday 12 Nov. 1909
My own dear Janet
What do you think this
picture tells about the mali's
little girl. I think it I thin

10. Helen's letters include this picture of their mali or gardener, Suggan, who, after his wife had died, carried his motherless daughter everywhere with him.

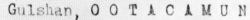

Gulshan, O O T A C A M U N

14th. August, 1 9 1

My dear Day,

    I do not believe any of you

will be able to tell what this picture is

about.   It is like one of the horrid pro-

blem pictures that are fashionable at pres

11. Once all Helen's children had left India, and were in Edinburgh for their education, a common evening's entertainment was skinning rats. This was done on the dining room table after it had been cleared (see page 133).

known for his development of a cholera vaccine, and asked him urgently to come to Bombay to work on a plague vaccine. They also set up a committee of medical men to try to combat the disease.[70]

Energetic sanitary measures were embarked on. Squads were sent round whitewashing, cleaning choked drains and insanitary alleyways and thousands of gallons of disinfectant were poured down such sewers as there were. The difficulty was that no-one knew which measures were effective against plague. A connection with rats was popularly acknowledged, but at this point no-one knew of the role of the rat flea in the cycle, or that only one species of rat was involved. Some doctors believed that the disease arose from insanitary vapours; others felt it came from rotten food and dates. As Will put it:[31] 'Thousands of pounds were wasted on disinfectants, which experiment has since shown are utterly useless, and innumerable lives were lost through ignorance of the proper precautions to adopt. As panic passed off, the Government established laboratories and organised bands of medical men whose business it was to study the disease: but it was only after years of observation and of laboratory experiments that it was discovered how plague really spreads.' It was to be Will's task to conduct these experiments, and, after he was put in charge of the laboratory at Parel, to mastermind them. It was during these years that the work done at Parel established for the first time and beyond doubt just how the disease was transmitted, and it was this which paved the way for effective control.

Haffkine arrived in Bombay on 7 October 1896 to find shops and bazaars closed, and streets in the poorer quarters deserted. He immediately established a makeshift laboratory, and filled a veranda with cages of rabbits and rats. Within three days he began work on developing the first plague vaccine. He applied the same principles which had led to his discovery of the cholera vaccine – the isolation of the bacillus, the development of a culture in which it would reproduce, and the selection of a method of killing it without destroying its immunising properties.

Waldemar Mordecai Haffkine was an extraordinary man to find experimenting on plague vaccine in Bombay. He had been born in 1860 in Odessa, and had left Russia under a cloud as a young man because of his revolutionary activities. He had gone to Paris and worked with Pasteur at the Pasteur Institute, and had there developed his cholera vaccine. He had then gone to India and undertaken an extensive anti-cholera vaccination scheme, travelling round administering the vaccine himself in infected areas. By putting enormous effort into his plague research, he developed a plague vaccine in the incredibly short time of three months. It was a dangerous exercise. Popovsky described the rigours of his work: 'Only a thin panel of

21

brittle glass stood between the staff and the millions of deadly doses of plague swirling in the test-tubes and flasks of the laboratory. Seemingly inevitable death menaced Haffkine and his assistants at every stage. It could have appeared as a hairline crack in the wall of a flask, or as the bite of an infected rat, or as any one of a hundred different accidents which it would have been impossible to foresee or guard against.'[32]

The vaccine was tried first on some rats at the end of December 1896. It proved effective, so on 10 January 1897 Haffkine tried it on himself. He developed all the symptoms of plague, with considerable pain in the area of the inoculation, but he recovered completely within two days. He then read a paper to the staff of Bombay's Central Medical College, and asked for volunteers to come forward.

The results impressed the medical authorities. In February 1897 the Madras Government – frightened that the plague would spread next to Madras – sent Will to Bombay to study Haffkine's methods. Helen and their daughters moved with him. Janet was then four. She recalled living in a tent on the sea shore, 'because no accommodation was available'. It may also have been that Will preferred to live there, away from the city and its disease. It was quite common for the Public Works Department, who were responsible for providing accommodation for the I.M.S., to house officials in tents; Janet remembered it as very comfortable. 'It had double tops to keep off the sun and various flaps which lifted up to admit air and light.' It cannot, however, have been easy for Helen to live there without running water, with a four-year old and a six-month old baby.

Helen and Will spent just over a year in Bombay at this point, then Will returned, with his family, to Madras in April 1898, to organise his own plague inoculation scheme.

It was against this background of plague and plague research that Helen brought up her two daughters. Quite apart from plague, there were other hazards for them. In those days, European children often failed to thrive in India. After the age of five or six they would grow thin and listless, without appetite and become very pale. They were subject in hot weather to prickly heat, an itchy body rash guaranteed to make the best-tempered child irritable. They kept getting stomach upsets, picking up parasites, and were at risk from various fatal tropical illnesses.

One of the things that did improve the health of such children was to take them to the hills. The hill station that Will and Helen went to most from Madras was Kodaikanal. It was neither so near nor so fashionable as Ootacumund, but it was much favoured by missionaries, giving rise to jokes about the two communities there, known as Kodai spiritual and Kodai carnal.[13] Helen and Will were always more on the side of the angels than of the Indian Civil Service, and Kodai became a second home. They had their own house there, called New Abernyte after Will's parents' country house in Perthshire. A picture of it that Helen painted shows it red-roofed, set on a wooded slope, with a tennis court and luxurious garden. Once, when she came back from a long home leave, they had to clear all sorts of creeping plants and cut down a jungle of trees and shrubs.

Spending the hot weather up in the hills, though, put Helen in a dilemma. If she was to be there with the children for the entire season, she would be away from her husband for four or five months. For some women, of course, this was a delightful thought – as for example, Kipling's siren of Simla, Mrs Hawksbee. But Helen never enjoyed being away from Will for long, and her solution was to leave the children with their Ayah at Kodai while she spent short spells with Will in the heat of Madras. The accepted wisdom in those days was that a man needed his wife more than children needed their mother.

It was on one of these journeys between Kodai and Madras that Helen wrote *The Story of Little Black Sambo*.[33] As Janet explained,[34] describing the same journey but going from Madras to Kodai, this trip was quite an undertaking:

After spending the night in the train going steadily South towards Ceylon, we arrived early next morning at Amayanayakanur, a small railway station about 20 miles from the foot of the Kodaikanal hills. Its name is now changed to Kodai Road. Here we got out with all our servants, horses, luggage and went to a travellers' bungalow for the day. Here we could get meals cooked by servants in charge of the bungalow, water for baths and cots to sleep on. But in both train and bungalow one had to be supplied with Keating's powder to keep off bugs and lice. And there would be small black or red ants crawling on the floor, lizards catching flies on the walls and occasionally snakes crawling into the bathroom through the outlet pipe to escape the heat and drought outside.

In the evening, carts drawn by two bullocks arrived and we were put in, lying down on rugs and sheets spread on straw and grass. The luggage was also put in, in front of the sleepers, and there was a covering of woven palm leaves to keep off rain or sun. The carts had very large wheels with iron rims and cows or bulls yoked to a long pole on which the driver also sat just where it touched the cart.

We children, in spite of heat and possibly mosquitoes, usually slept comfortably on the straw and did not waken till the carts stopped at Periakulam (the Big Tank) in the early morning. It was only about 20 miles journey but bullocks do not go more than about 3 miles an hour. The driver probably slept too, for the bullocks knew the way and kept to the proper side of the road without guiding . . .

In the morning, after some sort of meal, possibly in another travellers' bungalow, we were met by porters with chairs, hammocks and ponies for the ascent of about 6,000 feet to Kodaikanal. According to age and sex, one went riding on a pony, sitting in a chair mounted on two long poles and carried by four men, or in a hammock lying down with something over one to protect one from the sun.

As the footpath began to climb we passed through thick jungle with many trees and shrubs, often with beautiful flowers, sweet scents and lovely large butterflies around. There were places where we crossed lovely streams and waterfalls and gradually the air got cooler. A bit more than half way up we stopped at a place called the Tope, where we had a delightful picnic meal supplied by an Anglo-Indian in Kodai called Mr Tapp. The porters also had a meal of curry and rice which they had brought and which they warmed up on a picnic fire. Then on up and up along a path zig-zagging where the ground was very steep, the vegetation rapidly thinning but there were still many beautiful plants, grasses, wild rhododendrons, ground orchids, lilies, bracken and other ferns.

Now we began to feel cold and put on more clothes to keep warm in spite of the bright sunshine.

Some time in the early afternoon we reached Kodaikanal. It is centred on an artificial lake made by damming a stream, and there were bungalows all around belonging to missionary societies, government officers and to an Indian Prince. A road ran round the lake and there were rowing boats and a boat club. Above the path by which we came up there was a road called Coaker's walk from which you had a marvellous view of the plains stretching away to the sea and Ceylon in the South. Our house was on a hillside on the other side of the lake and higher up. You could go up by a steep path or by a road in a rickshaw or a dogcart.

It will be seen from this that the journey from Kodai to Madras, which was the direction in which Helen travelled when she wrote the book, was a long way removed from a suburban train journey of half an hour or so. For Helen the entire journey took two days and two nights. As she travelled farther and farther from her daughters her thoughts were with them, and she wanted to do something for them. She had enough time on her hands to work out the story, and then to perfect it. One of the noticeable things about it is the economy of language and the perfect match between text and picture. The consistency and unity of the book may well have been helped by a long spell of uninterrupted concentration. It is likely that Helen worked out the book during the journey then finished the pictures and wrote the text out neatly when she got to Madras. She was careful to make the volume small enough for her daughters to hold easily in their hands themselves – something she had always wanted from books when she had been a child.[35] Then, since she had her own book press, she bound it herself and sent it off to her daughters as a present.

With its pictures in bright primary colours and Little Black Sambo always on the point of being eaten, Janet and Day – then five and two – loved it. When their mother was there to terrify them with stories about tigers, they preferred her;[13] but in her absence the little book was some sort of comfort and a reassurance to them of her love.

Other people who saw the book admired it too, particularly a friend of Helen's called Mrs Alice M.E. Bond.[33] She thought it ought to be published and she asked Helen if she could take it with her on her next home leave to see if anyone was interested. Helen had not written it with any thought of publication, but, rather doubtfully, she agreed. She remembered from her childhood being told by R.M. Ballantyne, when he visited her parents' home in Edinburgh: 'Don't sell the copyright of your first book. That's the one,' he said, 'that you make the most on.' R.M. Ballantyne knew what he was talking about. He had suffered from the loss of the copyright of his early books,[9] and the subsequent history of *The Story of Little Black Sambo* was to prove him right in the advice he had given to Helen when she was a child. Remembering this advice, Helen made one request to Mrs Bond, that she would not sell the copyright.

In London, Mrs Bond took the manuscript picture book to a publisher who was trying to bring in some quick income from a series of small books for children called The Dumpy Books. These were edited by E.V. Lucas, who was then a columnist on *The Globe* as well as the compiler of *A Book of Verses for Children* and literary adviser to Grant Richards. Grant Richards, later one of London's leading publishers, was to be known in the years ahead for issuing the works of George Bernard Shaw, H.G. Wells, A.E. Housman and John Masefield. It was to Grant Richards that Shaw wrote, in connection with Grant Richards' autobiographical volume *Author Hunting:*[36]

You should call your book *The Tragedy Of A Publisher Who Allowed Himself To Fall In Love With Literature.* The publisher who does that, like the picture dealer who likes pictures or the schoolmistress who gets fond of her pupils, is foredoomed. A certain connoisseurship in the public taste is indispensable; but the slightest uncommercial bias in choosing between, say Bridges' *Testament of Beauty* and a telephone directory, is fatal.

25

Grant Richards was at that time a young man of twenty-seven. He had only been in business on his own for two and a half years. He had begun with a capital of £1,400, but by this time he had, as he put it, 'made intimate acquaintance with anxiety'. When shown Helen's bound and illustrated book *The Story of Little Black Sambo* he immediately offered Mrs Bond £5 for the copyright.

This put Mrs Bond in a quandary, as a letter[37] she wrote to Grant Richards on 20 June 1899 shows:

> Could you manage to wait 6 weeks for an answer? I should very much prefer to ask my friend in India to decide about her own book, but, in case this would make the publishing of the book at all doubtful, I should have to make up my mind to decide something alone, but would *infinitely* prefer not to. Please answer me by return as, in *any* case I must write by next mail to Mrs Bannerman . . . In case of your obtaining the copyright, would Mrs Bannerman lose all future chance of a share in the book?

The question of copyright is of great importance to any author, not only because a royalty is paid to the holder of the copyright on each copy sold, but also because it is through the ownership of the copyright that an author can keep control of his own work. This loss of the copyright was to work substantially to the disadvantage of the book and to the disadvantage of Helen's reputation. Not having an indisputable claim to the copyright she was unable to pursue the many versions, paying no copyright fees to anyone, which flooded the United States, adorned, in some cases, with damaging illustrations.

Grant Richards, however, was not prepared to move an inch on the copyright. His letters to Mrs Bond have not survived, but obviously he merely repeated his original offer. Two days later Mrs Bond wrote back to him. 'In answer to your letter of 21 June I have no option but to accept your offer, without reference to Mrs Bannerman, as I am anxious not to jeopardise the success of the little book.'[38]

On that basis Grant Richards went ahead and prepared *Little Black Sambo* for publication. Helen, however, wrote to Mrs Bond indicating that she was reluctant to sell the copyright. This letter has not survived, but Mrs Bond wrote again to Grant Richards on 9 August 1899:[39] 'I am sorry to find that Mrs Bannerman is somewhat disappointed as to the copyright, which she is most anxious to keep. She says, of course, if it is too late, she will abide contentedly by my decision but she would prefer you to pay her nothing for the book, and make what you can out of it, and let her retain the copyright. Can this be managed? If not, as I have given my word, the present arrangement must remain.'

Here was the germ of what could have been a fascinating legal dispute, which might have been worth pursuing in view of the book's phenomenal success. It would have centred on the question: can an author's copyright be sold without his or her express agreement? How far did Helen hand over power to Mrs Bond to act on her behalf, and how explicit was she about instructing Mrs Bond not to sell the copyright? A legal case of this kind might have brought Helen a fortune; it would certainly have fattened a few lawyers. Helen, however, was not by nature inclined to embark on law suits; nor was she even particularly interested in money. So there the matter rested for many years – a *de facto* sale of the copyright for £5 by Mrs Bond, a sale to which Helen had never signed her agreement.

Helen also objected to her name on the title page. Mrs Bond had raised a doubt about this in her letter to Grant Richards of 22 June:[38]

It did not strike me before leaving India to ask Mrs Bannerman any details as to what she would wish done and I am not *sure* if she would wish her real name on the title page or merely a nom-de-plum. I will write to her today and ask this, and if you are able to wait for so long, I will let you know at once on receiving her answer, but if you cannot wait, even for this, then, I think, you had better put "Helen Bannerman" on the title page.

By 9 August, after Helen had replied, Mrs Bond wrote to Grant Richards:[39] 'She says she would *prefer* not to have the name of Bannerman printed on the title page, but if it seems best, she will leave this also, otherwise, I suppose, you had better merely put the initials H.B.'

Three other matters were discussed in the correspondence between Mrs Bond and Grant Richards: a possible preface, the use of Indian words, and question of presentation copies for Helen herself. Grant Richards had asked for some biographical detail to use in a preface. Mrs Bond told him:[37] 'Mrs Helen Bannerman is the wife of Major Bannerman of the Indian Medical Service, and a great authority (Major B) on the plague. Mrs Bannerman is in the habit of telling her two little girls stories, which she illustrates in little paintings as she tells them and she told me that the story and illustrations of "Little Black Sambo" just came into her head during a journey, evolved by the moving of the train.' Grant Richards pressed Mrs Bond for more details. After she had heard again from Helen she replied:[39] 'As to preface, Mrs Bannerman says nothing more than I have told you already. It was written for her own little girls and "just came into her head".'

Mrs Bond then asked Grant Richards to tell her if he was 'intending to explain (in footnotes) any of the words, only common to Anglo Indians', and whether he needed any help in the matter. Publication of the book, however, was pushed through very fast, and no footnotes appeared. The question of Anglo-Indian words was to be yet another source of disagreement between Helen and Grant Richards in the future. Then there was the question of copies for the author. Mrs Bond, in her first letter, dated 20 June 1899, had asked: 'in case it is printed before we start for India on October 4th, would you send our presentation copies to her by me and if so, how many?' By her second letter dated 9 August she asked: 'As to the original copy of "Little Black Sambo" which I left with you, I imagine that when it is done you will return it to Mrs Bannerman by me. Her children will value it in the future . . . Please note, I leave for India at the end of next month.' No trace now remains of this manuscript book.

The date recorded at the Public Record Office for the first publication of the book was 31 October 1899. It was offered for sale at the low price of one shilling and six pence. In a review of 'Modern Nursery Books' in *The Spectator*[40] on 2 December 1899, *Little Black Sambo* emerged a very economical buy. It was the second cheapest in a group of ten nursery books reviewed; the most expensive was six shillings.

That *Spectator* review criticised some of the other books available that Christmas which, it said, suffered dreadfully from the 'one-eye-on-the-parent' complaint and went on:

Very different must be the verdict on that most attractive little book *The Story of Little Black Sambo*. It has been briefly noticed in these columns before, but no comparison between old and new fashioned nursery books would be quite fair without allowing Little Black Sambo to give his protest in favour of recent books. His history was not written with one eye on parents and guardians, or the inconsistency of mixing up the African type of black with delightful adventures with tigers in an Indian jungle would never have been allowed to pass. As it is, Little Black Sambo makes his simple and direct appeal in the great realm of make-believe without paying the slightest attention to the unities or caring in the least about anything but the amusement of the little boys and girls for whom he was so obviously created. Every parent should at once get the book and give it both to the nursery and the schoolroom. It is impossible to deny that among this year's Christmas books *Little Black Sambo* is, to use his own classic phrase, far and away 'the grandest tiger in the jungle'.

SEPARATIONS AND 'SAMBO'

The geographical inconsistencies of Helen's books – singled out in that review – have been subsequently widely criticised. The confusion which was already there was made worse by the other illustrators in the U.S.A. One American critic, Selma Lanes, adds a further geographical twist by bringing Madeira into the picture. In *Down the Rabbit Hole*[41] she claims that Madeira, being off the West Coast of Africa, has 'a certain African population' and adds:

> A proper English gentlewoman of the '90's, one of the sustainers, if not the builders, of the British Empire, she no doubt saw one dark-skinned non-Englishman as looking much like another. Indian and African blacks were readily and innocently confused in her mind.

Madeira, however – unlike the Cape Verde Islands, which have been extensively settled from mainland Africa – was occupied in the fifteenth century by the Portuguese and has remained ethnically Portuguese ever since. And Helen's letters make it clear that far from being so ignorant as to confuse an African with an Indian she was able to distinguish between the racial groups within India.

Why then did a person who was both well travelled and scholarly write a book which contains aspects of both Africa and India? The explanation is that she was writing, not for publication, but for her own daughters. She wanted to set her story somewhere far away and exotic; she chose an imaginary jungle-land and peopled it with what were to her daughters a far-away kind of people. To have made the setting India would have been too humdrum and familiar for them. Then, because she had a liking for terrifying tigers, she brought them in as the villains. She was far too good a naturalist not to be aware that tigers are found in India but not in Africa; no matter. Her jungle-land was an imaginary one, and tigers, which for her were symbolic dragons, were essential to the story.

The most Indian aspect of her books is the language. This again stems from the audience for whom they were written. Her daughters understood Hindustani words like 'ghi'; the English equivalent, 'clarified butter', would have been a mystery to them.

A question which has stimulated a lot of discussion in the U.S.A. is: why did she choose the name Sambo for her hero? As has already been indicated – and the question is gone into fully in the last chapter – it is a name which came to have unfortunate connotations through its use in the United States as a generic title for any black male. It is difficult to pinpoint the moment when the word moved from being a name to being a label. In[43] *Uncle Tom's Cabin* (first published in serial form in 1851–52) it is used as a name; the indications are that it came to be used in a generic way well after this. If it was used generically before 1899,

Helen had no knowledge of this. She used it as a specific name. She was fond of puns and verbal jokes and many of her characters have names derived from common phrases such as – 'Mumbo-Jumbo'; 'Rag Tag and Bobtail'. In this she was following in the footsteps of authors such as Charles Dickens, who invented amazing names for his characters and places, plucked from everyday words – for example, 'Dotheboys Hall' the wretched academy which did down its pupils.[43]

Helen's original publishers had no qualms about her use of the name Sambo, but they did dislike her use of Indian words in the text. Nor was this the only source of disagreement. A letter from Grant Richards indicates that Helen had written to him asking if he had sent out review copies, suggesting he should also sell the book in Canada and criticising the cover. In March 1900[44] he wrote to her clarifying an earlier remark that she suffered from misconceptions about his role.

> I referred to misconceptions because it seemed to me that you were under the impression that I was neglecting my various duties connected with the publication of your book. In especial I referred to your writing and asking whether copies had gone out for review. If I undertake the publication of a book at all you can be quite certain that important details of this kind will be adequately dealt with.
>
> In the same way you asked me to write and see if it would be possible to place copies on sale in Canada. I have done so, but have had no favourable reply from any Canadian bookseller until this moment. Your friends in Canada must create a demand, and then the booksellers will speculate, but not, I am afraid, before.
>
> For the rest I must confess to being very disappointed at your dislike of the cover, which I may tell you I like extremely myself and which every other competent critic has expressed admiration for, its simplicity being its chief attraction.

Despite the cover, the book sold extremely well. According to Justin Schiller in *The Book Collector*[1] of Autumn 1974, the first edition of October 1899 was followed by a second edition within a month. A third and fatter edition appeared a year later, in September 1900, followed by another edition that October. This fourth edition advertised the book as being in its 21st thousand. By May 1903 eight British editions had appeared, and in 1904 came a large-type version.

From these Helen made nothing – apart from her original £5. Nor did she make anything from sales of the book in the U.S.A. or from any other parts of the world. Her motive in asking her publisher about the promotion of the book and possible sales in Canada cannot have been financial. The American rights to the book were bought from

Grant Richards by Frederick A. Stokes of New York, and he published the book there in 1900. It was a duplicate of the Grant Richards version but with a different cover.

From 1905 onwards, when Reilly and Britton included the story in their Christmas Stocking Series, along with *Peter Rabbit* and *Uncle Tom's Cabin*, a variety of unauthorised versions, with pictures by other illustrators, began to appear in the U.S.A. More than fifty of these were published in the United States, and many of them made no mention of Helen as author. But as she had lost the copyright, there was little she could do.

The question of the validity of the sale of the copyright, however, was still lurking in the background. It became acute in the late 1930s, when the possibility of film royalties arose. The publishers – and by then Grant Richards' firm, after many vicissitudes, had been incorporated within Chatto & Windus – offered Helen an ex gratia payment for the film rights. In reply her lawyer asked for evidence of the sale of the copyright. This the publishers were in no position to produce, though they could argue that Mrs Bond's letter substantiated their claim that Helen had in fact agreed, albeit reluctantly. In 1940 an offer came from Hollywood. The publishers offered Helen half the film rights. Throughout the 1940s negotiations were initiated by a number of film companies but for a variety of reasons they all fell through. In 1963, however, as a result of a new agreement with Chatto and Windus, royalties began to be paid to her heirs on each copy sold in Britain, in exchange for exclusive U.K. publication rights.

Although Helen herself saw only £5 from the book, she was very pleased with its success, especially as she had tried, and failed, to get another book published the previous year. This was a book of poems, which she had sent, ironically, to the same publisher, Grant Richards. He had offered to publish it if she paid thirty five pounds. 'I should ask,' he added, 'that the money be paid on the day the manuscript goes to the printer.' The letter,[45] dated 21 July 1898 was presumably not followed up by Helen. There is no sign of the book, and no trace of the poems – though 'Far Away Far Away Over the Sea' may have been one of them. The warm welcome for *Little Black Sambo* turned Helen's energies away from poetry towards what she now knew was a success – writing books for small children.

Chapter Three

Muggers and Mangoes

While all the correspondence about *Little Black Sambo* had been passing to and fro between Helen and Mrs Bond, Helen was settling into a new house. Will had been transferred in March 1899 from Madras back to Bombay. Haffkine was about to go on leave and Will was needed to take charge of the Laboratory in his absence.

After Haffkine had gone on leave, Will moved the Laboratory in August, 1899 from the Central Medical College to more spacious premises at Old Government House, Parel, on the outskirts of Bombay. Test tubes, cages full of rats, and flasks of plague culture were set up in the once elegant rooms. A contemporary visitor[46] described rows of great bottles spread out in a, 'vast and cavernous apartment from which the light is completely excluded. You peer into it from behind a single flickering candle, and see the dim shapes of huge tables stretching away into the darkness, and innumerable decanters faintly shining. You ask what the room is and are told it was once the ballroom.' Bombay society had once danced there in a blaze of light; now the room was given over to the cultivation of plague, the germs of which, Will said, 'love the darkness rather than the light because their ways are evil.'

Will and Helen and their two daughters moved into a bungalow in the Laboratory grounds. It had been previously the house of an A.D.C. The only problem was that the Laboratory had embarked on a rat extermination programme and the captured rats kept escaping. Despite the rats, however, Helen enjoyed Parel. Groves of date palms and coconut palms separated Parel village, with its railway workshops and mills, from the Fort area of Bombay.[47] The road between was a dust-track, and people travelled along it on horseback, in horse-drawn carriages, or on bullock carts. There was also a rail connection with Bombay. Now swallowed up within Bombay, Parel at the turn of the century was an isolated and pleasant spot.

Parel House, or Old Government House, had a strange history.[48] On the site originally was the Hindu temple of Parali-Vaijnath. Then in 1673 the Jesuits put up various buildings. After Bombay was ceded to the British, Parel House was taken over by the Governors of

32

Bombay, who used it from 1719. In 1855, however, Lady Ferguson, the wife of the Governor, died there from cholera, and it was abandoned. When the plague epidemic was in full spate, Parel House was reopened as a Plague Hospital. Its next role, as we have seen, was as the Plague Research Laboratory. In 1906, the name was altered to 'The Bombay Bacteriological Laboratory', and in 1925 the name was changed again to 'The Haffkine Institute'. It is under that title that it is known today as one of the world's foremost bacteriological institutions.

Helen drew innumerable pictures of the house and gardens and the Laboratory staff and their household servants. Within the gates of old Government house was clearly a little community that lived and worked together. She had been used, in both Madeira and in Edinburgh, to households with a nanny and a cook, but in India, where labour was very cheap, a wide range of servants was customary. It was also, to some extent, obligatory; there were some functions which a cook could not, for example, be asked to perform, and equally so with other servants. Helen's establishment was, for its day, a modest one. She mentions a bearer or head servant – called by the custom of the day 'the boy', (a term which, like the word 'native' which was then in universal use for an Indian, is now unacceptable). Then there was a 'matey' or a houseman, to look after the cutlery and the lamps, a cook, an 'ayah' for the children, a 'hamal' to sweep the corridors and verandas and, lowest in status, a sweeper to remove what was then called the 'night soil' from the commodes to take it away to an appropriate spot to be buried. Helen lived at Parel without drains, without electricity and without refrigeration. Water was heated in large containers and tipped into the bath; cooking was done on a wood fire in the kitchen. Meat was either killed on the premises, if it was chicken or duck, or bought fresh each day.

Outside the house, there was a 'mali' to tend the garden, a 'syce' for their two horses and a 'gharri-wallah' or coachman as well. Helen would use the services of a 'dhobi' to wash their clothes and a 'dherzi' to sew them. It was a labour-intensive economy; and it was the memsahib's role to supervise it and see that it all ran smoothly. Unlike some British women in India, Helen indulged – while her children were young – in very little social life. She visited rarely, dined out occasionally and hardly ever entertained. Pat Barr, in *The Memsahibs*,[49] describes some women who lived a hectic social life, leaving their children so entirely in the care of the servants that they could hardly speak English. Helen took her duties as a mother seriously and spent nearly all her day with the children.

The kind of establishment which Helen ran was not exclusive to the British in India. Mrs Vijaya Lakshmi Pandit (sister of Jawaharlal

Nehru) who was born in 1900 describes in her autobiography *The Scope of Happiness*[50] a childhood with considerable similarities. She tells of waiting in the garden as a three-year-old, with her ayah, for her father to return from court. He would arrive driving himself in a dog-cart, pulled by his pure – blooded Arab mare called 'Queen of the Road', and when he saw her, would stop and lift her onto the seat. 'Afterwards I fed lumps of sugar or a carrot to the "Queen" and trotted along by Father's side to his room where, after thanking him in flowery Urdu, I received a kiss and went back to the nursery.'

Mrs Pandit explains that Allahabad, where she grew up, was divided into English and Indian quarters, with, however, some rich Indians living in the Civil Lines, as the English sector was called. Her house was in the Western section and was a happy bustling home.

> Everyone seemed to be involved, and happily so, in work and play or whatever the interest might be, and the sound of laughter was what guests always associated with Anand Bhawan. Anand Bhawan stood in the midst of a spacious garden, which was Father's special joy. It had tennis courts, a riding ring for the children, an orchard, and an indoor swimming pool. In the middle of the building was a big, square open courtyard with shallow steps leading up to a deep veranda running all the way round and onto which opened the bedrooms. A tiered fountain in the centre of the courtyard was used during the hot summer evenings and kept the temperature bearable. Sometimes, when there was a party in the courtyard, the tiers of the fountain were filled with chunks of ice and sweet-smelling flowers whose scent wafted into the bedrooms. Parties in Anand Bhawan were very popular whether they were informal ones in the courtyard or formal ones in the dining room.

> Dinner parties were occasions to be remembered, with the table set with crystal and silver and flowers to match the dinner service.

Life with Helen and Will was much simpler. Their home, like the Nehru's, was a happy one, but on a more modest scale and their life at that time was particularly quiet. After she had been in Bombay for a month, Helen was expecting a baby again. She stayed within the Laboratory grounds with Janet and Day. She was helped at that time by her younger sister Elspeth, who was not married and came out for a few months to give what assistance she could.

Helen's first son, Pat, was born on 25 January, 1900, in the house at Parel. Janet remembered[13] a white cot being painted before he arrived and being taken to see him – by this time she was seven – shortly after his birth. While she was expecting Pat, and after he had arrived, Helen continued to tell stories to Janet and Day. She would make them up, and sometimes draw pictures for them as she went along. 'She used to entertain us every night', Janet recalled, 'with exciting stories of all kinds, when we were in bed.' For this reason, Janet explained, she and Day never cared so much for their mother's books as other children did. They were at the source of the tales she invented. 'I think,' Janet added, 'that she would have given her life to writing if she had not had her children to bring up. She felt she could not do both.'

Nevertheless, five months after Pat's birth, on 8 June 1900, Helen wrote to her publisher, Grant Richards, in London to say that she had started work on a second children's book. He wrote back[51] on 26 June to say that he was very pleased to hear the news. 'Acting on the assumption that I shall publish this book in the autumn, I want to ask you whether you won't at once begin to think of a successor to it for next year. One ought, to keep up the success of the books, to have a new book every year.' He dealt with Helen's inhibitions about her name appearing on the cover, assuring her that if she wished, the new book could simply be labelled as by the author of *Little Black Sambo*.

On one other question, Grant Richards was less accomodating. 'To be quite frank with you, I should be unwilling to part with the copyright of "Little Black Sambo". Having the book my property enables me to sell comparatively large numbers at specially low terms which I could hardly do if I had to pay a royalty: but this will all be to the advantage of "Little Black Mingo", which will be helped by the success of its predecessor.'

The success of *Little Black Sambo* meant, however, that Helen was in a position to negotiate over *Little Black Mingo*, and she did. In a letter from Grant Richards[52] dated 29 November 1900, it is clear that she was prepared to publish her second book elsewhere unless she could get back the copyright of *Little Black Sambo*. As Grant Richards put it:

I have just returned from Edinburgh where I had two interviews with Mr J.P. Bannerman (Will's elder brother). As you suggested in your last letter to me, he told me you were very anxious to get back the copyright of 'Little Black Sambo', saying that it was not so much the financial value of the copyright that you wanted to secure but that you wanted the book in your own hands, to stop the publication of it if at any time you desired to do so, and generally to control it. He told me that if I would give back the copyright he would be glad to allow me to have all the profits of the first edition of 'Little Black Mingo'. I was sorry to find it impossible to accede to your and his request, but I assured him that any suggestions that you might make I could always very carefully consider, and if at any time I wished to dispose of the copyright I should first offer it to you. I am sorry to say, however, that this did not satisfy him, and he ended our interview by telling me that unless I would agree to return 'Little Black Sambo' he would have to treat with some other publisher for its successor. As you had not said this or suggested it in your letters to me, I asked him if he would give me time to communicate with you on the matter, and to this he kindly consented.

These consultations did not turn out favourably for Grant Richards, and when *The Story of Little Black Mingo* appeared in October 1901 it was published by James Nisbet and Co. Ltd. Possibly Helen had been riled by further remarks by Grant Richards in his letter of 29 November 1900 indicating pained surprise at her attitude over the Sambo copyright – an attitude she had made clear to Mrs Bond before entrusting the book to her, and that Mrs Bond had made clear to Grant Richards in her letter[39] of 9 August 1899. What Grant Richards had written,[52] a year after his negotiations with Mrs Bond, must have infuriated Helen:

If, on Mrs Bond's return to India or as soon as you heard from her that she had sold me the copyright of the book, you had as urgently desired me to return it to you, I believe that I should very seriously have considered doing so, but your letters asking this did not arrive until the middle of last summer, when already *Little Black Sambo* was a success, and some part of that success, I am sure – not the chief part but some part – was due to the fact that, having to pay you no royalty, I was able to induce booksellers to take and push the book by offering them extremely good terms.

Helen kept the copyright of all her subsequent books, though none of them – as she had feared – did anything like as well as her first one. Changing publishers to James Nisbet and Co. Ltd. also suited Helen over another matter in which she was in disagreement with Grant Richards – the question of unfamiliar words. This second book was, like *Little Black Sambo*, an adventure story, set in Helen's imaginary jungle world. The hero, unusually for those days, was not only a girl, but a black girl. The villain was a crocodile or, to use the word used in India, a 'mugger'. As Grant Richards had written to Helen on 29 November 1900:[52] 'You strongly urge the retention of certain Indian words, pointing out that your little Indian friends think that the English words are poor substitutes. Your contention, I think, would have more weight if the book circulated mainly or even largely, in India, but it does not, it circulates in England and on this account I shall very much prefer, if I am to publish the book, to translate the words.'

The Nisbet version of *Little Black Mingo*, when it came out in 1901, had the full range of Helen's original words, such as 'chatty' for a water pot, 'dhobi' for the man who washes the clothes, the familiar word bazaar and the word 'mugger'. Apart from the word 'mugger', these are words without an exact English equivalent, but a child could tell precisely what was meant by the accompanying picture. If readers were to enter Helen's world, they had to acquire a few new concepts – as, for example, the existence of a servant such as a dhobi. While acquiring a new idea, they might as well use a precise name for it, rather than use an English translation which carried different overtones. The wisdom of Helen's approach is seen in the unsatisfactory version of her later book *The Story of Little Degchie-Head*, published in the U.S.A. as *The Story of Little Kettle-Head*. The title conjures up a picture of a kettle with spout and handle, whereas what Helen was talking about, and what her pictures showed, was an Indian cooking pot without handle or spout. That sort of cooking pot could go on a child's head, as happens in the story. A kettle, however, would be too small and totally inappropriate.

The use of Indian words puzzled those adults who liked books to observe the unities of time and space. The words and animals placed the story in India but the characters were, once again, African. Black Noggy's house, to add a further dimension, looked like a croft in the Scottish Highlands.

As Helen wanted, there was a picture on the cover but not her name. The first edition shows a sympathetic drawing of Mingo, in black on a pale green cloth cover, with the title in red. It was more attractive to a young child than the plain, lightly-striped cover of the first edition of *Little Black Sambo*. Inside, the book made no mention of Helen Bannerman, but credited it to the author of *The Story of Little Black Sambo*.

Some adults find the pictures in *Little Black Mingo* excessively violent. There are two of the explosion in which Black Noggy and the mugger are blown to bits. Children, however, especially those from a secure and loving home, can delight in those pictures. Their understanding of pain in anyone other than themselves is very limited, and they can find Black Noggy's well-deserved fate very satisfying. Perhaps concern about violence is a modern obsession; the picture leading up to the explosion was one of the ones singled out by *The Guardian* for a favourable mention in a contemporary review.[53]

> We do not think this is quite as good as *The Story of Little Black Sambo* but then Little Black Sambo was one of the most delightful aquaintances we ever made. Some of the Mingo pictures are excellent, especially the one showing the arrival of the mongoose, and

the later one of the Mugger, Black Noggy and the kerosene tin.

Other reviews were also complimentary. *The Glasgow Herald* quoted *The Bookman*[54] of November 1901: 'The text is irresistibly funny, and the illustrations – all coloured – are to match. *The Scotsman*[55] on 14 October described it as, 'a sort of companion to *The Story of Little Black Sambo* . . . It is full of amusing pictures, cleverly drawn and coloured, which illustrate the humours of the text admirably. It is a book that will amuse any child from two years upwards.' *The Spectator*[56] praised it too, but felt it could not match up to its predecessor:

> It is almost as diverting as *Little Black Sambo*, but not quite, for from the nature of the case it is impossible that the second story should possess the virtue of absolute freshness and originality which distinguished the first.

The creatures featured in the book were familiar to Helen from her life at Parel – in some cases all too familiar. On one occasion she and Will went on a picnic to Vehar, the source of Bombay's water supply; just near where they settled down was a dead mugger. 'It had been shot by someone', Will wrote,[57] 'and there it was quite close to our drinking water, lying on its back with its legs in the air, smelling horribly. However, fortunately it was lying to leeward. . . .' The Laboratory, too, was an excellent source of information about unpleasant animals and how they bred. *Little Black Mingo* contains detailed and accurate drawings of muggers hatching. There is no record in Helen's letters of her sketching muggers hatching in the Laboratory; but in the years ahead she was to draw many pictures of lizards' eggs, turtles' eggs and snakes' eggs hatching in the Laboratory.

It is easy to see why Helen's books were far less 'vicarage tea party' than those of her contemporary, Beatrix Potter. Helen's life was a good deal less genteel. The Ulysses of *The Story of Little Black Mingo* is a mongoose; Helen knew quite enough about the species to avoid making him too much of a hero – unlike Rudyard Kipling, who, in *Rikki Tikki Tavi*,[62] almost canonised a mongoose. The mongoose, Helen knew, had its unpleasant side:[58] 'I bought four nice young ducks', she was to write it a letter home, 'and two days ago the cook told me they were nearly ready to use. And then yesterday the boy came and asked me to come and see. A mongoose had got in beside them during the night, and it had killed a poor duck outright and sucked its blood, and it had bitten a hole in the neck of another. I don't know if it had sucked the second one's blood, but it was still alive, only poor thing, it was quite lost, and when the houseman put it down, it threw its head up, staggered and fell over on its side and could not walk a step. So I just had to send it to be killed too.' Then she added more cheerfully, 'We are to have it for dinner today.'

By contrast, Beatrix Potter came to know the realities of farm life in her farm at Sawrey; but until she was forty seven she had lived with her parents in their house in Bolton Gardens, South Kensington, in London. Her delightful pictures of animals are idealised and romanticised; compare her elegant Jeremy Fisher, a frog who sits on a water lily, fully clothed and sheltering under an umbrella, with Helen's natural frog in *The Story of Little Black Quasha*. Helen's animals are never dressed in clothes, are never anthropomorphised. The monkey in *The Story of The Teasing Monkey* makes himself a cloak or covering out of coconut husks; but this is in keeping with what a monkey could do. Nor do her animals have names, apart from Jacko the monkey. They are the frog, the snake, or the tiger. They also show in their behaviour the obsession of the real animal world – eating their prey, or at least trying to do so. It has been argued that to clothe animals in human garments, and tuck baby rabbits into little beds with sheets, and feed them with spoonfuls of castor oil, is misleading and harmful to a child. My faith in the power of children grow out of any misconceptions such books may induce is total; but Helen Bannerman, though her animals do talk and show human emotions such as rage, portrayed them very firmly as animals and not as pseudo-humans.

After she had finished *The Story of Little Black Mingo*, Helen became seriously ill. Elspeth had gone home by this time and Janet recalled:[34] 'I remember that Dr and Mrs Scott of the Wilson College took us all into their home. It was there that my mother had her operation for a liver abcess, caused by dysentry. After the operation a tube for the drainage of pus was inserted in the wound for a number of days. A characteristic incident at this stage was my mother's desire to see the wound which the nurse naturally would not allow. But the next day when her hair was being brushed my mother got hold of a hand mirror which she slipped under her pillow. Next time the wound was dressed she slipped out the mirror while the nurse's back was turned and inspected it to her satisfaction. She had suffered a lot of pain and the operation was a great relief, though it took her about a year to get over it.'

Helen's next book, not surprisingly, was about a mother who is ill and a child who makes her better. *The Story of Little Black Quibba* is a very reassuring book to read to any child whose mother is unwell – not least because the mother is quickly forgotten as the child goes off to search for the mangoes that will bring about her recovery. The mother is only remembered at the end when the child triumphantly runs home with a mango in each hand: 'Even the sight of them made her feel better.'

In the garden at Parel was a mango tree which Helen looked at as she lay ill. 'Just outside my bedroom,' she was to write three years later,[59] 'stands a great mango tree, and we had been watching it, and thinking what a lot of young mangoes there were on it, and the gardener used to keep his pots under it and great mounds of earth and sand and leaf mould that he mixed when he filled the pots. Well, the other day, when I was in my room, we heard the most fearful roaring noise, and down came a hugh branch, right on top of the pots, and just where the mali might have been sitting . . . Now we find all inside the branch is rotten, and every bit of the tree will have to be cut down before it is safe . . . All the mangoes will be made into pickles or mango fool.'

If the mangoes in the story were based on an everyday fruit, something which sounds improbable in *Little Black Quibba* is the episode where the snake eats three frogs, who, after the snake's death, hop out alive and well. Yet something strangely like that is recorded in one of Helen's letters – though it happened a year after the book was published. 'The other night', wrote Helen,[60] 'Dad and I were walking from the gharri to the house with the hamal carrying the lantern. As we got near the house we heard a little voice crying "Ow, Ow". Said Dad, "What's that?" "It's a snake swallowing a frog", said I, for I had heard the noise once before. "I'll go and see", said Dad and took the lantern from the hamal, and I went too, to see if it really was a frog calling. As Dad went along I expected the noise to stop, but it went on, and presently Dad called out, "Here it is!" and held the lantern near, and sure enough there was a snake with a poor frog half in and half out its mouth. "Is it a poisonous snake?" said Dad. "Never mind whether it's poisonous or not, kill it", said I, "I don't like any snakes so near the house". But Dad poked the snake with his finger and it dropped the frog, and began to crawl away and Dad shouted to the hamal to bring a stick and Dad beat it till he killed it . . . and then Dad forced its mouth open and looked at its teeth and said it was a harmless snake. And then the silly frog jumped back just as if it liked being eaten, right onto the snake. Wasn't it stupid?'

Helen got away from snakes and frogs, however, when the time for her second long leave from India came round in June 1901. She had been by that time in India twelve years, and her previous long leave had been from December 1894 to April 1896. She was now thirty-nine and Will almost forty-three. They set off for Edinburgh with Janet nearly eight, Day nearly five and Pat aged fifteen months. After Helen had been in Scotland for a few months she was again expecting a baby, and she stayed on in Edinburgh for the birth. Her second son and last child, Robert, was born on 6 June, 1902 at her parents' home at 11 Strathearn Place. Will stayed for the birth and then left immediately for India.

MUGGERS AND MANGOES

Helen stayed on in Edinburgh for a further six months and it was while she was there that *The Story of Little Black Quibba* was published (written when she had been ill with a liver abcess after Pat's birth). It appeared in October 1902, 'by the author of *Little Black Mingo*', and was published by James Nisbet and Co. Frederick Stokes and Co. in New York published it there the following year. Although she was no longer writing for Grant Richards, Helen followed his advice and was managing, despite two births and a severe illness, to produce a book a year, in time for the Christmas trade. Grant Richards would not have been pleased, however, by the star role for an Indian word – mango – in the text, nor by the picture of Quibba on the cover. Yet Helen had her fans for whom the Indian flavour of her books was welcome. When she arrived back in India, just in time for Christmas, she found a favourable review in The Times of India waiting for her.[61] The reviewer took the opportunity of putting Helen's book into the context of all the books by British authors published in India:

It used to be the fashion to sneer at Anglo-Indian authors. *The Saturday Review*, eighteen years ago, noticing a book by a new writer, now very well known, commenced with these words: "There seems to be something depressing and bewildering to a naturally funny man in the narrowness and monotony of Oriental life. His wit loses its edge, he trades upon his ideas and the order of his mind becomes provincial." This tone is no longer possible with Rudyard Kipling and Sir Ali Baba in the hold, and it was never very just. If we take into account how small and how busy the English population of India is, the surprising thing is that it has produced so many clever writers in many veins. The latest of these is not an Anglo-Indian only, but a Bombayite, who has given us, within three years, three of the most successful creations in the domain of child literature which it has been our hap to come across. To write for children is the gift of few: to believe they can do so is the delusion of many. But when *Little Black Sambo* by Helen Bannerman appeared about three years ago, those parents who were lucky enough to fall in with it felt at once, or soon discovered by experiment, that the authoress was one who knew the road to a child's mind and head. To quote the words of Goethe it was "complete enough to satisfy, fragmentary enough to exite, barbarous enough to arouse, tender enough to appease". .... and now Little Black Quibba is published just in good time for Santa Claus . . .

Her latest book was a success in India, but the return to India was a sad one for Helen. Janet and Day were now nine and six – old enough to be thought better off in Britain where they were less exposed to tropical illness and could receive a better education. Helen returned in December 1902 with only Pat and Rob. Janet and Day were left in Edinburgh with Will's sister Ata and were not to see their parents again for three years.

Separation from her daughters was a source of grief and anxiety for Helen. Separation had brought forth the song 'Far Away Far Away Over the Sea', and had been the trigger for *Little Black Sambo*. Now it was the impetus behind weekly letters to her daughters, each with a watercolour illustration. It was normal for parents separated in this way to write each week to their children at home. Such letters are usually scrappy and infinitely forgettable. Helen's are different. With pictures about four inches by three at the head of each letter, they have a certain quality about them. When sufficient letters had been gathered, they were bound into volumes and those volumes were there in Ata's house for the children to browse through and to look at. As the volumes grew from one to ten, to seventeen (and probably eighteen or nineteen with one or two volumes now missing at the end of the series) they turned into a continuing family book. It was a more sophisticated version of a story book to compensate for her absence; but the motivation was the same.

In Edinburgh, Janet and Day settled down to the serious business of their education. They faced the separation with resignation. As Janet recalled: 'We just accepted it. We had to'. As well as staying with their Aunt, they were surrounded by an extensive family circle of uncles and aunts and grandparents and cousins. Looking back, Janet and Day spoke warmly of Ata: 'She was very, very good to us. She gave all her time to us. But of course we did miss our parents.'

If small children had to be left in another country in the care of others, this was the way to do it – in contrast to Rudyard Kipling's largely autobigraphical experience which he described in *Baa Baa Black Sheep*.[62] His parents left him in a hostile household, contacted through an advertisement. They sailed back to India and left their son a victim of bullying and spite. Only when a friend of the family visited the young Kipling and his sister a few years later was it discovered that he was almost blind through neglected eye problems, lied frequently to keep out of trouble, and cringed when he was approached, expecting blows.

Janet and Day in contrast already knew Ata well. Life with her was never dull.[63] She was prepared to take the children anywhere that promised to be interesting. She maintained that she could not afford a carriage, so she travelled around Edinburgh on a large tricycle. She was of substantial build and had never managed to master a bicycle. On expeditions with Janet and Day she went more prosaically by tram or on foot. Edinburgh then was small enough to walk almost everywhere, and Ata was a vigorous woman.

Some of the other relations were unusual characters too.[64] One of Helen's brothers, Charles, was an engineer who kept a boat of his own design on the Edinburgh-Glasgow canal. It had a sail as well as paddles. He was also interesting for his encyclopaedic knowledge of old Edinburgh. Then Helen's parents were always ready to welcome their grandchildren. Christmas tended to be a grand family occasion with twenty or more sitting down to eat. Also part of the family circle were a number of servants who had been with the family for many years. 'Nainie', for example, had been with Helen's parents in Madeira, and stayed with them till her death. She loved telling fortunes from tea leaves, though she would never read them on a Saturday: 'Owre near the Sabbath', as she put it. Even after successful prophecies, 'Here's Willie tumbling free an elephant!' – which he duly did – she would be inclined to add 'But ye ken it's a' a heap o' lees!'

Ata's house, with a nanny and servants, was 50 Ann Street. It is a small and intimate street near Edinburgh's West End, not far away from Robert Louis Stevenson's childhood home in Heriot Row and Sir Walter Scott's town house in Castle Street. It is a little valley in the heart of Georgian Edinburgh, almost unchanged from the time when Janet and Day first went to live there in 1902. Irregular terraced houses run along each side, with long gardens in front and a narrow road down the middle. There are still cobbles, paving stones, iron street lamps and grey stone buildings each of an individual design.

Ata's house was particularly irregular. Since it was on a corner, and still part of a terrace, not one room was rectangular. Even the panes of glass in some of the windows were curved. In the basement were the servants' quarters and kitchen. On the ground floor was the dining room and schoolroom. Next came bedrooms and on the top a drawing room with a view past the tall houses of Moray Place and Ainslie Place, over the low lying Dean Gardens and across the Firth of Forth to the hills of Fife.

It was to the children in Ann Street that Helen's mind constantly turned when she got back to Bombay. As she put it in a letter to Janet after she had been back with Will for a fortnight, and was spending the Christmas holiday with him at the nearby hill resort of Khandala:[65] 'There is a steep jungly hill up behind the house, and Daddy and I walked up there yesterday and looked at the view. But we were not talking about the view, we were talking about our little girls, and wondering if they were having a happy New Year's Day and what they were doing.'

Helen's feelings for her absent daughters shines through her letters. 'Do you know what Pat's favourite story is just now?' she asked Janet on the sixteenth January 1903, 'It's about a Dad and a Maam that hadn't any children, and then a wee girlie came, and they called her Janet, and then another wee girlie came and they called her Day, and then a wee boy came and they called him James Patrick, and then *another* wee boy came and they called him Robin.'

This was a reassuring letter for Janet to receive. It stressed the essential unity of the family, not their actual disunity, and it also showed Pat as thinking about his sisters, not just receiving all the attention of their mother. Helen was often to write of the interest of Pat and Rob in pictures and stories of Janet and Day; it was a sound instinct on her part to try to keep possible jealousies to a minimum.

Helen's letters take the reader into the world of her nursery. For most mothers the nursery stage does not last long, and is soon displaced by the reality of large and growing children. In Helen's case the fleeting world is preserved, and for those who have been through the experience of the daily care of young children, her accounts spark off memories – memories of exhaustion, repetitive routine, constant questions, and the emotions in the children of delight and despair and rage.

When they first arrived in Bombay, Helen reported,[66] Pat was very cross. He was not very well and had got rather disobedient on board ship. He would grin at Ayah when she wanted to kiss him, and 'as poor Ayah is just in raptures about seeing her rajah again she wants to kiss him pretty often.' Rob, however, took to Ayah straight away. 'He never minded her giving him his tub or anything. The only thing that makes him a little cross is that he wants her to walk about with him, and she, being new to him, finds him so heavy she has to sit down pretty often. But he is very fond of her and sometimes gives her one of his gaping kisses.'

The day after that letter Helen met Rob in the Laboratory gardens with Ayah. 'I offered to take him from Ayah, but no, the wee roguey turned his head away, and would not come. He sends you a wee wet kiss,' Helen wrote to Day, 'and Pat sends a kiss and your own Da and Mother send you a hundred.'

Helen apologised[67] for not having painted the pictures in her first few letters. They were simply pencil drawings. 'By next week', she said, 'I hope to unpack the big box, and get it out so you will have to think of me as diving into a big box, and getting out dusters and tablecloths and books and photographs and last, but not least, my bookbinding press.' This may have been a hint of more books to follow, to be sent to Janet and Day. It is not known if she sent any, which she illustrated and bound, just for their use. No such book survives today. In the middle of 1903, however, she was to work on *The Story of Little Degchie Head* and it would be published in October of that year.

As they settled down in Bombay at the beginning of 1903, after their brief Christmas holiday in Khandala, Helen and Will and the baby slept in one room in their bungalow and Pat and Ayah shared another. After Helen had been back in Bombay for a fortnight came that milestone which may mean nothing to some readers, but which is of the utmost significance to any mother. Helen reported:[68] 'Baby is beginning to sleep right through the night now. He gets his last supper at about 11 then does not wake again till nearly six, but when he does he is so hungry.' This comment, in January 1903, meant that Helen, who was breast feeding Rob, had been through seven months of continuously broken nights. Nowadays, with the fashion of giving even very young babies cereal, they tend – mercifully – to sleep through the night a good deal earlier than seven months.

If Helen's nights became more restful, her days grew busier and busier. Pat was three years old, and exceptionally demanding. He was not a clinging or insecure child. His problem was excessive curiosity and a highly developed sense of mischief. He was completely carefree – and very endearing. A personality like that meant that he had to be watched every minute of the day. Rob, in contrast, was wise and careful; from babyhood Helen recognised in him a streak of common sense which was a relief after Pat's wildness.

A child such as Pat could have been bullied into submission, but this was not Helen's way. Here is her description of how she got him dressed in the mornings:[69]

I am sure you would laugh if you could see the way I dress Pat every morning. As soon as I get off his pyjamas, off he scurries. Then I get his little vest, and run after him and we have a bargain that when he is caught he must stand still till he gets it on. Then off he scoots again, while I get his wee bodice, and I chase him with that till I catch him. Then he must stand still again till that is put on, and then off again, till I catch him with his breeks. Then comes a frock, then shoes, and then his red jacket – 'my pocket coat' as he calls it – for it has been very cold in the mornings. Then he only needs his topi – such a dirty topi it is now – and then I dress myself as fast as I can and collect all the crusts and plantain skins that are left from chota hazri.' These remains from their early morning tea and fruit were then taken by Helen and Pat to the stables and fed to their two horses, Cuddy and Bob.

Observing Helen dealing with Pat in this permissive way – and clearly not resenting him – it might be thought that here was a relaxed and happy young mother, enjoying the company of a lively child. The truth was more complex. When Helen had arrived back in Bombay at Christmas 1902 she had found Will facing a crisis in his career. The month before there had been nineteen deaths at Mulkowal in the Punjab following the use of plague prophylactic prepared at the Laboratory. Had there been any lapse in the purity of the preparation? If there had, was this the fault of Will, the Superintendent, or of Haffkine, the Director? Haffkine was responsible for the method and principle of the process; Will for carrying it out. A Commission of Enquiry was set up. On its findings would depend Will's future. If it were to find him guilty, it would be likely that he would have to leave the Indian Medical Service, and that he would then have difficulty finding a job elsewhere.

The surprising thing is that with all this anxiety, Helen's marriage does not seem to have come under strain. Haffkine was so deeply affected by the difficulties caused by the disaster and the enquiry that eventually he became far from normal in his behaviour. Will, however, is shown in the evidence[70] preserved in the India Office Library in London to have remained rational and courteous in all his dealings. All witnesses combine to emphasise that the marriage of Helen and Will was an exceptionally happy one. Will's neice Craigie, who visited them in India a few years later, called it one of the happiest she had ever known.[25]

Helen's letters show no sign of strain. There was no jealousy between the two boys. Pat was unthinking in his actions, but he did not go in for sulks or tantrums. There are references to Will being tired and occasionally suffering from headaches, but he was there with the family on outings to the Bombay zoo, or the Governor's Sands or to Vehar for picnics. He was also very much in evidence laughing at Pat's antics, and conspicuous in his tolerance of them.

The evidence is that Helen and Will were both able to separate their anxieties about Will's position from their family life. They were not so insecure that they had to take out their anxieties on those around them. This must have needed considerable inner assurance and strength. Both had enjoyed happy childhoods. Helen may have been particularly helped by the example of her father in his triumph over the loss of his money in his late middle age. Their religion was a comfort to them. Helen, in particular, was completely powerless; all she could do to affect the outcome of the Enquiry was pray. It is noticeable that as the years passed she became more and more fatalistic in her attitude to the future. 'If God wills', became her approach – an attitude both very Indian and at the same time Calvinist.

Helen must have needed all her inner strength to get through those days. She was presumably not yet fully recovered from Rob's birth and she was still breast-feeding him; she missed her two daughters in Edinburgh; Pat was running round the house cutting the leaves off plants with scissors, and unscrewing her sewing machine and pouring his milk on purpose onto the floor. His table manners, Helen wrote with moderation, left a lot to be desired. He was a 'plowterer,' who enjoyed putting his hands in his food and spreading it about. He was given his own small table and chair and left to himself. Helen found this more satisfactory than having him on her knee, when she got covered in his food as well.[71]

Pat had no idea that mid-day rests were designed to give the mother a rest as much as – or even more than – the child. He always wanted a good jump-about on his bed before he settled down. As Helen wrote to Day:[72]

Do you remember how you used to love to jump on the bed? Well, Pat's in a spring bed here and he just loves to jump on it. At about half past twelve I say "Time for bed sonny" and he says 'I want to jump a little first, maam'. So I say "Yes, you can jump for a few minutes." Then he says 'I want you to see me, maam' and I say "All right, Baby, come, and we'll see big fella jumping" or else I say "I'll come in a minute, just wait till I change my shoes and then I'll bring Baby" for I find I don't get nearly so tired standing with Baby in my arms if I wear a pair of shoes with no heels. Then we go to the nursery and Pat gets into his bed and jump, jump, jumps, and falls down and picks himself up and jumps again and Baby is just as delighted and jumps in my arms. Sometimes I lay the two little brothers side by side in bed and jolt them up and down saying "jiggy jiggy, jiggy jiggy, jog jog jog" and Baby thinks it is such fun he just laughs all over his wee face and he always rolls over and looks at Pat, just as if he wanted to say 'Isn't this fun?'

Even once he had been put down for his rest, Helen often had no peace. She sent home many stories of how Pat would throw all his bedclothes on the floor or get into the dirty clothes basket and throw everything out and play at houses inside it.[73] She must have been very relieved, most evenings, when his bathtime came, and she would hear his prayers and tell him a story, and finally settle him down for the night, tucked inside his mosquito net.

It is easy to understand why Helen had little social life at that time. She did, however, sometimes go out in the afternoon,[74] leaving the children with Ayah, and pay some calls. For this she would dress up in her best blue muslin dress and a grand hat. She would wear her second best shoes, because the path to the ghari was sand and sea shells which scuffed her best ones. She took a spare pair of shoes with her in a bag which her daughters had given her, and changed them, and her gloves, just before she arrived.

Helen was not comfortable in high society. In 1903 she and Will were invited to a large reception to meet the Duke and Duchess of Connaught who were visiting Bombay. 'I was so frightened that I would not be able to curtsey properly that I got another lady to show me how to do it the week before, and I practised before the looking glass. And I was so busy curtseying that I never saw the Duchess hold out her hand and so I missed a handshake.'[75]

Occasionally, however, she had to go out with Will to a dinner party. She described one in detail, held in November 1903.[76] It was held at the home of the Chief Justice of Bombay, Sir Lawrence Jenkins, who had been Chairman of the Committee of Enquiry into the Mulkowal Disaster; at that time he had delivered his report but it had still not been published. Helen, however, made no reference to the Mulkowal background lurking behind the dinner and told her daughters about the Jenkins' unusual household. It consisted of Sir Lawrence and Lady Jenkins and Lady Jenkins' pet monkeys. At the dinner table were twenty guests. There were pale yellow flowers and pale yellow table napkins. One guest, however, had to change his chair because it was about to collapse – it was ricketty from the monkeys playing on it, their hostess explained. When the guests got to the stage of eating ices, one of the monkeys (which were hooloos, a very black furry kind with white eye-brows, short legs and long arms) was brought in. It sat on the arm of the hostess's chair and she fed it with little spoonfuls of ice and talked to the guests about it. '"He's very fond of ice," she said, "but he likes hot pudding better – but you're too late for pudding today, aren't you dear? He and his sister come in evey day after lunch, and have such games in this room, they're not naughty but only very wild. No, she doesn't come to dinner, her manners are not good – No Hooloo, don't lick, put your tongue in. Salaam, make salaam, that's it. I have three but the little one is too sleepy to come in, you can't rouse him. This one is wakened to come in. Now dear, you must go to bed. Say goodnight. Kiss me. No, you must not hold on. Go with David, goodnight dear."'

As Helen commented, she and Will felt very rich when they reflected on what they had at home instead of hooloos.

Chapter Four

The Mulkowal Disaster

The Commission of Enquiry into the Mulkowal disaster, chaired by the Chief Justice of Bombay, Sir Lawrence Jenkins, contained two medical men – Lt. Col. Bomford, Principal of the Medical College of Calcutta, and Major Semple, Director of the Pasteur Institute, Kasauli. They heard evidence from all the people involved, including the I.M.S. doctor who had carried out the inoculations and the Indian compounder who had assisted him, and Will and other Laboratory staff who had prepared the batch in question. They reported relatively quickly to the Government of India; though in the way of official reports, it was not published in full till some four years later in 1907. The findings,[77] however, were communicated privately to Haffkine as Director of the Laboratory, and he refuted them vigorously. The Commission found that 'the contamination had in all probability been introduced into the fluid before the bottle was opened at Mulkowal'. This pinned the blame firmly on the laboratory rather than on the doctor in the field. The Commission went even further in apportioning blame, and accused Haffkine rather than Will. They criticised a new mass-production process Haffkine had devloped while Will was away in Scotland on his long leave in 1902. This involved leaving out carbolic acid which had hitherto been included as a defence against contamination – and relying on sterility. The commission commented that the carbolic acid 'was a valuable agent in restraining tetanus growth when added to plague prophylactic', and they therefore thought its omission a grave mistake.

Haffkine found this unacceptable and fought to overturn the verdict. From Will's evidence[78] it is clear that he felt carbolic ought to have been included and that he had earlier, on his return to India, argued against the new method: 'I expressed surprise to Mr Haffkine when I found that carbolic acid was to be omitted, but he argued that we had the sterilising process of heat. . . . Working with a big staff it is, in my opinion, impossible to work safely without carbolic. I think carbolic would have controlled the amount of contamination. . . . I think the change was a mistake under the circumstances.'

The evidence was the basis of a bitter divide between Will and Haffkine. But it was not only Will who gave evidence criticising the absence of carbolic acid: all the other medical staff at the laboratory also felt it should have been included. Not unnaturally, Haffkine began to feel he was up against a united front of the Indian Medical Service. Possibly he felt there were shades of the Dreyfus case about the affair. He was isolated both professionally and socially – professionally in that he was a bacteriologist and his colleagues were all doctors, and socially in that he was Jewish and a bachelor. His first language was Russian, but he was very much in the mainstream of European culture, speaking excellent French and German and enough Norwegian to translate a textbook on botany from Norwegian to German. He was extremely musical, played the violin and adored opera. His colleagues, by contrast, were Scots whose knowledge of French, German and opera were limited and whose relaxed conversation often centred on rugby football.

Helen and Will made no reference to any social relations with Haffkine in any of their letters to the children; in fact there is only one reference to the disaster which must have played such a large part in their lives. In December 1904[79] Helen referred to a lecture Will gave to the Industrial and Agricultural Exhibition. To her the significant thing was that Sir Lawrence Jenkins took the chair: 'You won't understand why that was so delightful,' she wrote, 'but he was the Chairman – no President – of the Commission that came down to find out why nineteen people who were inoculated in a village in the Punjab died of tetanus, so his introducing Father, when he was to lecture about inoculation, was just as good as saying that he knew who was to blame and it was not Father.' From those who did not understand the niceties of the division of responsibility within the laboratory Will had to endure comments such as that from one cheerful guest who arrived on his doorstep saying, 'Well, Bannerman, been killing off any more people recently?' As Janet recalled many years later with a degree of understatement: 'It was a very trying time for my father and mother.'[80]

While the inquiries were dragging on, relations within the laboratory were reaching breaking point. Haffkine soon ceased all personal communication with Will, and with other officers working in the laboratory, and instead wrote notes. There was an extraordinarily bitter quarrel with Captain W. Glen Liston – a close friend and respected colleague of Will Bannerman – over who owned some rats for experimenting.[81] Plague-free rats had to be caught in ships arriving from plague-free countries, and were always in short supply. Liston had made his own arrangements to get hold of some plague-free rats, but Haffkine thought they ought to be in the general pool. Notes began flying to and fro.

THE MULKOWAL DISASTER

Mr Haffkine, C.I.E.   13 May 1903
Sir,
May I have the thirteen rats which I had specially arranged to be sent
to me from a ship just out from England? They are to be used for
minimum lethal dose experiments.

W. Glen Liston.

On receipt of this note, wrote Haffkine in a long complaint about
Liston's conduct, 'I despatched the same messenger to the head clerk
to get the daily animal stock report and see what our stock of rats on
that day was; and while I was waiting for the report I received in suc-
cession the following notes:

Mr Haffkine, C.I.E.,
Sir,
I am waiting for the rats. May I have an answer to my note of this
morning?

W. Glen Liston.

Mr Haffkine, C.I.E.,
I am waiting for the rats. This is my third note this morning.

W. Glen Liston.

Liston ended up by claiming that a fortnight's observation had been
wasted through Haffkine's actions, and that his experiment had been
spoiled. Liston's final barb in the series of notes was to request a pen
for black ink – presumably for writing yet more notes.

There was another quarrel over which office Liston should work
in. Haffkine at one point refused to see Liston about the matter. Liston
sent an orderly back requesting an interview. Haffkine then takes up
the story:

When I reiterated my reply, Captain Liston sent me a slip of paper
asking to speak to me; then another asking to be informed at what
time of day I would see him; and then walked up briskly to the door,
gave three hammering knocks into it, and burst into the room,
saying: "I came to demand a reply to my question." I rang for the
orderly and asked him whether he had informed Captain Liston of
my being unable to see him. Before he had time to reply, Captain
Liston clenched his fists and shouted out: "I shall not leave the room
until you reply", and planted himself in the middle of the room. The
sepoy hurriedly left the room. I rang for him again and asked him to
call in a clerk. When the latter came, I ordered him to take down

Captain Liston's words.

It was quite apparent to the senior officers of the Indian Medical Service that normal relations within the laboratory had broken down. It was not as if Captain Liston's claims could be easily dismissed. He was a doctor and scientist of high repute, later to become Director of the Parel Laboratory and to run it with distinction from 1911 to 1923.

Haffkine accused Will, in a confidential report, of lukewarm support and adverse influence on junior members of the staff. Will defended himself[70] against those charges by pointing out to his superiors that Haffkine wrote the report after hearing the evidence that Will gave before the Commission of Inquiry into the Mulkowal Disaster. Will felt it necessary to write: 'I would request the Government would extend to me that protection which is accorded to all witnesses in a court of law against detrimental effects arising from evidence given by them.

An inquiry was set up into Haffkine's behaviour. In October 1903 an I.C.S. officer, the Honourable Mr E.L. Cappel C.I.E., was appointed to look into whether Mr Haffkine had locked Captain Liston out of his or the superintendent's room, whether he (Liston), was using the superintendent's room in evasion of orders, and whether there was any justification for Mr Haffkine's statement that Captain Liston's account of the incident was untrue and misleading.

The report[81] was complete within a few weeks and found against Mr Haffkine. 'There was no justification', it concluded, 'for the remark that Captain W.G. Liston's statement that he had been locked out of his room at the Plague Research Laboratory at Parel was an untrue and deliberately misleading one.' As Mr Cappel explained, it was admitted by all that relations became strained after the Mulkowal disaster and the inquiry into it; for many months Mr Haffkine had ceased all personal communication with his staff and at the same time he had required his express authority before any changes could be made. 'This order', said Mr Cappel, 'led to the most trivial details of business as well as more important matters, being thereafter settled, not verbally, as they should have been amongst a staff working together in one building, but by correspondence. This correspondence moreover assumed a distinctly hostile tone on both sides, and must have entailed a great waste of time and efficiency.'

It was not a situation which could be allowed to continue. Will had already asked if he could be posted back to his original base of Madras; Captain Liston was prepared to move to the Central Provinces. But transfers of this kind could not be arranged overnight. While the administrators shuffled their papers, Mr Haffkine and Will and the rest of the Laboratory staff sweated it out, communicating only by note.

Will's professional position was not his only anxiety: he was also worried about the health of his children. By the end of August 1903, when Rob was fourteen months old, he developed a kind of glandular fever.[82]

> All his poor little neck is lump with hard glands, some that seem to be sore, and some that he does not mind us touching, and we suppose that he has something the same in his throat for he seems to have so much pain when he swallows, and Ayah has to feed him by force, and he just cries and cries till sometimes he makes himself sick. You would almost have laughed if you could have seen us the other night: Ayah offering him soup, I offering him a rusk, and Dad up at three in the morning cooking away at his Nestle's food, and poor baby refusing everything, and yet not able to sleep for hunger.

They decided to take the sick child away from the heat of Bombay, so Helen set off with the two children, and presumably also Ayah and one or two of the servants, for the not too distant hill station of Khandala. When Will joined them there for the weekend he was able to write home that,[83] 'Rob is quite on the mend now, and getting fatter every day. I found him sitting up and smiling, and quite a different boy from the pinched wee thing I had left two days before. God had been very good to us in giving us back our wee lad that we prayed so much about.'

At the same time, Helen and Will had the anxiety of hearing that both Janet and Day were ill in Edinburgh with scarlet fever. Their father wrote to them:[84] 'We were so glad to get your postcard last mail but still more glad were we when on Monday evening arrived the telegram to say you were well and up. That night you may be sure Father and Mother gave thanks for "goodness and mercy" and felt very much as though they had been led into green pastures and beside still waters. Please thank Ata for sending that telegram.'

Helen was also ill in August 1903. She had a fever which was possibly malaria. Both children were rather cross. Pat had what was described as a sore tummy and was given quinine and castor oil and chemical food (an iron tonic). He objected – unusually for him – when she took Rob on her knee at the piano in the drawing room. 'Some days ago', she wrote,[85] 'I was afraid Pat was going to be really ill, and would have to be kept in bed, and as I have a little fever myself, I did not know how I was going to keep him happy but I am glad to say he is much better, and so hungry that Dad had to say "No more to eat just now" at breakfast and at tiffin,' (tiffin being Hindustani for a light lunch).

As they got over their illnesses, their normal life at Parel resumed. It was the rainy season now, and sometimes it was so wet that Pat could not get out. Eventually Helen let him run out in the rain with nothing on for a few minutes, just to enjoy all the water.[86] 'He ran about and frolicked and came in just running with water from head to foot. It was really like a bath it was so wet.' When their clothes got wet it was a struggle to dry them, the air was so moist. They had to be dried over charcoal burners, or 'siggris', and even then they sometimes went mouldy. In the middle of August Helen and Will set off through the downpour in their carriage to a wedding:[87]

> For ever so far the street was just like a river and at last we actually came to a place where the children were regularly bathing by the roadside, and the ones that were sitting down were covered up to their waists, and one child, who was leaning back, was in up to his armpits! The water was right over the tyres of the wheels and you could not see where the foot pavement ended and the road began. And all the time it poured, poured, poured, so that there was not one dry minute the whole day. However, we enjoyed it very much, and as there was a porch both at the Church and at the Wilson College House it was only running from this house to the ghari and back that we got a little wet.

As the weather improved there were evening strolls for Will and Helen.[88] There was a big tank, or artificial lake, behind the laboratory, and they would go up there to watch the water plants being cleared. One evening they saw a man in a boat planting something in the water. Will asked what he was doing and he told them he was planting singara, the fruit of which is roasted and eaten. This is a kind of water chestnut, and Helen, with the attention to detail which characterised her, reported that he paid 250 rupees to the government to be able to grow this crop in this Government tank.

The month or two after the monsoon was over were clearly a pleasant time of year in Bombay, unlike the month or two before it broke. In September they went off to the nearby resort of Vehar, which supplied Bombay with water. It was quite an undertaking:[89] 'We went by train to a station called Bandup (you must pronounce it "Bun-doop") and then walked over beautiful low grassy hills and under the big bridge for the water pipe and down to Vehar Lake, where boats were waiting for us and we rowed across to the other side where there was a biggish bungalow – at least it was big enough to hold us all.' They took with them five servants and twelve porters to carry their luggage, besides which they had sent out two carts and two servants beforehand. 'But you see we had to take out even beds and tubs for some of the party and all the things we needed for food for four days.' This expedition was not for themselves alone; they went jointly with the family of Will's friend and colleague, Captain Liston.

By October the holiday was forgotten and Will was in bed with malaria.[90] As a result, he ordered the whole household to take quinine. To make sure that all the servants took their dose, Helen had them up to the dining room every evening after supper. They were shy about drinking in front of her, Helen explained, so, 'they stood just outside the door, and I saw a black hand come forward, and take a full glass, and in another minute it came back and handed back an empty glass. When the cook was told to come for his dose, he shouted back that he was quite well and did not need any medicine, but I said it was Master's order so he came meekly too and drank his glass, and I am glad to say they have none of them any more fever.'

When Rob was sixteen months, Helen proudly drew a picture[91] of him standing up by himself. As she admitted, it was not particularly good progress – many babies stand a few months earlier than that – but he had been so ill, and had not even been able to crawl for the previous three months. So they were all full of praise for him, and delighted to report that he was getting plump again. With his health had returned his good temper: 'He is such a sweet wee boy. When he comes in from a walk, I hear him in the nursery saying "Mum, Mum" and as soon as Ayah puts him down he starts to crawl to me as fast as ever he can. He always thinks I am in my bedroom and if I am in the dressing room he will crawl past without noticing me, he is in such a hurry to get to the next room. But if I speak he turns to me with a roguish wee smile and come tumbling over his own little arms in his haste and he is not content till I have picked him up and hugged and kissed him.'

By November Rob was staggering across the room. Pat meanwhile was also progressing – to letting down tyres of his father's bicycle.[92] 'Was that you Pat?' he was asked. 'I don't sink so.' 'Think a little,' said Helen, 'You know Jesus does not like us to tell lies, so think and little and then tell me.' So he thought a little and then said 'Yes, I think it was me.' Helen's approach to parenthood can be judged from the fact she did not scold Pat for being naughty, but praised him for his honesty. By her choice of words she also defused a possible confrontation. If her second question had been the standard: 'Well, did you, or didn't you?' Pat would have had no get-out. By the phrase she used, however, she offered him a way of telling the truth without appearing to climb down. This bears all the marks of a person skilled at personal relations, and adept at dealing with small children.

Despite her preoccupation with Pat and Rob, she still made time for her next book, doubtless partly for Janet and Day and perhaps also for a wider audience. This was *The Story of Little Degchie Head*, published by James Nisbet and Co. Ltd. in October 1903. Helen was still coy about parading her name, and it appeared as 'by the author of *Little Black Mingo* and *Little Black Black Quibba*'. *Little Black Sambo*, not being a Nisbet publication, was ignored.

On the cover was a picture of the heroine, though not in colour, and the book was subtitled 'An Awful Warning To Bad Babas'. The subtitle is the clue to the book. Helen's previous tales had been conspicuous for their lack of a moral precepts or advice on how children should behave. In this book Helen poked fun at the 'awful warning' books which were so common and so popular in her day by offering a tale which was so improbable that not even the most credulous child could take it seriously.

The book shows, as *The Scotsman* of 12 October 1903 put it, 'the terrible punishment that befel a naughty little girl who was too fond of poking the fire'. It is an improbable and comic moral tale rather in the genre of *Struwwelpeter*, and received an appreciative review in the *Sind Gazette* of 18 December 1903:

This differs from its predecessors in that the heroine, Little Degchie-Head, is not black but white and her name is Mary. While disobediently poking a fire in the cookhouse she gets her head burnt off. This cook, for fear as we are left to surmise, of that bugbear of all native servants, a Police enquiry, promptly repairs the damage by clapping upon the vacant place that utensil of his trade from which Mary derives her name in the story, and having decorated it, *secundum artem*, with a nose, mouth and eyes, he sends her back to her parents. Mrs Bannerman is too skilful a story teller to offer any explanation of the success of the imposture. Children do not want such matters explained. It is assumed that nobody knew, and the inconvenience and shame that Mary suffered in evading observation are narrated with historic simplicity. Tears and laughter will play at see-saw while this part of the tale is being told. But joy comes on Christmas Day, for Santa Claus, after some natural perturbation at the strange creature which he finds in Mary's bed, draws a beautiful doll's head from his wallet and puts it into her stocking. By far the happiest part of her toilet next morning is the substitution of blue eyes and golden hair for the hateful degchie. Nothing even in *Little Black Sambo* equals the comic absurdity of the picture which shows the headless Mary standing before the looking glass so that she may see to put the gum properly on her neck before fixing the new head in its place. needless to say, Mary lives happily ever after and never wants to poke fires any more.

THE MULKOWAL DISASTER

As that review points out, this is the first of Helen's books to depart from her imaginary jungle world. The setting is a British household in India at the turn of the century. The pictures of the mother and the father and the Indian cook are similar to Helen's drawings of herself and Will and her cook in her letters. In both, Helen is shown with a long skirt, a high-necked blouse, and hair piled on top of her head. Will and the father in the book are both shown as large, with drooping moustaches. Though the setting is real, the story is fantasy of the most improbable sort; but doubtless it appealed to children in the days when babies arrived in the doctor's bag or by stork, and when moral tales were packed with children who starved to death when they refused to eat their dinner, or blew away in a high wind, or drowned when they did not look where they were going. The story has a macabre side to it; but that is to take it seriously. It was nothing like so ghoulish as the widely read *Struwwelpeter*,[93] the English version of which was published in 1848. In this the foolish Harriet had been warned not to play with matches, but of course she did:

> And see, Oh! What a dreadful thing!
> The fire has caught her apron-string;
> Her apron burns, her arms, her hair,
> She burns all over everywhere . . .
> So she burnt, with all her clothes,
> And arms and hands, and eyes and nose,
> Till she had nothing more to lose
> Except her little scarlet shoes
> And nothing else but these were found
> Among her ashes on the ground.

Helen's heroes and heroines always managed to escape their fate through their own cleverness; Heinrich Hoffman's children show not a spark of intelligence and are defeated by bogeymen – as for example Little Suck-a-Thumb and the great long red-legged scissor man:

> Snip! Snap! Snip! the scissors go
> And Conrad cries out Oh! Oh! Oh!
> Snip! Snap! Snip! They go so fast
> That both his thumbs are off at last

In contrast, Helen's heroine Mary has successfully learnt her lesson by the end of the book, and, as the book puts it in its last line: 'that is how her head has never been burnt off again'.

Psychoanalysts such as Dr Marjorie McDonald, who discusses the book in her article *Little Black Sambo* in *The Psycho-Analytic Study of the*

Child,[4] sees the story as being about the guilt that follows playing with exciting forbidden fires and the ensuing castration. The child's head however, was burnt off; some might think this castration comparable to the proverbial operation which was successful though the patient died.

The book was published in the U.S.A. by Stokes in 1904, and was included in *The Jumbo Sambo* volume which was published in America in 1942. It was not, however, included in the boxed set of Bannerman books produced by Chatto and Windus in 1972. It lacks the timelessness of those of Helen's books which are set in her imaginary jungle world. Perhaps because it was a take-off of a Victorian type of book, it now appears exceptionally dated.

In the real world of the laboratory, meanwhile, Haffkine had still not accepted the findings of the Committee of Inquiry into the Mulkowal disaster. Throughout 1903 he had pressed on with experiments to show that including carbolic in the vaccine was irrelevant and that his new method was less liable to contamination than the old because it involved less handling. He demonstrated that his vaccine was made totally sterile by heat. Such sterile vaccine is in fact what is used today, without antiseptic in it; but the argument of Will and his colleagues was that, in the light of the techniques of the day, and the comparatively untrained staff available, total sterility was an unachievable ideal. Those differences of approach were fundamental and irreconcilable. Will was relieved when a transfer back to Madras came through on 26 November 1903 and he was told to take up the appointment of Superintendant of the King Institute of Preventative Medicine on 10 December 1903.

Helen and Will and the children were on holiday at Mahableshwar when the news of the transfer arrived. They interrupted their holiday and left the next day for Bombay to pack up all their things. Inevitably they had gathered a lot of belongings in their time in Bombay and felt they could not take them all to Madras. A large rocking horse was sent to the Scottish Orphanage and unwanted toys were distributed to the eight children of the servants. They lined up – apart from the sweeper's children who, Helen was sad to see, stood to the side – and were allowed to choose one toy in turn till they all got three each.[94]

Helen gave no indication in her letters of any regret at leaving Bombay. They arrived in Madras on schedule and stayed at the Connemara Hotel. After a week they moved into a house in St Thomas' Mount, a hilly district some eight miles south of the city. Their baggage from Bombay and some new furniture they had bought in Madras was due to arrive that same day.[95] By nightfall nothing had come. All that was in the house were two chairs and a table, a little china and a box of stores sent over by the wife of a colleague of Will's,

THE MULKOWAL DISASTER

Mrs King.

The boys were bathed in a basin and two mats, or 'resais', were laid on the floor for them. No one was worried about the discomfort: what did bother Helen and Will was the lack of protection from mosquitoes. Will went out in the dark to see if he could hurry anything along. He met the cart trying to deliver their new furniture, quite lost, and guided it home. Very shortly, both boys were tucked up into one of the new beds, with Pat's feet on Rob's head, and curtains over the mosquito-net poles. Helen and Will relaxed and sat down at last to their first dinner in their new house.[96] Helen's chair collapsed underneath her. She commented wryly that, when she tasted the food, she wished it had been the table which had collapsed.

Helen disliked what her new cook offered. All the food was flavoured with kerosene and sometimes the porridge was black from using a dirty cooking pot. Until the plate and silver were unpacked and sorted out, the vegetables were served in soup plates; Helen did not mind that nearly so much as the 'queer colour' of all the food. As, there is no reference to the dismissal of the cook, it seems that Helen either got used to his style or ceased to notice what she was eating.

There were two batteries of artillery near the house and one regiment of Indian artillery.[97] The Bannerman's day was punctuated by bugle calls, and like people living near a railway, they all came to live by the noises they heard at regular intervals. As they settled in, Helen had time once again to enjoy playing with Pat around his bedtime:[98]

After we have had our bit of chapter – this would be a Bible reading and he has said his prayers, and I have dressed for dinner, I sit in a chair and shut my eyes, and he creeps up softly. Then I open my eyes and I say: "Who are you?" – No answer. "Who are you?" – No answer. Very loud – "Who are you? Can you speak? Oh I know you, you are white and you've got pink eyes and you won't speak when you're spoken to, you're a ghost. But I'll tickle you, tickle you, tickle you." Then I lean forward and try to tickle him, but he always shrieks with joy and runs away and I sink back in my chair and pretend to go to sleep again. He thinks this great fun and we do it over and over again till the trumpet at the mess close by begins to blow "Puddings and pies for officer's wives" and then off he goes to bed. That trumpet is always the sign for him to go to bed at night and he has another sign for the middle of the day, for a gun always fires at 12 o'clock and then I send him off for his midday sleep.

There were by now games which Rob could join in, and the house echoed to shrieks of gleeful fear when they got down to the serious game of 'tigers'.[98]

They turn down two of the cane chairs in the drawing room so that the arms and backs make a den and then they creep inside and roar and growl. Baby can make a tremendous noise when he roars. Then Pat changes his mind and turns into a "ticket master" who stands between the legs of the chair and gives out tickets for all the people who want to travel, and then Baby usually comes out of his den and runs about and tumbles down in fun and they make a great noise and laugh a great deal.

After some years of this, one can perhaps understand the custom of even doting mothers sending quite young children to boarding school. All the evidence is, however, that Helen's principles in bringing up her children were to leave them to find things out for themselves and to restrict them as little as possible. She even preferred them to read for themselves as soon as they could. If they were always being read to, she felt, they had less incentive to learn to read.

At Christmas they set off to Chingleput to spend the holiday with their old friends the Andrews, who ran a school there for Indian girls. On Christmas Day[99] they went to a service in a village called Vallam which was gathered together from several small villages. As Helen explained: 'the Hindus would not give the Christians work, so Mr Andrew gathered them into a little Christian village of their own and they are going on very well.' Mr Andrew preached in Tamil on the text 'A Saviour is born' and the congregation sat on the floor and listened earnestly with 'such nice happy faces.' Helen went on in a way that seems very dated to us today: 'Perhaps it was my fancy, but the poor heathen people who were standing outside looking in at the windows had a sort of hungry longing look compared to the happy Christmas people inside.'

Helen and Will then left the two boys with the Andrews and went to Trinchinopoly for two days to visit their friends the Bonds[100] – the same Mrs Bond who had taken the manuscript of *The Story of Little Black Sambo* to London. Clearly there was no ill-feeling over the loss of the copyright; there are a number of affectionate references in the letters to the Bond children, Mary and Bobby. Like most of their friends, the Bonds seem to have been Scots; Will refers to the Bonds going on leave and the possibility of Janet and Day meeting them again. The best laid plans, however, as Robert Burns had good cause to know, 'gang aft agley'. Instead of arriving back in Chingleput on the Thursday their train from Trinchinopoly was delayed by floods and they did not arrive till Saturday. Helen drew a graphic picture[101] of the train almost surrounded by water; it had to go back to Trinchinopoly and then get to Chingleput by a much longer route.

Back at Chingleput, Helen wrote, they were sitting on the veran-dah when some visitors arrived:[102]

"Who are they?" said Dad, but I had guessed so I jumped up and said "Oh, Danakoti! How do you do". Helen then explained that Danakoti 'was once a poor little village girl, who did not know how to read or write and had only a ragged little frock to wear, but Mr Andrew thought she would learn well and be able to teach others about Jesus, if she went to school, and pay for her till she had finished learning. And when she grew up she married a teacher and now they live not far from Chingleput and they have a little boy and a little girl. The little boy is a little younger than Pat and the little girl is a year old. "And what are their names?" said I. "This one," said Danakoti in Tamil, "is Anba Bannerman" – "and the little girl?" – "She is Jessie Bannerman". Then Mr Andrew explained that Anba means 'love' in Tamil. "Can you guess", Helen asked her daughters staying with Ata in Edinburgh "who they were called Bannerman after?"

Janet and Day would have known that it was not Helen but Ata. Ata's visit to Madras, when she had undertaken to pay for Danakoti's education, had been in 1893, eleven years previously, and here was Danakoti, hearing that Helen and Will were visiting Chingleput and coming with her children and her brother to see them. 'They looked so happy,' Helen went on, 'and Danakoti and her brother asked how Ata was and how the two little girls at home were, and they thought it very nice, when they heard that they were with Miss Bannerman. And they asked us to tell Ata they had not forgotten her, and they prayed to God to bless her.'

Helen then asked Janet and Day whether they would like to take on the responsibility for paying for the education of a girl at the Chingle-put mission school. She and Will would pay the appropriate amount each month and Janet and Day would be expected to write to the girl who they sponsored and take an interest in her. Janet and Day wrote back to say they would like to do so, and two months later, when Helen and Will were next at Chingleput, they chose a girl call Paran-jodhi, who said she was eight but who Mr Andrew thought was prob-ably six. 'I hope she will bring you much happiness', wrote Helen[103] 'and some of the greater blessings which God keeps for givers'.

In the middle of January 1904 the children's Ayah left, presumably to return to Bombay, and a new one arrived. Helen reported[104] that Rob liked the new Ayah, Ilanda, but loved to tease her. For a few days, both Ayahs were there, and Rob seems to have enjoyed all their atten-tions.

When he tumbles down of course he cries, so the old Ayah invented this way of stopping him. When he falls she pretends he is picking up pice – that is pennies – and she comes and begs for some and he is so much interested, pretending to give her pice, that he forgets all about the tumble. Then Ilanda comes and says "*Humku paisa do*", which means "Give me pice", but no, the wee rogue turns his back and waves her off and says "Nay, nay" and gives all his fun-fun pice to the old Ayah. And when he thinks she is getting too many he comes and hunts for one and pretends to put pice into my hand, but he won't ever give poor Ilanda one.

Each stage in Rob's development was lovingly reported. He was not quite talking but had a vocabulary of single words which grew every day. Sometimes, though, they were hard to recognise. Helen was puzzled one morning[105] when he pointed to the door of her room and said, 'sheen, sheen'; eventually she realised he was trying to say 'machine' and wanted to turn the handle of her Singer sewing machine. He often doubled his words so that, 'chocolate' for example, came out as 'lock, lock'. He was even sophisticated enough – at 20 months – to enjoy a verbal joke. He began to say words after Helen so she would say to him:

"Say sorry, Baby" – "Toddy"
"Say Pussy, Baby" – "Pooshee"
"Say mousie, Baby" – "Ma-shee"
"Say Doggie, Baby" – "Bow-wow"

"Wasn't that rather neat of him?" Helen asked. "And he knows it's a joke and he laughs so much. Now when we ask him to say doggie, he always says 'Bow-wow'."

She also sent home a discription in April, 1904 of how she spent her mornings:[106]

Even in the early mornings the sun is very hot now, but poor father just has to cycle to office through it. I am more fortunate, for we have a splendid Baobob tree in the compound; it is really as large in the stem as a little house, and though branches are rather leafless just now, the stem makes a delightful shady place. Here the boy puts me a little table, and I generally do the pictures for your letters, and write a good many of my letters or do some sewing or work the type-writer, because I want to learn to use it properly. When he comes in from his morning walk Pat joins me here, and after he and Baby and I have inspected the stables and given the horses their bread [still the same horses, incidentally; they had been brought in padded horse-boxes by train from Bombay] and Baby has said

"Ed-medshun" and the coachman has salaamed and said "very good sir", Baby goes off for his bath and Pat and I return to what we call our little garden.

In the evening, Rob used to have another bath and then come into the drawing room to play with his parents before they had dinner and he and Pat went to bed. Some of his play was quite elaborate.[107]

He pulls a cushion off one of the chairs and lies down and puts his head on it and says "Bow bow", holding up one wee finger. Now what do you suppose that means? Well it really means that he is pretending to go to sleep, and a dog is barking outside and disturbing him. So then I say "Doggie, don't say bow-wow, Baby's going to sleep," and Baby gives a little chuckle of satisfaction and says "Mow" and I say "Pussy, don't say Miaow, Baby's going to sleep," and then he chuckles as before and says "Tock" and I say "Boy, don't talk, Baby's going to sleep." Sometimes when he is really very sleepy I carry him in to his bed and sit down beside him, and go on saying these things over and over, then if he is not quite asleep and I stop, he says "Bow wow' in a sleepy voice and usually he drops asleep before I have sat long beside him.

Sometimes Helen's days were enlivened by a rare excitement such as a moonlight cow hunt.[108] She had brought some Eucharis lilies in pots from some people who were leaving India and was very proud of the way they brightened her bare brown garden. There were in fact 580 pots with a variety of plants and she had them arranged in rows and little round groups. One night some of the neighbours who had cows drove them in at the gate and next morning some two or three hundred of the pots had lost most of their foliage. Will arranged for their own cow to be tied up with a long rope, so that they could be sure she was innocent, and gave orders that if any other cows were seen they were to be taken to the pound. One evening Helen and Will happened to sit up later than usual. When Helen at last went to bed she heard a soft munching noise outside. She looked out in the moonlight and saw about a dozen cows. She called to Will, Will roused their Bearer in the back verandah and he roused the syces and another servant and the matey and they rushed out together and caught one cow and a calf and tied them up. These were sent to the pound, and from that time on there was no further trouble.

Another excitement, almost as rare, was going into Madras for some shopping.[109] By the end of April 1904, Helen was preparing to go to Kodai for a holiday to get away from the heat. They planned to take three of their servants with them – the Bearer, Poonoosawmy,

Ayah and a sweeper, and needed to buy blankets for them for the cold nights there. The heat of the shop almost rises off the page of Helen's description: 'Oh dear! How hot those blankets looked, in that hot shop, with the boy in his shirt sleeves and the electric punkah whirling over our heads.' Will arrived in the shop to help her. He had been at a function and wore his hot-weather full-dress uniform, with sword and belt and helmet, gloves and spurs. He must have broken out in a sweat even thinking about such a uniform.

A few days after this shopping trip, on 20 April, 1904, the steady continuity of Helen's life in Madras was broken. A telegram came for Will asking him to report to Bombay on 1 May to take charge of the plague laboratory. This was unexpected. Only eight days previously Will had taken up an additional appointment in Madras, that of Professor of Hygeine and Bacteriology at Madras Medical College. In addition to his research work he was looking forward to setting up his classes and teaching his subjects to the students, mostly Indian, who were coming forward for the courses at the college. What lay behind his transfer was that relations within the Bombay Plague laboratory had become intolerable and Haffkine had been relieved of his duties as Director. Haffkine left India almost immediately and carried on his campaign to clear his name in Europe; it was the start of many years of disappointment and frustration, as anyone who has had dealings with official enquiries will appreciate. Two further independent enquiries were set up as a result of his pressure, and the evidence from these and the original report of the Commission (which had still not been published) were sent for comment to the Lister Institute in London.

Meanwhile, in Madras, Will prepared to go to Bombay and take charge of the Laboratory, and Helen packed up their things for the holiday in Kodai for herself and her children. Will hoped to spend four or five days at Kodai himself, but could not take more, partly because of the tight shedule and partly because, as he explained to his daughters, he wanted to save up as much leave as possible to be able to go back to Edinburgh the following year on home leave. Helen's description of the journey in May 1904, and her picture,[110] shows that on this occasion she rode up the hills side-saddle on a pony. Ayah was carried in a canvas chair, holding Rob, and the sweeper was carried with Pat in another. Helen's picture shows Ayah reclining and holding a parasol over Rob's head – no idle luxury this. With the air so clear as they got up into the hills, European infants would burn quickly and seriously if they were unprotected. There were also, in addition to six porters for each canvas chair, some twenty-five porters for all their boxes and bags and bundles.

Will was only able to stay two days; by 6 May 1904 he was at work in the Laboratory in Bombay. His first act, explained in an official letter[111] dated ten days after he started work at Parel, was to change the method of manufacturing the vaccine. He reverted to the original method which included carbolic acid: The object that Mr Haffkine had in view in the manufacture of the 'new prophylactic' was to obtain a fluid with more dead microbes in a given bulk than formerly. He originally believed that by this means the size of the dose would be diminished, and that therefore a larger number of doses could be sent out in each bottle, and that

It could be manufactured with less apparatus and a smaller staff. It was with these ideas that he undertook to supply the Punjab with 70,000 doses a day by October 1902. Mr. Haffkine's original assumptions, however, proved incorrect when put in practice. He nevertheless continued to manufacture prophylactic on this principle, stating now that he believed the addition of young plague microbes to the material grown in the old way would increase the protective power of the prophylactic. He had, as in the previous instance, performed no experiments to prove whether this assumption was correct or not.

Apart from these considerations, however, I believe that there are other and graver reasons why the manufacture of this material should be discontinued. I believe that there is danger to those employed in the transference of live plague germs in large open pipettes from one flask to another (which is one of the operations in the process of manufacture of this new material), as it is impossible in this way for even the most skilful to avoid spilling the fluid containing live plague germs upon the work tables. Transference of the germ to the worker these circumstances is an almost certain sequel.

He went on to add that the men doing this work were not trained bacteriologists but British soldiers, assisted by Indian labourers.

Having changed the method by which the plague prophylactic was made, Will set out to try to persuade the public that it was safe. Naturally confidence had taken a severe knock. In the Punjab, where a big inoculation programme had been embarked on, 24,268 people had been inoculated in September 1902, and this had risen to 111,337 in October. Then had come Mulkowal and the programme had been abandoned. 'In the meanwhile', commented a Report on Plague in the Punjab 1902–3,[112] 'not only the people but many officials became distrustful of inoculation. It was common to find officials, who had formerly earnestly advocated the measure, declare that they could no longer do so, now they themselves so distrusted it that they would not consent to submit to the operation. It was thus that even after a supply of prophylactic prepared by the original method and subjected to additional tests as to its purity was obtained, it was only in those districts of which the officials enjoyed in an exceptional degree the confidence of the people or had managed to reassure themselves of the safety of the phrophylactic that the people came forward at all freely for inoculation. In no district, however, did the number of inoculations performed approach the number estimated, and in no large town were more than a few hundred people inoculated.'

Because of this crisis in confidence, the Government of India decided to clear the air and publish some information about the Mulkowal Disaster in time for an Industrial and Agricultural Exhibition which opened in Bombay on 26 December 1904. They issued a press communiqué[113] which sketched the background to the disaster. The Government of India gave full credit to Waldemar Haffkine for developing the plague vaccine but then pointed out that he had changed the method of manufacture on his own authority. Their communiqué gave a summary of the findings of the Commission of Inquiry and a summary of the conclusions of the Lister Institute in London.[114] The Lister Institute favoured including carbolic acid and added the rather ambiguous comment: 'In all probability the tetanus was at the time of inoculation in the fluid contained in the bottle,' but they went on, alluding to the evidence given by the doctor who had performed the inoculations, 'the fact that a bottle presumably tightly corked (vide Dr Elliot's evidence) should contain enough tetanus growth to destroy 19 people, and yet not be accompanied by sufficient smell to arouse the suspicion of Dr Elliot, who, according to his evidence, remembers smelling this particular bottle, is difficult to comprehend.'

The communiqué then went on to say that the method used in preparing the prophylactic was such that it was impossible for any germ to enter the fluid from outside. Carbolic acid was once again included and the purity depended, 'not upon chemical or bacteriological conditions but upon a mechanical device, the working of which will be publicly demonstrated at the Exhibition.' In an attempt to promote the vaccine Will gave lectures and demonstrations every evening at the Exhibition, missing his Christmas leave.[115]

Restoring public confidence, however, was a slow business and people were still dying – for lack of inoculation – from plague. Will and Helen's coachman, for example, came to them in great distress to tell them that his little son had died of it in the Plague hospital.[116] He had been to visit him in the afternoon and had brought back good news of him, but at about nine o'clock in the evening a telephone message had come from the hospital to say that he had died. 'I am very sorry for him', Helen wrote, 'for Sankar was the only remaining son.

THE MULKOWAL DISASTER

An elder brother died about a year ago. Poor Tukaram (that is the coachman's name) goes about looking so sad. He has only one big daughter now, I think.' Vaccination had been available to this coachman's family, but they had not taken advantage of it. Perhaps – who knows? – this family had been influenced by the gossip and bad publicity for the plague inoculation which had followed the Mulkowal disaster.

Chapter Five

In Their Mother's Pocket

While Will was establishing the new vaccine, using the old method of manufacture which included carbolic acid, Helen was enjoying the cool of Kodai with the children. When she and the boys arrived there from Madras in May 1904 they found various forgotten toys were still in their house, Abernyte, and the boys gleefully played with their sisters' tea set and immediately broke some of the cups. The cool weather meant that instead of being listless and lethargic, they were exceptionally energetic:[117] 'I wish you could see the wee brothers here', Helen wrote, 'In their warm red coats and hats we think they look just like wee Scotch laddies and they are so merry, and run about so actively that it is just a treat to see them.'

But the fun in Kodai, with walks and carriage trips and a large garden for the children to play in, only lasted for a month. By the middle of June 1904[118] Pat was seriously ill with scarlet fever: 'He lay in bed and would hardly speak at all, and cried miserably when we said "now it is time for your medicine" or "now you must drink your milk". And all the change he got was from lying in somebody's arms, he could not play, and could not talk, he could only listen to stories and hold a little elephant that I brought up with me in his hand.'

Rob was kept quite separate from Pat, to save him catching the infection. While Helen nursed Pat, Ayah took complete charge of Rob, and would bring him round the outside of the house each morning to wave to his mother and brother. Helen would wrap Pat up in a quilt and take him to the upstairs window of his bedroom:[119]

Pat drums with his wee fingers on the glass, and says, "Baby, baby", but I am sure Baby can't hear him, for his voice is rather weak. Then usually I pop Pat back into bed, and open the window, and call to Ayah, to know how she is, and how Baby is, and why he was making such an outcry in the early morning, and the answer is always the same: "Baby don't like put on clothes, wash face, Ma'am". And Baby says "Upee–Mummee" and Ayah pretends to throw him up to me, and I pretend to catch him, and he laughs and is quite merry. At first he used to cry to come to me, but now he understands that he can't, and only cries if he sees me in the garden.

68

It was some three weeks before Pat was up, even in his dressing gown, and another week before he could go out of doors, wrapped up in a blanket and pushed about in an ancient pram. All his clothes were sent to Bombay to be disinfected, so when he went out with his mother during his convalescence he wore his dressing gown and an old shawl round his head.

As he got better, he took to rolling down the hillside dressed like that, but his mother was thankful when he stopped, as the grass was long and she was afraid there might be snakes in it. After six weeks, it was thought to be safe for them all to be in contact again.[120] Rob came in and gave his mother a big hug and settled down on her knee, but when Ayah came to take Rob for his walk all she got from him after her weeks of care was: 'Go away'. Poor Ayah.

When he had been ill, Pat had been a difficult child to amuse. His mothers' pictures show train sets, fishing rods, scissors and paste and various other diversions. In addition to those, Helen had passed the time in telling him stories. Among these had been one which was to be published in the autumn of 1904 – *Pat and the Spider*. Alone among Helen's books, the hero is clearly her own child. Pat is named, and shown in the actual clothes he then wore – the sailor suit illustrated in the book is shown in a letter to Day on 15 August 1904. Those who are troubled by Helen's caricatures of black people should take a look at the caricatures of her own son. To caricature was simply her natural style of drawing; there was nothing racial about it.

Pat and the Spider appeared in time for Christmas 1904. It was published by Frederick Stokes and Co. in the U.S.A. the following year but was never particularly successful. It was included neither in the *Jumbo Sambo* published in the United States in 1942 nor in the boxed set issued by Chatto and Windus in 1972. The books selected for *Jumbo Sambo* were: *The Story of Little Black Sambo, Sambo and the Twins, The Story of Little Black Quasha, The Story of Little Black Bobtail, The Story of The Teasing Monkey* and *The Story of Little Kettlehead*. The boxed set by Chatto and Windus included: *The Story of Little Black Sambo, Sambo and the Twins, The Story of Little Black Quibba, The Story of Little Black Quasha*, and *The Story of Little White Squibba*). Like her previous three books (though unlike *The Story of Little Black Sambo*) there was no mention of Helen's name on the cover of *Pat and the Spider*. There was a picture of Pat on the outside printed in blue and white.

Pat and the Spider was, like Degchie Head, not set in Helen's particular jungle world, but in a strange country which had an equally puzzling geography. It had both brambles – as blackberries are known in Scotland – and bamboos. Apparently Janet and Day enjoyed reading it in Edinburgh, and Helen made a number of references to it in her letters at the time it came out. On 18 November 1904 she wrote to Janet: 'I am glad you like "Pat and the Spider". I am sorry to say Father had not had any time to put in any bit except "the Biter Bit" in the title, but I laugh and say "Yes I will with pleasure, said Pat" in his, because he is so fond of that bit. It is what Pat really says if you ask him to do anything'. This indicates just how far Helen's books were a family affair, arising out of her own experiences, rather than academic exercises written in a vacuum. Will apparently was in the habit of contributing something to each book, and in this case he provided the spiders for the illustrations. As he explained to Day on 19 November 1904: 'The only thing I had to do with it was to send two large jerry-mangalams to draw the spider from. Only the spider in the picture cannot be a jerrymangalam because they don't have any webs. But if you don't tell anybody that nobody will know and so it will be alright! Don't you like the poor tiger with its tail all twisting with fright at the spider? I like that and the green tiger best, I think.'

Helen also mentioned the book in her letter to Day of 18 November: 'Do you know what we call "Pat and the Spider"? We call it "Padder" because Baby called it that one day. He is very fond of it, and keeps asking, "Wa's date?" and pointing at things. His favourite picture is what he calls "Pit-Pat-poodee eating a bramble" but what I like best is where we get a bit farther on and he says in a solemn voice "Tiger coming" and then he always wants to hurry on to see the tiger.' Like *Little Degchie-Head* it is something of a moral tale, though the biter who was bit turns out to be one of the villains – a tiger who turns a poisoned green when he eats a spider. There is something of an air of science fiction about the story, for it involves Pat creeping through a bamboo stalk which makes him the same size as a small spider, and also the spider crawling through in the opposite direction and growing as large as a tiger.

In August 1904 Will joined Helen and their sons at Kodai for a brief holiday. He found Rob looking so well that he hardly recognised him, but Pat gave cause for some anxiety. As Pat recovered from his scarlet fever, he was not quite the carefree child he had been. Helen described,[121] in September 1904, how he was very much afraid of things. She admitted that this was partly her fault. She had said in his hearing at Kodai that a panther could easily get in at the downstairs nursery window. 'So for a while,' she reported, 'he would hardly cross the lobby alone.' However, she talked to him,

> about how Jesus takes care of his own children and we prayed about it and he got much braver. But at Vehar the other night the wind and rain were so strong we had to shut all the doors into the upstairs

verandah except one door to the north end, and we had to fasten the doors between our bedroom (the little boys and mine) and the sitting-room, and then the only way of getting from one room to the other was along the outside verandah, which was very dark. So the first night when I told Pat to run round and get his supper he did not want to go, and begged me to come too. "Oh" said I "you're not a coward now, you know who'll take care of you. Run along, and show me how brave you can be." So off he went, and while I was calling words of encouragement, thinking he was lingering just outside, a cheery little voice halloed to me, through the door. "I'm here mother. Weren't I a brave boy?" So my next night, when he had finished supper (I happened to be in the sitting room) he shouted "I'm going to bed. I'll show you how brave I am," and dashed out of the door. But alas! Poor boy in the dark he did not see a long arm chair and the next minute he came back howling having just knocked his eye on the shoulder of a chair. It was slightly cut at the outside corner and next day it was swollen and black and blue.

Three weeks later Pat was still clinging to Helen. He was now four, almost five, and in a letter of 7 October 1904 Helen gives an example of a certain degree of regression. Rob meanwhile was at the stage when he would not eat when Helen was there. As Helen said of Rob: 'I say he would like to live in my pocket'. Pat after his scarlet fever, was much the same: 'Today, when Pat fell down the back stairs from the nursery bath room and cut his head, when I cuddled and petted him, he said "Baby and me are dust the same, sometimes I like to live in your pocket too."'

Rob's devotion to Helen at this time was such that she resorted to various ruses to ensure that he took his food from ayah:

The other day, right in the hottest part of the day I was busy putting Pat to sleep, and when I got him over (in the hammock) I was surprised not to hear Baby's voice anywhere. So I looked into every one of the seven rooms in this house – they have names painted above the doors, Aden, Zanzibar, Kandahar, Sibi, Quetta, Kohat and No. 7 which is the drawing room – and Baby was not in any of them. 'Where *can* he be?' said I to myself – 'Is he in the go-downs?' So I went to the drawing room, which has windows to the back and here was my wee roguey, sitting in the swing and being swung to and fro in the thick thick shade of an old mango tree. (Only I have made one mistake [in my picture] I have forgotten his topi which he had on, otherwise I'd have had to call Ayah to get it.) I only smiled to Ayah, and waved my hand, for if Baby hears my voice he shouts at once. "I want to come to you, Mum. I don't want Ayah" and he is so fond of me that nothing Ayah can offer him will coax him to stay with her. The only way I can get him to go for his tiffin is to pretend I want to eat it. I go along the verandah, and I call "Boy, don't give Baby any tiffin. Give *me* tiffin today." Then Baby runs past me on his sturdy wee legs and calls "Boy, bring *my* tiffin!" and he is so busy getting it from the boy that he does not notice me slip away to my room.

Helen was worried about the boys falling off the verandah.[122] It was raised eight steps from the ground and had a horizontal bar just at the level of Rob's head. She was frightened that he would run onto the verandah and straight over the edge. He was not the least afraid of falling, but would swing round on the pillars in a way that made Helen's hair creep. He was careful about the steps, however, and would sit down, like an old man, if they were steep. Then he got covered in insects which had a painful sting. At certain times of the year these 'poochies' as Helen called them, were all over the house – on the dinner table, on the chairs, on the towels, in the bath. If they had not had mosquito curtains round them, Helen said, they would have been in the beds too. Helen must have asked their landlords – the Public Works Department – to do something about the verandah, for a month later she described[123] the railing they put up all the way round the house. By then, Helen reported, the boys were flying up and down the verandah, pretending to be trains or birds or tigers, and the new railing made it much safer for them.

While writing about what the boys were up to, Helen always made a point of bringing Janet and Day into her letters as much as possible. She thanked[124] them for some heather they had sent. She had it in her drawing room in a green glass and often sniffed it and thought of, 'two girls who are tramping about among miles and miles of it and breathing that same smell and getting all their feet dusty with the sweet yellow pollen.' Her daughters were at that time on holiday in Aviemore, and Helen added: 'And then I think I'd change all the heather in the world for a peep of those two happy little girls.'

·When Janet's eleventh birthday came round on 13 October 1904, Helen described[125] how she and Will and Captain Liston drank her health at dinner.

Father made a speech, beginning "Lady and gentlemen" then I broke in "Eleven years ago, I was pacing the platform of a little wayside station."

"Exactly so" said Father.

"When a telegram was handed to me which informed me that I

was now the proud father of a fascinating daughter." And here the speech broke off abruptly, for Father began to tell us in colloquial language that he had been reminded of that telegram just the other day by a native clerk, whom he met again at Guindy. He was on the platform when Father got the telegram "And 'Sir'" he said to me 'do you remember you were so pleased that you gave a rupee to the juggler on the platform?'"

So that was how the speech ended, then Captain Liston said "Health, long life and prosperity to Janet" and we all emptied our glasses.

Images of this kind are the cement of families; Helen was a master at recording them.

She also recorded[126] the reaction of her own son Rob to *Little Black Sambo*. At the age of two, his views were firm and his enthusiasm was not uncritical: 'He comes into my room and says "want to lie on your bed, read Bamboo, Mum." He calls Black Sambo "Bamboo". He is very fond of the blue trousers, but he won't be bothered with the middle of the book, so we generally jump from about the third tiger to the "cakes" as he calls them and in the last picture he always looks to see if all three have "spoons".' There is also a reference to the boys dipped in ink till they turn black, featured in Heinrich Hoffman's *Struwelpeter*.[93] Helen drew a picture of Pat and Rob dancing naked out in the monsoon rain. They were just as wet, she said,[127] and nearly as black as great Agrippa's little boys. As Selma Lanes has suggested, the picture of the 'little blackamoor' striding out with his umbrella could well have influenced Helen's drawing of her Little Black Sambo.

By November 1904, when he was two and a half, Rob was climbing on walls and drainage ditches as actively and dangerously as Pat.[128] There were a number of deep ditches in the laboratory gardens, some with cement walls. One, in particular, was in a very shady place. Helen used to sit there in the early mornings while the boys would climb and jump over them. 'Along side this ditch,' Helen wrote, 'is a narrow little channel down which the malis used to run water for the garden, but of course it is not used now. Baby is very fond of crossing the old ditch but till two days ago he had to have a hand – now he shakes us all off and says "Don' touch me, I step across all mysoff." (he doesn't really say myself but mysoff). He very nearly tumbles every time he does it, but as he never quite does, I have got used to his doing it now. Sometimes he and Pat get down in the ditch and pretend to be tigers or bears, but I am not very fond of letting them go in, for there are bushes growing at the bottom and lots of dead leaves, and there might easily be scorpions and centipedes among them. Baby is getting very big. Yesterday he said to me "I not wee boy mum, I great big 'trong boy" and it really is true. Sometimes I feel quite sorry for myself when I think of the four nice babies we have had and think that soon there won't be one left, they've all turned into big girls and boys.'

Rob had all his baby curls cut off by his father and Captain Liston[129] and was bought new shoes.[130] He was very proud of himself, but, as a letter of 16 December 1904 shows, he still had a long way to go before he was really as big as he thought:

Today in my tub I heard fearful howls – I could not think what was the matter, so I hurried out, and found Father trying to howl fearfully – oh what a silly mistake! I meant trying to comfort Baby who was howling fearfully, and would not tell why. But presently Ayah told me that Master Pat had given Baby a white chilly and poor baby had bitten it. So I made Ayah bring some butter and I put a lump into his mouth and after a while he began to cry not quite so hard. So then to distract him I said: "Come Baby I'll show you a picka". He did not stop crying but he began to look about, as if he wanted to see a picture, and I showed him this sheet. "There's naughty Baby" said he, and stopped crying altogether. "Look" said I, "There's Ayah coming along the verandah, she's just going to say "Come to bed now master Robert" and naughty Baby sees her and he's running out of the other door crying "Daddy I want you!" (That is what the little rogue really did. He was playing with me very merrily in the drawing room and suddenly he ran out of the room calling "Daddy I want you" and it was only when I saw Ayah coming along that I knew why.) "Naughty Baby running out anuvver door – saying Daddy, want you," said he, and then he gave a great guffaw of laughter and looked up at me with the tears sparkling on his cheeks and his poor wee nose and forehead all red and blotched but a beaming little grin spreading his mouth and showing his little teeth.

Pat, that December, 1904 had his first visit to church. Helen took him to a short prayer meeting in Bombay.[131] They went in by train, which Pat enjoyed a good deal more than the service. Helen thought he behaved quite well, though he said 'Mum' loudly twice and then, 'he began poking at my face with his naughty little fingers and I had to scold him energetically in a whisper and then he fell to kissing my hand and then he held the hymn book upside down, and studied it earnestly, so he disturbed nobody except me, and he did not worry me much'. Helen's comments seem remarkably mild. The nearest she got to criticism of the hyperactive Pat at this stage was to comment wistfully to Janet: 'I must say by the time you and Day were his age you were quieter.'

Helen and Will held certain church services at their house at Parel, and Helen played the harmonium. One day in that December,[132] Helen wanted to practice so she told Pat to go out with Ayah. He went a little way, then reappeared. She sent him away again and played on till it grew too dark to see. She then went on to the verandah and called out for Pat. A little voice answered 'Yes Mother' from right above her head. She looked around, and there was Pat perched on the roof.

"Come down, you rascal" she said.

"I climbed up the ladder" said Pat "and got on the roof, and when I were coming down again the ladder slipped, and began to wobble, so I just stayed up till you came out and called me".

And indeed the ladder, Helen found, was ready to slip at the lightest touch. It was a good thing, she reflected, that he sat down quietly and had not tried to come down or he could have been badly hurt. Helen's approach of letting her children work things out for themselves was beginning to pay off. And possibly this was a magical experience for a child who later turned out to be very musical.

Pat was not always sensible however; nor was he often quiet. He and Rob had wild games playing at being coachmen, sitting on Helen's book binding box and her trunk of spare china. At Christmas time, a pony arrived for them – 'my pony' as Pat called him, or 'dat donkey' as Rob put it less respectfully. They were taken out on it together by the syce, and on one occasion they all ended up – in a heap – with Ayah as well.[133]

That particular accident was probably more the fault of a passing car than of Pat, but it was strange that wherever Pat went, some sort of disaster followed. As Helen put it,[134] he devised new kinds of mischief every day. Pat tried to make holes in the bottom of some flower pots but as he tried to make them with a croquet mallet, they turned out rather large. Then he cut the heads off the sun flowers, and someone put a bit of hoop iron in Will's bed. He snipped the ends of his pyjamas with scissors and emptied the earth out of a favourite pot of his mother's. After a midday rest in his father's bed, alongside Helen, he dived headlong over the end of her bed, straight onto the tray of after-noon tea, scattering it everywhere. But the last straw was one day when Helen kissed him and noticed his hair was sticky. 'What have you been putting on your hair, Pat?' she asked. 'Plague prophylactic that I got at the laboratory.'

With the boys running in and out of the laboratory they had to be regularly inoculated against plague, and other diseases too.[135] Apart from pulling his arm away so that he had to be redone, Rob did not suffer, but when he was vaccinated against smallpox, Pat began: ' "I feel very sick." Father left Baby, Helen continued and ran to Pat and made him lie down on the floor and take a drink of water then he went back to Baby who stood steady on his high stool saying "I want Daddy to scratch my arm some more" and finished vaccinating him, and Baby did not feel in the least bit sick or shaky. I sat beside Pat and told him stories to keep him from thinking of the sickness and he put his legs up in the air but for a while he got greyer and greyer till he looked dreadful, then gradually his wee face got a little pinker, and by and by he was up playing with the things on Father's table.'

Two weeks later it happened again with the plague inoculation.[136] Five minutes after the process Pat was white in the face and grey round the lips and, 'Father had to sweep aside blotting paper and ink on the writing table and make him lie down there. Father put his legs up on a bookshelf and gradually his colour came back.' After all this, and his scarlet fever earlier, Helen reported that Pat had since been rather ill and miserable, with his arm very sore.[137] Rob claimed that his arm was sore too, but Helen could see from the way he used it that it was not.

Despite the lethal diseases around her, Helen was clearly fit – and happy – at this time. On the twenty-sixth of February 1905 she had her forty-third birthday. Will gave her a gold bracelet and the boys some eau-de-cologne; the girls sent some embroidery and Ata sent some progressive whist score cards. What a contrast Helen's full life at this time was with that of her contemporary and fellow-author Beatrix Potter. At the beginning of 1905 Beatrix Potter was thirty-eight, but had hardly ventured out of her South Kensington nursery suite.[137] She had published her first six tales (which Helen Bannerman was familiar with) but did not know London at all. Margaret Lane, in her biography, describes how, after visiting a theatre, Beatrix Potter wrote in 1905: 'I thought the drive there was the most interesting part of the affair. Extraordinary to state, it was the first time in my life that I had been past the Horse Guards, Admiralty and Whitehall, or seen the Strand and the Monument.' Beatrix Potter's father on some occasions prevented her from going to see her publisher, and her mother used the vapours and other forms of female blackmail to prevent her daughter developing an independent and fulfilled life of her own.

Helen was mistress of her household. She knew Bombay well, and moved around it in her carriage or by train for visits and shopping and Church activities. She handled her own affairs with her publisher, apart from the first publication of *The Story of Little Black Sambo*, when she had been helped – or otherwise – by her friend Mrs Bond. She went riding in the morning or evening with Will and was a keen gardener, growing lavender, basil and thyme in the heat and humidity of Bombay. Where Beatrix Potter suffered from depression induced by boredom, Helen was at this time healthy in a difficult climate, without air-conditioning and exposed to virulent infections. Beatrix Potter, who did so little, found herself always tired; 'How is it' Beatrix Potter wrote, 'that these high-heeled ladies who dine out, paint and pinch their waists to deformity, can racket about all day long, while I who sleep o' nights, can turn in my stays, and dislike sweets and dinners, am so tired towards the end of the afternoon that I can hardly keep my feet?' Helen did not dine out very often, nor did she 'racket about', but she did live a busy and fulfilled life. She and Will were interested in all new developments, particularly scientific ones. One evening, for example, they visited a steamer in the harbour,[138] and from it inspected a new light-ship, charged with gas, which burnt night and day. 'As we steamed away out into the "stream" as they call the middle of the harbour, the great light kept winking its bright eye at us and sending its deep sweet note across the water, till we were far away out.' It must have been on nights such as this – or possibly sitting out on the verandah in the dark, that Helen studied the Indian stars, and sent descriptions to her daughters at home describing the different position of the stars in India.

The scourge of upper-class women in Helen's day was nervous illness, brought on in many cases by not having enough to do. Helen was the embodiment of the principle that an active life is the best way to stay sane. She was fascinated by the Indian world around her. She observed it in detail – sometimes critically – and sent home detailed descriptions of festivals, kite-flying, street sellers and any incidents that occurred. When she travelled as a tourist she was enthusiastic about all she saw. In the early part of 1905 she and Will and the children visited Bijapur; descriptions of mosques, minarets and tombs poured from her pen. As she put it: 'I have been staring about me till my eyes are as large as saucers and my mouth gapes like a Church door.'[139]

Her enthusiasm for what she did and saw is infectious. The reader can share her excitement as she sets off to a party at the house of an Indian friend, to celebrate the wedding of his son:[140] 'We had a little trouble to find the house, but once we got near the long array of carriages, the sound of a band and lastly a house and garden all lit up with thousands of tiny coloured lamps, shewed us we were going right. So in we went and Father said "What kind of instrument's that?" I said it must ge some kind of a native zither, and then we moved on and saw what we had been hearing – a man playing with two slender little wooden sticks on a lot of little wooden bowls, tuned to what I suppose he considered a correct scale by having water poured into them. "Tink a tink a tink a tink" they flew backwards and forwards here and there ever so fast, and it was rather pretty.'

SAMBO SAHIB

Perhaps it was easier for a woman to live a really full life in India than in Bolton Gardens, South Kensington, where Beatrix Potter lived. In India there was no escape from the unexpected. One day Will experimented with a new way of killing bacteria in a go-down, or shed. The principle seems to have been that of a flash fire. He put saucers with bacteria on the floor of the shed and set fire to the kerosene he had sprayed inside. Helen and the children, who had come to watch, were almost incinerated in the blast; the bugs were unaffected. Rob on one occasion saved his Ayah by shouting out when she fell into a well, and on another when her sari caught alight on a fire. Helen frequently described unexpected household happenings. On April 14 1905, for example, she told Day: 'Ayah came running to me in the drawing room and asked me to come and see something in the dining room. And when I got there, here was one of the laboratory monkeys hiding between the blackwood almirah and the wall' (Helen obliged with a picture for the children). 'I threw it a plantain and a walnut, but it took no notice, and then I gave orders that all the doors and windows were to be shut, for fear it should escape altogether. And very soon Corporal Scott came over, and said he would catch it and he tried to go up to it gently, but, though generally it is quite tame with him, this time it tried to bite him, and then it jumped away into the pantry, where it smashed two lamps, and a big white goglet for drinking water. I could not help laughing, but I was sorry about the goglet, for it came from the Persian Gulf, and the neck was just broken off as if it had been cut with a knife.' (Another picture to show the two pieces and what a goglet was – a long-necked earthenware vessel). 'Then somehow or another it managed to slip out, though by this time there were three other men and a dog in pursuit, and he raced along the verandah and popped into the spare bedroom, and there he was caught and carried off in triumph, but he left a trail of destruction behind. But it's not only the monkeys that come in from the Lab' – she felt she had to add – 'that do *that*. We have a monkey of our own and its name is Pat, and it is the most destructive monkey that ever was seen. The other day it went out with a knife and cut a lot of the plants in the verandah, it pulled up one of my poor tarragon plants by the roots and threw it away, and a little tree that has sweet white flowers which was coming up in the grass was lopped off close to the ground and I fear it is dead.'

Despite it all, Helen painted her two watercolours each week for her letters, and sometimes did other paintings and drawings too. She played her harmonium, and tried without much success to teach Pat some psalms. She ran the household and saw to the welfare of her servants. That she also managed at this time to fit in a new children's book a year, and illustrate it, is impressive.

IN THEIR MOTHER'S POCKET

The next excitement that loomed up in 1905 was their next home leave. At the beginning of February Will wrote to the Government to ask how much leave he had due. On 11 February he booked their passages home on the Anchor Line *Britannia*, sailing on 18 May and arriving at Marseilles on 5 or 6 June. From there they would travel by train and ferry and train again and reach Edinburgh on 10 June. But he must have acted prematurely, for on 6 May Helen wrote to Janet and Day and asked them to pray that their Father would get his leave, or only she and the boys could come home.

The leave was not forthcoming; possibly there were problems finding someone to take charge of the Laboratory. Helen set off with the boys and their Bearer Poonoosawmy. Will did, however, join them briefly at the beginning of 1906. The boys were excited about the trip, and the week before they left, they pestered Helen to tell them a story they particularly enjoyed.[141]

> They like me to tell them a long story of how we go down and get on the ship and sail away and then get on another little boat and then into a train and then another boat and then one train and then another and then at last I say "Now, little boys, look out of the windows. There they are. Those are sisters jumping and prancing on the platform." (Of course, it may not really come true, if we arrive in the very early morning). And do you know the wee boys get so excited they begin to jump and prance too, and their eyes shine and they laugh, and when I have finished, right up to going up into the nursery and getting a hug from Annie' (this was the Nanny in Ata's house in Ann Street in Edinburgh) 'and some bread and jam, they both shout "'gain! 'gain!" One day I told them it three times straight on end, and they still shouted "'gain! 'gain!"

There were more stories once they got on board. Janet and Day had sent out a box of toys to help keep them amused. A journey of this kind, with active children with more curiosity than sense, could quickly become a disaster if they got too bored. In a letter headed, 'Gulf of Suez, 29 May 1905', Helen wrote: 'We passed Aden last Monday or Tuesday – Tuesday it was, and on Wenesday I told the wee boys a fun-fun story of how the gulls were so pleased at them for throwing bread to them that they flew away to their sisters at home and asked if they had any messages, and the sisters said "yes" they had a parcel, but they did not know how to send it, and the gulls said they would take it, and as they were a little shy they threw it in at the cabin window, and then I went down and found it and brought it up, and there was great joy when it was opened, and first the watches came out and then the pistols and then the bricks and then the puzzles, and the chalks and the books and they have been a great help in amusing the little boys ever since'.

They slept up on deck till they were through the Suez Canal. Then they had the excitement of their cabins with their upper and lower bunks. After that, Marseilles and the train across France, the cross-channel Ferry, the train to London and then probably a sleeper to Edinburgh. Helen must have been very glad of all the toys to help amuse the boys; and gladder still to see her daughters again after an absence of three years.

Chapter Six

The Mali's Pool

Helen's home leave lasted almost a year – May 1905 until February 1906. She stayed for some of the time with her parents at 11 Strathearn Place, Edinburgh, where a room was always kept for her,[142] and in the summer she rented the manse at Rothiemurchus and enjoyed a country holiday there with her children.

Until his brief leave began, early in 1906, Will was absorbed in the work in the laboratory. Although great credit must go to Haffkine for his development of the plague vaccine it was Will and his colleagues who then shifted the emphasis of the research and turned to measures which were to lead to the eradication of plague from India. The problem with inoculation was that while it protected individuals it left a reservoir of infection in rats from which a new epidemic could spring at any time. Will and his colleagues were determined to establish precisely how plague spread. With this information they could then set about eliminating the source of the infection. It was a daunting task; but they were to achieve it.

A high powered Plague Commission, with considerable Government funds, was set up to enquire into the cause of plague and ways of dealing with it. As it began its work Will published an assessment of the knowledge to date in the *Journal of Hygiene* of April 1906. He pointed out that the research should be directed into the unproved theories of transmission of the disease by the rat flea.[143] As his colleague Major Lamb put it in 1908 in his *Summary of the Work of the Plague Commission*:[144] 'So convinced were Colonel Bannerman and Captain Liston of the truth of the flea transmission theory that they had designed and built at the Plague Research Laboratory, Parel, special go–downs or cabins, in which it was proposed to carry out large series of experiments to prove this theory. These go–downs had just been completed when the Plague Commission began work, and, as we shall see, the experiments which were made in them by the Commission went far to prove that the rat flea is the only agent of transmission of plague infection from animal to animal.'

The results of those experiments were published in *The Journal of Hygiene* beginning in 1907. They were a breakthrough comparable to

Robert Ross's work on malaria – and as with malaria pointed the way towards an effective programme for getting rid of the disease: exterminate the rat or the rat flea. Studies of ways to achieve those objectives poured out of the Parel Institute over the next few years: new kinds of rat traps, poisons, gasses and insecticides; schemes for rat-proofing buildings and ridding clothing of fleas; academic measurements of how far a flea can jump and how effective oil is as an insect repellent.

When Helen and the boys returned with Will to Parel in February 1906 they found the laboratory was conducting its own rat extermination programme, offering one anna for two live rats and one anna for four dead ones. This brought in between sixteen hundred and two thousand rats a day. If any of these escaped they were likely to be harbouring the deadly rat flea. According to Helen's letters, rats escaped in huge numbers, especially at the point when they were being taken out of their cages and dropped down the old Government House well to drown. Then a new method of destruction was developed:[145] an early and primitive gas chamber. This involved putting them into a pit, cages and all, and then, as Will put it: 'we pour in some horrid smelly stuff called Hydrocarbon, and put the lid on, and in a quarter of an hour all the poor rats are dead. We put big stones on the top of the lid to make it air-tight so that the rats may soon be killed by the fumes, and it cannot take long to do this, for the squeak-squeaking of the rats stops almost at once and in 15 minutes all are quite dead.'

Rather than draw the memsahib's standard scene of a nice landscape, Helen used to send letters packed with pictures and descriptions of the rats. Accompanying a picture of a man with some eleven bundles supported on a pole Helen wrote: 'It is a man carrying forth some of the thousands of rat traps that are set every evening in Bombay. In streets and gullies, in shops and go-downs these traps are set at night, and then the man goes round and collects them in the morning, and – I think – crowds as many rats as he can into the trap and they are sent out here to be examined and destroyed. I think I have seen as many as fifteen rats in one cage.'

Helen does not seem to have let the rats bother her. They were a constant and casual topic in her letters. She became rather peeved when a pincushion embroidered 'Dad' by one of the children was eaten, and was uncharitable enough to hope that the rat had choked.[146] But on the whole she accepted rats with resignation, noting that it was always her Vinolia soap they went for; they did not seem to care for Pears. One week they would be among her clothes, the next week in the children's. Once they got into the piano[147] and ate the felt padding and part of the lid. Another time a rat began to eat one of Helen's best red curtains.[148] Will sent for the carpenter to take down the curtain, and for the rat catcher from the Laboratory to come with his forceps, and all the servants dropped everything they were doing and joined in the fun. They chased it around the room and out onto the verandah and down the steps into an old drain, and in among the flower pots, and at last they caught it and took it away.

Mostly, however, the rats were caught in a much more routine fashion in traps. Helen describes how one night she and Will were in bed when they heard their bedroom trap spring shut. They were too sleepy to deal with it there and then, but when they checked the trap in the morning they round that the captured rat had been eaten during the night by the other rats scampering around their room.[149] Every room had a trap set at night. Once one trap yielded two rats, one musk rat and two large toads. In accordance with the Presbyterian maxim 'waste not, want not', the rats were sent to the Laboratory and the toads to the fern house – to eat the caterpillars.

Rats not surprisingly played a part in Helen's next book – though the star role went to another laboratory animal, a monkey; the rats merely had a walk-on role. Monkeys were kept for vaccination experiments, though Helen wrote a number of letters about one particular one kept as a pet, tied up in the laboratory grounds.[150] She and the two boys were fascinated by it, and she sent home pictures very similar to the ones she drew in her book. Called *The Story of the Teasing Monkey, by the author of 'Little Black Mingo'* this has long been out of print and is now quite forgotten. It also seems to have made little impact at the time. It was published by James Nisbet and Co. in 1906 and by Frederick Stokes Co. in New York the following year. Although this is the only one of Helen's stories not to have a child as hero, it has a number of similar features to her other books. The hero is Jacko, a monkey, who is about to be eaten by a lion and a lioness and a bear; he outwits them and escapes. The real life Jacko, who had survived various experimental plague inoculations, was tied up on the steps of the verandah; he frightened and bit both children. Later, after the book was published, Jacko, on a chain, was tormented by three wild dogs and killed.

Rob may not have liked the real Jacko very much, but he loved *The Teasing Monkey.* Apart from Helen's books, and those of Rudyard Kipling, there were then hardly any children's books which took a setting which British children in India knew and understood, and set an adventure story there. This tale had trees and fruit familiar to the boys, such as banyan trees, whose roots Pat enjoyed climbing, and bananas and coconuts which were the apples and pears of their childhood. The reason for the lack of commercial success for this book may lie in just that; it must have seemed very weird – with its rats and trees with dangling roots – to any child outside India.

Helen filled the gap in children's books by writing her own; she also did the same over schooling. Pat was to stay in India till he was over seven and Rob till he was nearly five. They never went to school in India; Helen taught them, along with their bearer Poonoosawmy, who wanted to learn to read and write. Perhaps because she too had avoided school in Madeira she was quite relaxed at a slow rate of progress in the three r's. Occasionally she would comment that it was strange that a child who could identify a plague liver still could not read and write. It was Will who wrote to the Rector of his old school, the Edinburgh Academy, to which Pat and Rob were to go in due course, to ask for the names of some books which Pat should be looking at. He sent across a blackboard from the Laboratory and for an hour each morning Helen tried to teach them their alphabet.

Poonoosawmy was a model pupil, unlike the boys. Helen wrote that one of her pupils was very industrious, one was very intelligent and one very idle.[151] 'I am sure', she said 'that you will guess the idle one at once. He says in about 10 minutes. "Mum, I'm tired of doing lessons, want to scribble on my slate now." And I am thankful when he sticks to scribbling on his own slate and does not take the wet rag and insist on scrubbing out the letters the intelligent pupil is making on his.' Poonoosawmy made good progress and was very neat at copying After three months of lessons Rob could copy the whole alphabet in a recognisable fashion, and Poonoosawmy was able to write an entire page. Despite all the competing attractions outside the schoolroom, Pat also made some progress and by August he wrote his ABC on the blackboard every day and Helen commented: 'I hope soon he will know all the letters.'

The trouble was that life at the Laboratory compound was so much more interesting for Pat than the schoolroom. 'As soon as breakfast is over', Helen explained,[152] 'Father starts to office and the two bad wee sons fly off after him. At first I did not mind much, for I had the cook's account to take and orders to give, and they generally came back before I was ready to begin, but now they have so many amusements in the laboratory and so many friends that they are terribly apt to forget my command of "come back in half an hour" and to stay either till I send over for them or Poonoosawmy fetches them for their siesta. They learn a good many things in the lab. Pat knows what a vacuum is but they don't learn to read or write. But I hope by and by Pat will discover the use of reading and then he won't take long to learn.'

Helen's patience paid off; Pat in due course was to become a doctor. Both Pat and his brother were fascinated by the Laboratory. One of Rob's earliest memories[153] of his father is of seeing him and an Indian laboratory assistant milk a snake for its venom. 'The drill was to catch the snake just behind the head. You then held it in your left hand just

THE
STORY
OF
LITTLE
BLACK
SAMBO

•

HELEN ·
BANNERMAN

12. The cover of the first edition, published in London in 1899, by Grant Richards.

13. An enlargement of Sambo's head reproduced from the first edition. In later editions this sympathetic portrait degenerates into a dark blob.

15. The British edition — note how the picture is ill served by the quality of the reproduction.

THE ONLY AUTHORIZED AMERICAN EDITION

THE STORY OF LITTLE BLACK SAMBO

BY
HELEN BANNERMAN

14. The cover of the U.S. edition, with pictures by Helen Bannerman, published by J. B. Lippincott Co.

16. The first edition of Helen's second book, published in 1901 by James Nisbet and Co. Ltd.

17. The modern edition published by Chatto and Windus. Note how the modern picture is less attractive.

18. A little-criticised aspect of the books — their gory violence. ". . . and B A N G ! ! the kerosene exploded and blew the old mugger and Black Noggy into little bits." (see page 37).

19. *The Story of Little Black Quibba* (1902). The cover of the first edition (see page 41).

20. *The Story of Little Degchie-Head* (1903). The cover of the first. edition (see page 56).

21. *Pat and the Spider* (1904). The cover of the first edition (see page 69).

22. *The Story of the Teasing Monkey* (1906). The cover of the first edition (see page 83).

23. The model for *Pat and the Spider* was Helen's own son Pat. She had no hesitation in offering hideous caricatures of him.

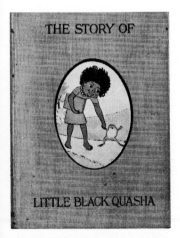

24. In 1908 Helen Bannerman returned to books about black children and published *The Story of Little Black Quasha*.

25. Once again, the modern edition is less attractive than the original.

26. In 1906 came the first edition of *The Story of Little Black Bobtail*.

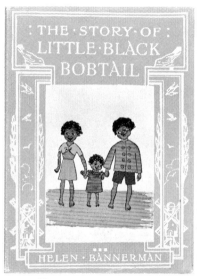

27. The present-day edition.

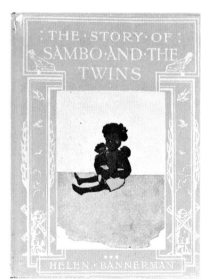

28. The modern edition of *The Story of Sambo and the Twins* first published in 1937.

29. Helen Bannerman's last book, published in 1966 after her death — a book for which her daughter Day must take the major responsibility (see page 152).

was not weary of 230 people a day. I should like to tell her anybody a like left out! to be so kind to leave them all kindest Helmie for Dr. Oller #3.

B O M B A Y .

Fr i . 31st. M a r c h 1911.

My own dear Robin

Dont you think it must be a very verrrry

bad set of children, who set their parents

on to fight ? Yet that is what you four have

done. Oh. I am shocked at you!! By last

week's mail you sent me out that delightful

Scottish Fairy book, and now Father and I

have the most fearful fights as to who is to

have it. He is much stronger than I, so he

can take it away from me, but then he has to

30. In her letters home, Helen delighted in offering caricatures of herself and her husband (see page 157).

31. Many of the animals and episodes in her books were drawn up from real life. Here she was visiting the old fortress of Chittorgarh. Will is on the left in the top.

Parel. Bombay
Thursday 28 October 1909.

32. Snakes and frogs keep appearing in her books — as they did in her life.

behind the head, you put your bare toe on its body on the floor and then you pulled the snake through under your toe until your toe was just holding the tail. This gave you room enough to manipulate the head of the snake. You moved your fingers so they grasped the sides of the snake's head just short of the jaws and pressed. Pressing here opened the snake's mouth. This erected the poison fangs and then with your other hand you drew the edge of a glass underneath the poison fangs and this caused the poison to be ejected into the glass.'

Sometimes the anti-venine made from such extractions was needed as a matter of life or death. As a doctor's wife, Helen had to deal with a number of snake bite emergencies:[154] 'When I came to get into the Victoria the boy handed me a chit: "Sir, the writer has been bitten by a snake, will you kindly do what you can for him." So I told him to say I was going to fetch father and drove off as fast as I could.' Will found the man, who had been clearing long grass in a cemetery, already very ill, but just able to say what colour the snake was. He described it as a dingy mud colour. From this Will guessed it would be a cobra, gave anti-cobra venine, and soon the man began to revive.

One anti-venine was no sooner developed in the Laboratory than it was urgently needed. This, Helen wrote, was for daboia bite:[155] 'Sultan, the man in the Laboratory, was catching one of the daboias, a very large fierce snake – they are wilder than the cobras a great deal – when its head slipped from under the stick he was pressing it down with, and it seized his finger in its teeth and held on. He had to give a fearful jerk with his arm, and flung the beast to a distance to get it off. Of course its glands were full of poison, as they were just going to extract it, so poor Sultan got a full dose. Fortunately they had in the Laboratory a small bottle of anti-venine for daboia poison, so Captain Lamb injected some at once, so he never suffered much from the poison, but the poor finger died from the bite up to the tip, and the two top joints had to be taken off. This is, so far as we know, the first time a man's life has been saved after a bite from a big daboia whose fangs were full of poison.'

The Laboratory was by now diversifying. Set up only a decade previously for plague research, it was becoming a general medical research laboratory, and taking on responsibilities for public health and health education. Will took the health education side seriously and spoke frequently on plague control, anti-venine for snake bite and other medical topics. He was a good speaker, in demand to give talks at the Bombay Literary Society, where he spoke about Lady Nairne's songs, and to give the address at St Andrew's Day dinners. His leisure interests were either scientific or connected with Scotland. He was an elder of the Scots Kirk in Bombay, and in 1907 was Chairman of the Committee for the Scottish High Schools. These had been founded many years previously by the Scottish community in Bombay because, Helen explained, they were not satisfied with the education their children were getting. They were run on Scottish lines and managed by a committee chosen from the two Scottish congregations in Bombay. As the wife of the Chairman, Helen had to give out the prizes at their annual prize-giving.[156] 'Very grand (and rather stiff) I felt as I stood on the platform with the Governor and Father behind me and handed book after book to girl after girl and boy after boy. These children had such pretty manners, they took their books so gently and all, except some very tiny tots, gave such graceful bows. Three of them said "Thank you" in very soft little voices. One little boy was so astonished when his name was read out, that he could hardly move, he had to be called twice, and then he came with wide eyes, and seemed half afraid to take his prize, but once he got it he hugged it tight as if he meant so say "nobody else is going to get it now."'

Another school that Will visited, to lecture on plague, was at Alibag, near Bombay.[157] There had been dead rats there for some time so the population had moved into huts in the palm groves along the sea shore. The school, where the lecture was to be given, was temporarily in the open air on the shore. Will took a magic lantern with pictures relating to plague and gave his lecture by the sea in the dark. 'It was very strange', he wrote, conjuring up the peace and beauty of the evening, 'speaking to the people in the dark in the open air, with the moon shining through the leaves and the sound of the surf on the shore.'

There is the same quality of delight and wonder in some of the letters describing their holidays, and in some of the pictures. In April 1906[158] they went for a few days to Sagargadh and stayed in a tent with a view across the plain to the white surf of the sea in the distance. There was a cool breeze from the sea and the tents were set in the shade of great fig trees. Admittedly the tent had been pitched on a heap of red ants, whose stings felt like burning needles. But if you wet the bite, Helen said, it soon stopped hurting. There were walks round the Fort. One evening – almost as in Helen's stories – they went for a walk in the jungle and came upon six or seven Katkaris waiting for the dark to go out hunting. 'These Katkaris', Will explained, 'are aboriginal people who live in the hills here. They are very black with curious long-shaped heads, and they had no clothes except a small piece of cloth rolled round their loins. They had bunches of leaves in their hair behind the head and they looked very weird and uncanny sitting on the stone wall round the well.' They allowed Will to try their bows and arrows and shoot at some trees with them. The children were unable to bend the bows at all, but tried using the arrows as javelins.

After this brief break, it was back to civilisation in Bombay, stopping on the way at a rest house at Dharamtar where they had breakfast with the Liston family in a room without walls, but a cool roof of palm leaves woven together.[159] Bombay was less pleasant; it was hot and a potentially dangerous situation was developing. 'Here in Bombay,' Will wrote,[160] 'We've been greatly troubled with ownerless dogs wandering about at night and fighting and barking, so we got the police to poison a lot of them and they killed 78. And Scott, one of the solders here, shot 14. So now we are pretty free of dogs. There have been a number of mad dogs going about Bombay and many people have been bitten by them, so it was time some were killed. If you look up hydrophobia in the encyclopaedia you will learn all about this dreadful disease and how a very clever man called Pasteur was able to find out a cure for people bitten by mad dogs. There is a place in India where people can be treated in this way called the Pasteur Institute at Kasauli.'

The monsoon came and went; the children suffered from prickly heat and stomach upsets. To get them away from the muggy weather after the monsoon, Helen took the boys up to Khandala. There the children found two playmates, staying at the same hotel, Freda Lesley Rogers, whose real name was Elfreda, and Edward Randle who was just six weeks younger than Rob. They played together very happily and Helen sent home a picture of the four playing with a goat and its kid.

The following week, however, after Will had joined them, Helen sent another picture, this time with only three children in it. 'The children in this part of the hotel', Helen wrote,[161] 'have been four happy little playmates, and now Edward Randle is not here any more. Last Friday he didn't seem well, and all Saturday he lay in bed though he talked to his mother of what he was going to do when he came over to play with Pat and Rob. But on Sunday morning he was much worse. He wanted water and then he couldn't drink it, and cried and pushed the water away. And then he got so ill that sometimes he didn't know his own father and mother. And on Sunday afternoon he died. Father was over a great deal all that Sunday helping to give him medicine to keep him quiet, for alas nobody could give him anything that would make him better. Sometimes he knew his father and mother and about half an hour before he died he said "Daddy, I want you to send me a big tiffin and I'll eat it, because once Rob came to Khandala and he ate a big tiffin and got quite well." His father had brought up a lot of fireworks on Saturday but he was too ill to enjoy them. Not long before he died he said "No more fireworks for me, Daddy."'

Helen then explained how it had all happened. 'He got a scratch on the face from their own little dog. And now it's supposed that the dog must have licked the scratch, for from that wee scratch he got hydrophobia. His father and mother sent the dog to a vet and he should have kept it to see if it was mad, but some of his servants killed it and so it was 10 days before he knew. And by that time, I suppose, he had forgotten the scratch. Anyway, he never told them the dog was mad. And now his father and mother have no wee son.'

Death came suddenly in India. Perhaps it was an awareness of that, or the certainty that Pat and Rob would not be with her much longer in India, that made Helen acutely aware that her part in their childhood would soon be over. When they were in Bombay they played for hours in the Mali's pool in the fern house. It was relatively cool there, when the ground outside was too hot to stand on. The water went everywhere and they got very wet and muddy. They found a tin bath and used that as a boat, which they used to anchor by putting one of its handles over a water pipe that stuck up in the middle of the pool. As Helen said,[162] 'perhaps it is not very good for the pipe, but when I feel tempted to scold them I remember that it's not very long till they go home now, and probably they'll never have the chance to boat in a tub again, and so I hold my peace'.

Growing up in the shadow of a plague laboratory is an unlikely setting for an idyllic early childhood, but with these two boys it was. There were rides every day, with Rob on the old horse Bob and Pat on the lively pony which Will, keen to see that the boys took exercise in the open air, had bought for him. There were swimming lessons in a swimming bath, with bicycle tyres round their necks as an improvised buoyancy aid, and play in the gardens either by themselves or with the children of the Lamb and the Liston families[163].

Perfect for children; but how was this life-style for Helen? There is every indication that she enjoyed it. She had two of her children with her and Will. By now she had a new piano, a semi-grand. She had her painting, her letters, her books, and her Church activities. A guest, whose husband lived in a remote posting, came to stay with Will and Helen to have her baby in their house. That sort of life was never dull, never isolated, but full of people and unexpected happenings. Helen not only took in people, she usually had a few unusual animals in her household as well. While Will bred rabbits and vipers and crocodiles in the laboratory and hatched turtles eggs in the Governor's bath, Helen at one time kept a pet squirrel and a little black buck deer.[163] She also went out, now and then, to parties and receptions, as for example in February 1907 when the Amir of Afghanistan came to Bombay. Helen had by then learnt to curtsey but on this occasion she forgot to put on high-heeled shoes and nearly fell over her dress.[164] Relations with the Amir were so cordial that in his speech he said he would not call India Hindostan but Dostistan, which means 'country of friends'.

Less grandly – but she seems to have enjoyed it more – Helen also went to a missionary tea at the Red House, the home of some American missionaries. There she heard Dr Gurubai Karenarkis, an Indian missionary, speaking of her recent trip to Europe.[165] 'She told us about the voyage, the flowers in Cannes, the nice French people, the kind English and Scotch, the cold weather, the rain, the meetings at which she spoke, the parties to which she was invited, the Christian work she had seen. She spoke very well, but the most interesting words I heard from her were spoken in a private chat after the meeting, and they began, "I had the pleasure of seeing your two little girls at home."'

By May 1907 it was time for Helen to have the pleasure of seeing her daughters herself. She and Will and the boys – who were never to see India again – sailed in the *Olympia* on 4 May and were expected to arrive by 25 May at the latest. 'We can't be sure till we reach Marseilles,' Helen wrote to Janet, 'But won't it be nice when we do arrive! I'll have to spend one night in London, and then – and then – and then! Caledonian Station about 6 p.m.!!!'

Even in Edinburgh, however, they could not get away from plague. They arrived back in Britain to find the Mulkowal controversy being covered in the newspapers and learned journals. On 1 December 1906 the *Indian Gazette* had published a collection of papers on it, including the full report of the Commission of Enquiry.[167] This had been presented in 1903 but not published till this moment. Then in June 1907 this same material was published in Britain as a Parliamentary Paper.[168]

The significance of the publication of the evidence was that the most eminent experts of the day could now examine it and reach their own conclusions. In June 1907, writing in *The Practitioner*,[169] the widely respected Professor W.J. Simpson, Professor of Hygiene at King's College, London, reviewed the evidence and pinned the blame not on the Laboratory at all but on the inoculation process at Mulkowal. He gave great weight to the evidence of the Indian compounder at Mulkowal who had said: 'The cork at Mulkowal was not loose. I remember it was a very tight cork and the forceps fell out of my hand onto the ground. I swished the forceps in the lotion and then pulled out the cork with it.' The inoculations in villages were carried on out of doors, and tetanus would be prevalent on the soil. Professor Simpson also pointed out that Dr Elliot, who gave the injections, was quite clear that he smelt the bottle and there was no smell – as there would have been if it had already been contaminated with an established growth of tetanus. He quoted experiments to show that a minute impurity falling into a bottle can permeate the fluid immediately and can give tetanus to anyone inoculated with it. He showed that if the impurity had entered in the laboratory the tetanus culture would have been extremely toxic at the time of the injection and people would have died far more quickly. Accordingly he came to firm conclusion that the bottle became contaminated with tetanus germs at Mulkowal at the time of opening.

This was the authoritative exoneration Haffkine had been seeking. Simpson made no assessment, however, of Haffkine's decision to exclude the carbolic. Here the evidence of the original Commission of Enquiry still stood: if the impurity had got into the bottle in the laboratory, then the addition of 0.5% carbolic would have rendered it harmless by the time of inoculation. Thus the conclusion one is forced to is that while *in this particular case* the addition of carbolic would have made no difference, it could have been crucial if contamination had entered a bottle at an earlier stage. The carbolic would have been ineffective in this instance because it takes time to destroy tetanus, and, in this case the contamination occurred immediately before the inoculations.

Professor Simpson's exoneration of the Laboratory from any part in the contamination was enough to provoke a spate of correspondence in *The Times*, in which Haffkine was supported by the Nobel Prize Winner and discoverer of the malarial cycle, Ronald Ross. A letter was published on 29 July 1907[170] over the signatures of ten leading medical specialists ending: 'We should like to express our approval of the stand which Mr Haffkine is making to obtain justice in this affair ... We sincerely trust that, therefore, the Government of India will see fit ... to exonerate Mr Haffkine publicly from the imputations made against him.'

By October 1907 the medical authorities in India were prepared to admit that an injustice had been done to Haffkine. He was invited to return but he could no longer be Director of the Bombay Laboratory – as Will now held that post. Haffkine agreed to work in Calcutta, but according to B.M. Naidhu, who wrote his obituary for the Bombay Bacteriological Institute,[171] he was by then broken-hearted. His contemporaries, according to Mark Popovsky, described him as growing increasingly reserved and sullen. In 1915 he reached pensionable age and returned to Europe. He died in a hotel room in Lausanne at the age of seventy-one in 1930.

Now, however, there is an international memorial committee for Haffkine, headed by a number of eminent medical and scientific men on it, and a number of leading Jewish figures. In Paris on 21 September, 1972 a plaque to him was unveiled at the Pasteur Institute.[172]

It is sad to reflect that, had the commission of Enquiry's Report been published sooner, and the results of the experiments associated with it, Haffkine could have remained more honoured in his day. As so often is the case, the secrecy surrounding an official report prevented justice being done until – as in this case – it was too late. There remains, however, the continuing and worthy memorial to Haffkine in the Parel Laboratory, renamed the Haffkine Institute in 1925.

Mulkowal apart, Will used the long leave to work for a D.Sc., awarded in 1909, for a thesis on, 'The Action of the Bacillus Pestis on certain carbo-hydrates and allied bodies in liquid media, and on the advantages or disadvantages of employing such media for the manufacture of an anti-plague vaccine.'

Helen was also busy, preparing another book. This was *The Story of Little Black Quasha*, published by James Nisbet in 1908. *The Teasing Monkey* had not been a commercial success; with this next book she went back to the formula of *Little Black Sambo* and returned to her imaginary jungle world. But she was still inconsistent; those with an eye for racial characteristics might be puzzled to see that the barefoot bookseller looks a rather grimy white. Those who see sexism in nearly all early children's books are also in for a surprise. As in *The Story of Little Black Mingo*, and *The Story of Little Degchiehead*, the hero, Quasha, is a girl. She goes off by herself to the bazaar, buys herself a book and reads it out loud to herself, laughing at the jokes, under a shady tree in the jungle. Inevitably, tigers then enter the story, and Quasha, an enterprising girl, climbs a tree to escape them. The tigers, spurred on by a frog who is friendly to Quasha, fight over who is to eat her. There are then two pictures by Helen Bannerman at her gory best, showing not only the ground covered with blood, but torn-off limbs, decapitated trunks, severed heads, tails, paws and chunks of tiger strewn everywhere. Nor is this all. One surviving tiger is led over a cliff and drowns (picture of the corpse floating upside down with its tongue hanging out) and the other, stepping over the remnants of the torn-part tigers, is bitten on the tongue by the frog and his 'mouth began to froth, and froth and froth and at last he all just frothed away'. This development was appropriately drawn, with the frog hopping away unharmed. The original ending Helen had in mind was for Quasha to present the frog with the book as a reward for his help. Day, however, then twelve, thought the book would be too heavy for the frog and that he would prefer a saucer of milk; so he got his milk, and Quasha kept her book.

This latest book was reviewed sympathetically in *The Times of India* on 9 December 1908. It commented correctly that it, 'never truckled with probability'. This was a perceptive and accurate comment made, though the article was unsigned, by a friend of Will and Helen, E.H. Aitken, author of *Behind the Bungalow* and other stories about India. He was a well-known naturalist and a fellow member of the Bombay Natural History Society. He had helped Will with advice in some of his studies about the life cycle of the rat and the rat flea, and Will used to share a house with him as he was left working in Bombay while Helen was away. He also did a little journalism on the side, and it is not surprising, perhaps, that he was a fan of Helen's books.

In 1908 Will had completed the thesis and Helen had published a children's book. These, however, were not their only preoccupations. They went with the children whenever they could to the Highlands or the South West of Scotland. For Rob those holidays were a sheer delight:[173]

> The one that's in my mind more than any other is Benderloch in the West of Scotland. We used to go there annually for many years and when we were small at school we used to take a reserved carriage in the train and this was great fun. The whole family packed into one reserved compartment. We arrived at this little station, probably in the afternoon. In the meantime the domestics would have got the house ready for us and we settled down to two months' summer holidays. What did we do? Well we had a boat, we spent long hours in boats, and picnics of course and walks and usually in summer we went to Benderloch, but in the Easter holidays we used to go to Laggan Farm which is near Strathyre. Not only ourselves, but our cousins and aunts used to come to the farm and we had quite homely parties there.

Shades of the prison house, however, were beginning to close over the growing boys. They were already at school, but the time was coming for Helen and Will to set off again for India and leave them with Ata in Edinburgh. Ata was fifty five and getting on in years to be looking after such energetic and free-spirited children. Janet was almost sixteen, and Day almost thirteen; Pat was nine and Rob seven. The arrangement had worked well enough with the girls, but perhaps the boys were too young or Ata was too old; certainly Rob missed his parents deeply. Before she left in July 1909, however, Helen wrote one more book, specifically for Rob, called *The Story of Little Black Bobtail*. It was published in the autumn of 1909 by James Nisbet and must have been a comfort. It was not a great success commercially, but he loved it:[173] 'I think it is the best children's story ever written. It has ships and a storm and polar bears, an iceberg and a cannon – what more could any child want?'

At the age of seven, Rob enjoyed *Little Black Bobtail* as an adventure story, and loved the violent ending. 'Little Black Tag fired off the big brass gun with a tremendous roar, and the polar bear was blown to bits and was never seen again.' Unaccountably, Helen disappointed some of her young readers by omitting a picture of all the torn-off limbs. Nevertheless one contemporary reviewer praised the action-packed aspect of the book: 'The amount of adventure and incident that is compressed into this little history of Black Bobtail should satisfy any child, and the pictures – especially those of the polar bear – are equally thrilling'. That same review, whose source is not known but which is pasted without attribution into a first edition of the book in the possession of the family, makes something of a mystery about the authorship. The author of *The Story of Little Black Mingo* has produced another delightful little book of the same kind, called *The Story of Little Black Bobtail* (Nisbet and Co.) These books have a special interest in Bombay, where the identity of the talented lady who writes and illustrates these stories is well known, and in England they have attained an unusual but well-earned popularity.' Helen was still being modest about her authorship of the books; but the only one which was a runaway success was the one with her name on it.

Other children, however, were unlikely to respond to the material in it which was specific to Rob. Polar bears, for example, were a favourite game for him and Pat; in one of her letters Helen had drawn a picture of the boys wearing a polar bear skin and chasing her round the house and trying to eat her. The clothes basket that Little Black Tag, Little Black Rag and Little Black Bobtail sailed off in also has similarities with the tin tub in the mali's pool. The tie-up between play and imaginings as a child and later interests or obsessions is expressed in Rimbaud's *Le Bateau Ivre* – the theme of which is the search made by all of us through the journey of life for that pool on which, as children, we launched our frail little boats:

> Si je désire une eau d'Europe, c'est la flache
> Noire et froide ou vers le crépuscule embaumé
> Un enfant accroupi plein de tristesses, lâche
> Un bateau frêle comme un pappillon de mai.

In Rob's case, exactly this search was to go on. He was to spend his adult life as an irrigation engineer in the Sudan, designing waterways and canals, as he had done for so many hours in his childhood at Parel. Pat and Day were to be unable to forget their early fascination with the medical secrets of the Laboratory and were both to go into the world of medicine. Janet's later life, too, when she was to return to Madras as a missionary, tied up with one of her earliest memories – riding to Church on her mother's knee through the woods at Kodai.

Chapter Seven

The Empty Nest

When Will and Helen returned to Bombay – without any of their children – in July 1909 Helen was forty-seven and had lived in India, apart from home leaves, for twenty years. Will was fifty-one and had spent twenty-six years there. Helen's pictures show that they had both aged. From this time onwards she draws herself as rather stooped, using spectacles for reading and needlework, and Will as heavier and with even less hair than previously. Their life without children was different. Helen now went out with Will when he visited hospitals, leper asylums and various medical projects and took a more active role in church and Y.W.C.A. activities. Reading her letters home, however, it is clear that Helen's horizons were still those of her home. She did not move out into the wider world of India and participate in its development. For a woman in that age, this would have been quite exceptional; but it is noticeable how seldom there are references to any of the political or social developments of the day.

This is equally true as regards British politics. These were years of great upheaval in Britain, with the landslide victory for the Liberal Government in 1906, Lloyd George's Budget in 1909, which introduced old age pensions and health insurance, the continuing debate over Irish Home Rule and the campaigns of the suffragettes. It may be that Helen and Will felt such topics were not particularly interesting for the children; most parents, however, are not over-solicitous about their children's interests but unthinkingly impose their own. Using this line of reasoning, both Helen and Will were absorbed in the problems of plague and malaria and snake-bite and leprosy but let the political world pass them by.

There were also interesting developments in India. After the reforms of Lord Curzon, which had included the partition of Bengal, amidst great controversy and upheaval, and changes in agriculture and administration, Lord Minto arrived as Viceroy in 1905. Between then and 1910 he presided – with a deceptively casual approach compared to that of Lord Curzon – over substantial developments. Curzon had set his face against appointing Indians to the highest reaches of Government in India; Lord Minto, backed by John

94

THE EMPTY NEST

Morley, who became Secretary of State for India in the Liberal administration which took office in 1906, favoured bringing Indians onto the Viceroy's Executive Council.[174] He discounted fears that such a step would seem a concession to what was called 'agitation'. He felt that the growing numbers of educated Indians were loyal and moderate, and deserved to participate in the Government of their country. Despite substantial opposition, especially from retired Viceroys, the plans for such appointments went ahead.

They were troubled times and political demonstrations continued. There were riots at Pandharpur and Nagpur in 1908 and an assassination attempt on a British official, when two Englishwomen were killed in Calcutta. Lord Minto tightened up on the publication of material which was an incitement to murder and he forbad seditious meetings, but at the same time he opened the higher reaches of the Indian Army to Indians. They already played their part in the Indian Civil Service and the Indian Medical Service, where entry was by competitive examination. Unrest continued; a bomb was thrown at the Viceroy and Lady Minto while they were on a visit to Ahmedabad. It failed to explode, but various murders of British officials did succeed. In December 1909 the British community in India was shocked by the murder of Mr Jackson, the collector of Nasik in the Deccan, who was shot at a theatrical performance held in his honour. It became clear that there were secret societies operating in Gwalior, the Deccan and Eastern Bengal, ready to use assassination as a political weapon. Lord Minto nevertheless pressed on with those reforms which he felt commanded sufficient support in his home base and generally encouraged the participation of educated Indians in the Government of India as far as was possible.

Little of the violence reached Bombay. The nearest the Bannermans came to being near a bomb was during a meeting in Bombay Town Hall at which the Governor presided to discuss proposals for a memorial to the King, who had died the previous month. 'There were a lot of long speeches', Helen reported[175] 'of which I could not hear anything and then, just at the end there was a sudden explosion – a little bang and a big cloud of smoke. We all looked round and people asked their neighbours what it was. I guessed right, I did not say a bomb. Lots of folk were a little wee bit startled because we have heard so much lately about native hatred of British rule and as you know several people have been murdered. Then everybody began to laugh, for it was only a flash light for a photo! Wasn't that absurd!'

Helen and Will put little faith in political measures to deal with such difficulties. As Helen wrote to Pat: 'I often think that Dad and I are kept so perfectly safe in India from bombs and accidents and motor smashes and diseases because we are so rich in dear people at home who pray for us, and it is very nice to think that our own children are helping to keep us safe from evil and from the fear of it, which is a worse thing even than the evil itself. I heard of one lady who was in Nasik who was afraid to go to sleep at night lest the natives should come and kill her and her two babies. Wouldn't it be dreadful to be so scared as that?'

The British authorities, however, were not so inclined as Helen to put all their faith in God. Some months after the Jackson murder a man was caught in Britain and charged with complicity in the murder and sent to India for trial. Helen, on a visit to Nasik where the murder had taken place, wrote home with all the details:[176] 'Here we are all greatly taken up about that man Savarkar, who escaped from the steamer at Marseilles. It was he who supplied the pistol that Mr Jackson was shot with at Christmas time and he was sent out here for trial. At Marseilles he contrived to wriggle out through the lavatory port and fell into the water. Thence he swam to the quay and there he was arrested by the men who were travelling in charge of him and taken back to the ship. But now there seems to be a question whether, as he had touched French soil, he will not have to be handed over to the French authorities and extradited before he can be tried.' Here was a story with shades of Lincoln, the Count of Monte Cristo and now a battle over extradition. It had everything. Rarely for her, Helen left its dramatic side and went on to explain to her children its political significance: 'Unfortunately there is a great deal of disloyalty and sedition in Nasik. The Brahmans don't like British rule, because it allows people to neglect them and keep their money to themselves, and so the Brahmans are driven to work, which they think quite wrong, so in places where Brahmans are strong sedition is apt to be strong.' Not an explanation which would appeal to the Brahmins, but this must have been how Helen's circle understood the troubles at the time. 'There were more than forty men in prison at Nasik', Helen reported, 'waiting to be tried for conspiracy. But the poor country people seemed very humble and polite and salaamed most profoundly to us as we passed along the roads. I don't think they care who rules over them, so long as they get enough to eat.' This was a common view at that time. It is echoed by Michael Brecher in *Jawaharlal Nehru: A Political Biography*[177] who points out that political consciousness among Indians was still confined to the intelligentsia; 'the peasant masses', he says, talking of the years 1909–1912, 'slumbered in a state of political apathy'.

Within Helen's world – the laboratory compound – there was a pecking order based not so much on race as on class. Among the doctors at the laboratory was Dr Avari. His son Jal played regularly with Isabella, the daughter of Will's colleague, Captain Liston.[178]

THE EMPTY NEST

There were also two children of Mr Scott, a former army sergeant, now a general handyman and overseer of the labourers at the laboratory. It is noticeable that his children, Jock and Arthurina, did not play regularly with Jal and Isabella. While the Bannermans had been on their home leave, the Listons – who had at one time been living in a big tent in the compound because accommodation was so short – had moved into the Director's house. When the Bannermans returned, they all lived in it together for a few months until it was time for the Listons' home leave. Helen enjoyed it, and shared the catering week about with Mrs Liston. Apart from liking the Listons, she liked having children about her, and was dearly indulgent towards them: 'Jal comes over from the Avari's house, just beyond the stables, before I am dressed in the mornings, and he and Isabella play together nearly all their waking hours. Yesterday was Jal's birthday and his mother sent us over a sort of birthday cake. It was made of stuff like thread all tangled up together (very like shredded wheat but not crisp), very sweet, and flavoured with coconut and cardamoms, and with roasted pistachio and earth nuts strewn all over it and here and there a roasted almond.'

Jal had a game with Helen by which he came into her room and asked, "Any crackers?" Sometimes she would say, "Go and see", and sometimes, "No". He would then go to one particular drawer of her writing table and open it and look. If she had said, "No", there would be none. If she had said, "Go and see", he would find two and he would seize them and rush off to give one to Isabella.

Helen also took an interest in the children of her servants. For some memsahibs, particularly those with too little to do, servants were the only topic of conversation. This was far from the case with Helen, but they do play a role in her letters from time to time. In one letter[179] she described a visit from the wife of Poonoosawmy, their Bearer who had gone with her to Edinburgh when she had travelled home without Will in 1906. She drew a picture of Poonaswamy's wife and infant daughter and explained that the family were Christian and the child's name was Helen. 'She and her mother came the other day, brought by Ayah . . . though Helen is 18 months old she can't walk yet. She has quite a lot of teeth and thick black hair but Ayah has cut it quite short, because it is easier to keep clean. I think the reason she cannot walk is that she has a grandfather, a mother and an uncle and an aunt, and they are all always willing to play with her and carry her about so she doesn't need to carry herself. She ought to have a Daddy too, but as you know Poonoosawmy was very rude to Mrs Liston and had to be sent away and he is working in Coloba now, in a house where there is only one room for *all* the servants, so they cannot have their wives.'

One other servant had also got into difficulties while the Bannermans were away. Pat and Rob must have been saddened to read about the gardener who had watched over them and played with them for so many hours. As she wrote to Pat a week after returning to Parel:[180] 'Bhugwan, the mali that you and Rob poured water over, has gone. He owed a lot of money to a money lender and they say he ran away because he could not pay. Poor Bhugwan. So Suggan is the head gardener now and he works very well. Do you remember he used only to sweep when we were here before?' Suggan, in the years ahead, was to have his troubles too. His wife died, leaving him with a daughter, at that time a toddler. Suggan kept her with him all day as he did the gardening, and she became a fixture in the laboratory grounds playing in the dust at his side.

It was the memsahib's responsibility to see to the welfare of the servants – a task that needed the wisdom of Soloman.[181] 'The dhobi reports a theft from his house. He *says* he was sleeping and some people came and broke open the window and took out a big box. But it was such a big box it would have taken 3 men to lift it, so it seems funny that he should have slept through it all.' Helen was not so dyed-in-the-wool an Evangelical that she was blind to evil where it clearly existed. She went on: 'They want to arrest my old dhobi Tika, and he is such a bad man I could easily believe he wanted to steal, only I doubt if he'd be brave enough.' Her letters fail to give the eventual outcome of this crisis: clearly her own instinct was that it was a put-up job by the victim.

Will's first task on arriving back at Parel – apart from his work – was to learn to drive a new car which was waiting for him. They called it, 'the Hummingbird' and it was to figure prominently in their letters in the years ahead. With no driving tests necessary, Will would drive it round the laboratory, filled with any women or children who wanted to come.[182]

'After tea Dad got the motor out almost every day and then Mrs Liston, with baby William in her arms got in, then I and Isabella and Jal and Mr Scott's little girl (Arthurina but they call her Appenah) all got in too and sometimes Mr Avari's big boy Memmy and then Dad set off driving out of the gate, as if we were going to the Fort, stopping just opposite the temple outside the gate, backing up the back road that goes round behind the tank, till we got far enough back to start forward again and turn in at the gate, and so run in nose foremost and back to the stable. Here we turned the same way, by running across the bridge and then backing out, so as to turn our back to the north gate, and then off we whizzed through the South gate again to turn at the temple and run back to the station. At first the car did all sorts of funny things, sometimes it whirred as if all its wheels were flying to pieces, sometimes it set off with a jerk that made Isabella and Jal nearly sit down on the floor, sometimes it cantered like a horse, sometimes it stopped altogether ... but by Wednesday Dad was able to take us out, along Vincent Road (the broad road that runs from near the West Gate towards Matunga) and yesterday he drove me into the Fort and the car went beautifully.'

The car ran well, and Will mastered its driving; but it was a recurring complaint that the ordinary people of Bombay had no idea about keeping out of the way. Within six weeks Helen had reported two breakdowns, two near accidents and one actual one.[183]

'Last Monday was Cocoanut day, when the fisher folk offer cocoanuts to the sea gods, to let them go fishing again after the monsoon, so that day we kept out of Bombay because it's not very canny to drive through great crowds of inattentive people. But on Tuesday we thought we were safe, and we went in to town. But Tuesday was a Mahomedan holiday and there were great crowds in Bhindy Bazaar and Abdul Rehman Street and in Abdul Rehman street we had to go very slowly, keeping the horn hooting all the time. But in spite of slow driving and continuous hooting and all of us shouting and screaming a boy got in front of the car and wouldn't get out of the way, he saw nothing and he heard nothing. Dad had to swerve this way and that to avoid people and gharis coming the other way, and at last the boy just dodged right into the car and was knocked down in the mud. Luckily he was not a bit hurt but a great crowd gathered immediately and we did not quite know what would happen next. But very fortunately for us a European policeman had seen the whole affair, and he came up and told Dad it was all right, and that he had seen it was not our fault. So Dad asked the boy to come near and asked him very carefully if he was hurt anywhere. And he said 'no', but the poor boy was very dirty, for it had been raining heavily and the road was a mass of mud! Of course at first we were dreadfully afraid one of the wheels had gone over him but Dad was able to stop the motor dead, the minute it touched him, and of course we were going *very* slow. Oh, I *was* thankful he was not hurt.'

At the time of the Gunputty processions at the beginning of August, Will had collided with another boy, who ran in to the road after his kite. He was also unhurt.[184] But a fortnight later Will was involved in a more serious accident which did involve some injuries. Helen's description gives a vivid idea of the choices facing a driver in those days before Highway Codes and innumerable regulations.[185] If one saw a way ahead, one took it. 'The road was simply crammed with people, but the tram lines were fairly clear. So Dad to save time kept on the lines, to pass a car which was going our way. We were almost past when suddenly a car came round the corner at a fearful pace just in front of us, and we had to run off among the crowd. The people next to us cleared away all right, but alas! a little knob never heard us or saw us and just as we came along closed up in front of us. Oh it was horrible! The splash board caught one man right in the middle of the back and lifted him off his feet, he knocked into another, who rolled down into the mud, and he upset a third who was carrying a framed photo. I thought the first two were right under the wheels but by God's goodness none of them was badly hurt. The first man had his elbow and skin bruised by his fall in the road, the second man was very dirty, but he smiled very good-naturedly and the third man had not even got the glass of his photo broken.' The injured were, as Helen put it, '*so* nice and good natured about it'. The Bannermans took the man with the bruised arm to hospital and arranged for a payment to him and for an anti-tetanus injection.

Some of the Bannerman's trips, however, were less disastrous. They used the motor to go to Vehar on an all-day picnic with the Listons and for Will's duty visits. Helen frequently went with him, and got to know various hospitals well and the leper asylum at Matunga. If she did not report in detail on the political developments around her, Helen gave her children their money's worth in covering the technological developments of her time. The installation of a telephone in their house (1906), the opening of a radio link between Bombay and London (1909) and the introduction of a new type of paraffin fan (1910) were written about in exhaustive detail. Even a new way of photographing the leprosy bacillus merited three sides of Helen's letter to Pat on 8 July 1910. She drew a picture of the equipment and described it in detail: 'The first thing you'll see is the lantern, for they take these "micro-photographs"' by oxy-hydrogen light. You'll notice one tube coming down to the back of it from the gas overhead (that's the hydrogen gas) and one from a long iron cylinder that's stuck in a stand (that's the oxygen). They burned together inside the lantern with a fierce hissing sound, which you must often have heard, and gave a most brilliant light. This shone out through a big bulls-eye window, through another lens, through a glass tank full of water (this was to absorb all heat from the rays of light, and you'll notice a little brass hose, by which they could let the water run out constantly if it was important to keep the light *very* cool – there was another on top to connect a pipe and let water in but I couldn't see that). Then another lens, then a flat yellow screen which somehow or other improved the photo, and then the microscope, which I have not made quite clear. It had a U-shaped foot so the light passed through and fell full on the slide, first below the nose of the microscope and into the nose of the camera which had another table, as long as itself, and was made in two halves, so that you could get the picture very far away. I saw the picture on the glass screen, of such tiny tiny bacilli, stained blue and pink.'

Is it fanciful to see something essentially Scottish in this preoccupation with scientific detail? There was a difference in background between the Scots and the English who served in India. Among the English there was a preference for the I.C.S. and the Army; the Scots were to be found in disproportionately large numbers as doctors, engineers, surveyors and in other occupations of a scientific kind. This was partly due to their educational system. The best English education, in the public schools, was of a general kind, encouraging verbal and written fluency and based on the classics rather than the sciences. The best Scottish education, on the other hand, included a grounding for all in basic science and a stress on the importance of 'gaining qualifications'. This was understandable in a society which was far from rich and which was used to exporting its brains to give them the opportunities they needed. The opportunities of Empire were a boon to able and ambitious Scots; they diligently acquired their qualifications and either emigrated to Canada, Australia, or New Zealand (or, outside the Empire, to the U.S.A.) or, if they sought careers in India or those other parts of the world which were under British rule, spent their working lives abroad and returned to Scotland to retire.

The Bannermans were able to live in Bombay in an almost exclusively Scottish society. Captain Lamb and Captain Liston, Will's colleagues in the laboratory, were Scots and were also related to each other by marriage. They attended the Scottish Churches, sat on the committee for the Scottish Schools and organised their annual St Andrew's Day dinners. They entertained each other in their homes and on picnics. Helen described in one letter how, after dinner in Bombay, she and Will and their guests, all from Edinburgh, chatted in the cool of the evening about that subject of such absorbing interest to the city's citizens – Edinburgh schools.

Without her children Helen's life had altered substantially. She was now able to live in an adult world, and to go out and about with Will to visit, for example, the centre in the foothills of the Himalayas at Kasauli where anti-rabies precautions were taken. This could have been the moment when she branched into writing for adults as well as children. She edited a magazine for the Young Women's Christian Association and, when necessary, wrote for it too. She wrote for adults with economy, pace and style. I have only been able to trace one short story, *My Friend Framji*,[186] published in 1906 in 'Flowers from The Manse Garden', Scottish Mission Industries Co. Ltd. Ajmer. (According to Day, the story was printed later in the magazine *Truth* purporting to be the actual experience of the author. Day wrote to the publishers pointing out that her mother had written it and that it was a work of fiction. The Publishers, Day reported, then apologised.) The story is a gruesome one about a diamond dealer who is held captive in the Towers of Silence in Bombay. Despite this, and possibly other short stories, she never broke through into the mainstream of writing for adults. Why was this? Forty-seven was old for a burst of creative energy; it would have been unusual in those days for a woman; or perhaps she lacked the strength – this was the moment when she became ill with sprue.

After she had been back in India for only a month she fell sick with the illness that was to stay with her till she left India finally in 1918. Sprue, a form of chronic diarrhoea, is one of the most debilitating diseases known to man. In her day there was no cure – except to leave the tropics. Sprue could make a person so weak that it was sometimes fatal, as Helen heard for herself, when, after she had had the disease for two months, she went visiting for the Y.W.C.A. She went to see a certain Mrs Coles:[187] 'When she came in I saw she was all dressed in black, and after we had talked a little, she told me she had lost a little girl. This little girl used to be very plump and rosy for an Indian child, and was always very merry, but she got ill, and they got one doctor to see her and he said it was her liver, and gave her soups and chicken broth and things like that, and she got much worse. Then they got another doctor, and he said she needed a change, so they sent her to Mahableshwar and that only made it still worse. At last they heard how many people Captain Liston had cured, and they asked him to see her. Whenever he saw her he said she had sprue, and he put her on milk and she began to get better at once. But when the monsoon came he said she would never get well in Bombay and advised them to send her home. Her grandmother was going, so she went with them, and from Aden and Port Said and Gibraltar they got postcards from her (she was only six but she wrote quite as well as Pat) saying she was getting so much better and that everyone was so kind to her. But when they got into the English channel they got very rough weather and the poor wee thing had no strength to stand it and died of exhaustion just six hours from Plymouth.'

Helen had the advantage of the best available medical treatment for sprue,[188] though she did not enjoy the treatment much. 'They have a horrible kind of patent sour milk which they prepare in the lab, and which is supposed to be very good for weak digestions. So every day, just after chota hazri, by Dad's orders, a bottle comes over, and I have half of the stuff spooned out into a saucer and the bottle sent on to Mrs Liston, who eats the rest of it. It is *very* horrid, and I think Dad might be content with giving me plain milk, but no, he grins and chuckles and spoons it out, as if life could give him no greater delight than digging sour milk out of a bottle!' Reading some of Helen's descriptions of the conditions in which they lived – and they must have been one of the most hygiene-conscious families in all Bombay – it is surprising they were not ill more often. The flies in the house were sometimes so numerous that they had to take tea with napkins spread over every bit of food. They put saucers over their cups and removed them briefly to drink, otherwise the flies fell into the tea and drowned themselves. And all the time the flies settled on their hands and faces and were constantly irritating.

Sprue meant that Helen stayed in the house more often, and went out very little. One consolation to her was her piano. It had been with friends while they were away, and now had been brought back. She had it repaired and re-tuned. Playing it was a constant source of pleasure to her. She was upset to find, however, that books which she had packed in tin boxes and left at Parel had been ruined by white ants.[189] 'You never saw such a mess, of eaten covers, ragged edges, loose leaves, unrecognisable scraps, and debris, half made up of paper, half of the mud the white ants had brought in to build their tunnels with. This mud was not even made of plain red earth, it was made of the white chunam out of the walls, and in many places where things are not eaten they are plastered over with this stuff that sticks like cement and looks perfectly horrible. Some of them *may* be rebound, but all the books that were in sets of several volumes are ruined and even those that can still be used will never look nice again. My beautiful Border Minstrelsy that Dad gave me on my birthday has *one* good volume out of five!'

There was a reference too, to her wooden book press being eaten by white ants. Helen consoled herself with the thought that, anyway, the Caxton press bound books better than she did. The first seven volumes of her letters home were bound in leather, presumably by Helen herself. The next ten, from 1909 onwards, were in an American cloth binding and have the mark of a bindery in Sussex on them – that of Mrs L. A. Vidler, Carmelite Bindery, Rye, Sussex. The presumption must be that the damage to Helen's press was so great that, from that time onwards, she stopped binding her own books.

One respect in which Helen praised the Listons' stewardship was over the garden. They had done a lot of work on it. Rob, now at seven, laboriously writing his own letters, and getting printed or typed letters from Helen in return, asked anxiously whether there were still two mali's pools. 'No', wrote Helen.[190] Uncharacteristically, her understanding of a child's mind failed her at this point, for she went on: 'There is only the nice one in the fern house. Captain Liston has got so many stand pipes put all about the garden that there is no need for the little muddy pool near the gate, and it has been filled up, and now a row of crotons and poinsettias runs right up from the gate to the porch. It looks much nicer without the old dirty pool.' Rob would have thought differently. Poinsettias were no substitute for one of his beloved muddy pools – gone, alas, as the song says, 'like our youth too soon'.

By the following week, the whole garden was a muddy pool, after eight inches of rain in two days. The Listons had put in dozens of roses, and a *Hibiscus rosamutabilis*. This last flower lasted only one day and changed colour from snow white in the morning to pale pink by noon and a strong dark pink in the evening. Unfortunately, a mould began to appear all up and down the stem and branches.[191] 'In the late fearful rain it has got worse and worse, and two days ago Dad said "That tree looks as if it was dying" – "Yes" said Mrs Liston "It's moulded through." "Well, we'll see what Plunas will do for it," said Dad. Plunas is a mixture of kerosene, soap and water (not very much kerosene) which they use for killing fleas and disinfecting floors, so he took the bottle and went out, and sploshed the tree all over, and, marvellous to relate, it has been looking much better since.'

But it was not only the trees which were drooping. If Helen was unwell, Mrs Liston was worse. Helen wrote that her friend looked so ill that she was glad, for her sake, she was going home. The Listons set off for Edinburgh in mid-September, with instructions from Helen to be sure to see the children, and to be sure to take Ayah with them to Ann Street too. This Ayah, who accompanied the Listons on this leave, had previously been Ayah to Pat and Rob in Bombay.

With her emissaries, her letters and her books, her children knew they were always in their mother's thoughts. She used to mark up their heights on the wall of her bedroom, and pin up any pictures they sent. When she went out she was constantly seeing a child who was the same height as Janet, or looked like Day, or was as naughty as Pat, or, as when she went to the Scottish Schools' Prizegiving in 1910, reminded her of Rob:[193] 'Big girls and little girls had come up for their prizes, lesser girls and lesser boys had followed and finally tiny tots had come and gone and now Mrs Service had sat down and everybody was waiting for the Chairman's remarks when a tiny wee boy scrambled down from his seat, and came to where the others had stood, waiting. There was nobody to give him a prize and apparently no prize for him, and everybody laughed, and I think we all felt a little sorry for the wee lad. But he just stood his ground, paid no attention to the laughter, and waited patiently. And then it was discovered that he had really been overlooked and there was a prize waiting for him so Mrs Service was asked to come and she presented it to him. The wee boy had been told by Mr Wilkinson that he would get a prize and though we all laughed he knew Mr Wilkinson would keep his word. And sure enough he got his book.'

Helen and Will had a brief break after Christmas at Ahmedabad, where they saw all the sights and enjoyed being tourists with Will's sister-in-law who was on a visit. This was quite overshadowed, however, by a trip that followed in the middle of January when she and Will set off for the foothills of the Himalayas, to Kasauli. Will wanted to visit Kasauli, the home of the anti-rabies centre for India, to see if he could set up a similar centre in Bombay. This was in due course achieved, though only after many years delay. As K. H. Dave, Assistant Director and Head of the Department of Viral Vaccines in the modern Haffkine Institute put it in 1974 in the Institute's Platinum Jubilee Commemoration volume:[171] 'As early as 1909, the importance of antirabic treatment centres and production of antirabic vaccine was recognised by Lt. Col. Bannerman, the then Director. Anti-rabic vaccine was not available in Bombay Presidency then and people had to go a long way to Kasauli or Coonoor for treatment; Bannerman proposed that a branch of the Pasteur Institute, Kasauli, be opened at Haffkine Institute. The proposal was approved by the Government of Bombay but technical difficulties and financial considerations delayed the formation of a separate Institute.' It was not until after Will's time, in 1922, that production of the first batch of anti-rabic vaccine went ahead in Bombay.

Helen loved the cool climate of the hills. She sent home a touristy watercolour of the snow-capped mountains and wrote rapturously from The Firs, Kasauli,[194] 'Here we are in Kasauli and this will give you a faint idea of the beautiful view we go out and gaze at every morning while the porridge is being brought in. We stand on a sort of shelf on the side of a very steep hill and we look across a perfect sea of hills which gradually melt from yellow to purple and from purple to pure deep blue, and away miles and miles beyond the blue hills – two hundred miles from Kasauli, Captain Harvey tells me – we see the snowy ridge of the higher Himalayas.'

Will described how the last bit of the road to Kasauli was very steep and people had to ride or walk or go in a rickshaw. He and Helen rode. They passed a lot of people walking, among them two policemen and a convict from Lahore jail. Will asked them where they were going. They said, 'To Kasauli', so he presumed that the convict would be appearing before the magistrate there. 'But the next day', he wrote,[195] 'as I was in the Pasteur Institute watching Captain Harvey inoculate the people who had been bitten by mad dogs and jackals, who should turn up but this convict led by the warders. He had been sent up because he had drunk some milk out of the same cup as a man who died of Hydrophobia. Captain Harvey enquired all about what had happened, and came to the conclusion that there was no need to treat him, so he was just marched off down the hill to Lahore.'

A hundred patients a day were then attending the Pasteur Institute. They came from every part of India and, while waiting, squatted in the sun in front of the house. While Will was there a man arrived from the frontier speaking only Pushtu; before he could be treated an interpreter had to be sent for.

Will explained[196] to the children how Pasteur had discovered that if a person bitten by a mad dog was injected with a little of the brain of a mad rabbit he would not get rabies. He described what you would see if you were to go inside the Institute: 'You would see a room with cages all round it on shelves, and in each a rabbit which has been given rabies by Captain Harvey, who is in charge here. After a few days the rabbits develope hydrophobia and become paralysed and die about the eleventh day. On the tenth day the sick rabbit is killed and its spinal cord is taken out and a small part of it mixed with water, and a small quantity injected under the skin of the patients. A very small dose is given at first, but each day it is increased, so that at the end of the treatment, 17 or 21 days after, a large amount is given, and the person goes away quite safe from rabies.'

Helen and Will enjoyed staying with Captain Harvey. He had a fire lit in their room each evening and provided two hot water bottles. Each morning the ground was covered in hoar frost, but, even so, magnificent roses were in bloom. Helen found it so cold out of doors that the skin at the tips of her fingers cracked. She repaired them with cotton-wool and Collodion and, with her hands quite numb, carried on sketching. She was delighted to hear that Captain Harvey was shortly to be marrying a Miss Sutherland from Edinburgh, and arranged for her to stay a night with them in Bombay when she arrived in March. In the event the couple were married from their house.

One of her Kasauli pictures[197] shows her being pushed up a hill in a rickshaw by four men. She and Will went out to lunch with Colonel Semple of the Royal Army Medical Corps. 'As The Firs is rather far down and the club where Col Semple entertained us is nearly at the top of everything we thought I would hardly be able to walk there, and Captain Harvey kindly got a rickshaw for me. But though I had four men and sometimes a fifth, when Dad lent a hand, I can assure you I felt very heavy going up and up and up. But it was wonderful how the men went on, never stopping, and never getting quite out of breath, though they panted a good deal on the steep bits. They must have taken me up about a mile and a half, and we must have risen about 500 feet, and when they were paid the next day what do you think they got? Twelve annas! Captain Harvey would not let us give them a rupee so they got 3d each and they were so pleased that they asked if I didn't want the rickshaw next day!'

On their way back from Kasauli to Kalka, Helen came down in a dandy, which was extraordinarily uncomfortable. This was a kind of boat-shaped chair, carried by four men. 'They went so fast that Dad's pony had to trot to keep up with them, and at first I thought there would be nothing but crumbs of me left by the time I got down to Kalka, till I discovered a way of rising a little, as if I were trotting on a pony.' After Kalka, she and Will broke their journey at Gwalior, where they enjoyed the Mohurram celebrations, then arrived back in Bombay at the beginning of February.

Her health improved after this holiday. She took lessons in writing Urdu and complained to her children that she had to use the simplest infant primers. She was delighted to hear that Pat, her own former pupil – and far from a star one – was dux (top) of his class at the Academy. Rob, in his letters, again wrote about the mali's pool. Helen understood how much of an effort it was for a boy who was not yet eight to write at all; in his early ones he had done two lines a day. She constantly praised him and told him she did understand the effort it was: 'If it is too much for you, dear son', she wrote, 'just write "I love you" and we will understand'.

Not all her letters were from her children or about them. Some letters must have been particularly sad to receive. On the 1 July 1910 she was to write: 'The mail has just come in today, and brought the news of dear Grandfather's "falling asleep". We could not have wished anything else for him, for I expect now his eyes that had got so dim are able to see clearly, and all the weakness and tiredness that had kept him always in the house, while all of you were able to rush about and enjoy all the loveliness of summer is swept away, and he sees and hears such lovely things that it would make him quite sad to be asked to come back.' This was her father, the expert in geology and in shells, who had spent part of his working life in India and then in Madeira; clearly it had been a long decline for a once-vital man. Helen went on to exhort her children not to forget him but to, 'fix his face and his kind words so well in your memory that when you see him again you will know him for your own grandfather. I know it's a long time since he was able to see you, even when he tried, or to say kind words . . . don't try to remember him lying ill in bed but think of the happy times before that'.

Helen advised the children to be extra kind to her mother. 'I don't feel as if any of you *could* love Grannie as much as I do, but as there are four of you I hope she just feels herself being smothered in love just now, and I hope you have all been remembering to pray for her.' Will praised Pat for representing the family at the funeral and wrote, in a little homily, that he hoped he would try to be a good man like his grandfather 'so that you may be honoured by all, as he was, when you too have to come to the end of life here'.

Chapter Eight

Will's Promotion

Without any children to take up to the hills, Helen stayed in Bombay through the hot weather of 1910, and through the mould and damp of the monsoon. Inevitably, the sprue got worse. Will prepared inoculations, and she kept writing home to say she was on the brink of being cured, but the illness persisted. Helen lived on milk and fruit and ate no meat – one of the side-effects of sprue is a sore mouth and a swollen tongue.[198] Because of that, she could hardly drink the milk she needed. Will supplied a long glass tube from the laboratory, like a straw, and she sent her children a picture of herself, with an exaggeratedly long nose and a look of distaste, sipping milk through this tube.[199]

Through most of the hot weather of 1910 she was unable to go out. She would lie in the gardens in a shady spot and sketch the flowers or the trees or a wasps' nest or do a very detailed picture of a tiny insect. She was a woman of great internal resource and the letters for those months are just as lively as those for any other time. She never ran low on interesting things to say. As Will put it: 'she was the kind of person who would take four sides to invite a person to tea'.

Will was then busy with a paper on hydrophobia and visited Poona in an attempt to get an anti-rabic centre in Bombay.[200] He also encouraged the study of leprosy in the laboratory. Helen visited the leper centre at Matunga and painted a gruesome picture of a patient to send to the children. Will, in his letter, pointed out the knobby appearance of the ears and nose and cheeks and the ulcers on the patient's arm and went on, 'We have a Captain Williams in the laboratory just now who is working at leprosy . . . he has found a microbe which he has succeeded in making grow on the laboratory media. It is got from these horrid modules on the lepers and it grows in long strings like hairs and then it breaks up into bacilli like those found in the bodies of lepers.' There were also experiments going on with fish, to see which were best to introduce into ponds to eat up mosquito larvae – an essential aspect of the control of malaria.

There was a development in Helen's works, too, at that time. She was delighted to get a letter from her publishers telling her that some of her books had been selected as school readers. She drew a picture of little Black Sambo[201] pointing with his rolled-up umbrella to the word Tiger on a blackboard in front of a class of white children. 'I wonder if you will be able to guess', Helen wrote to Rob, 'what this picture represents? It is not anything that I have ever seen, but still it is meant to set forth a fact, and the fact is this, that my little black books are going to be used to teach wee children to read. Only I have made one mistake, for I have taken Little Black Sambo as the teacher, and he is not really one of the ones that is going to be used, the ones that are, are *Little Black Quibba, Pat and the Spider* and *Little Black Bobtail*, but I am sorry to say that I have been so stupid all this week, that it is a wonder I remember I wrote any little books at all, or, remembering that much, that I have not invented quite fancy names for all of them. The publishers are going to bring out a series of readers, and they have written to tell me they are going to put these three stories into them, one into one book and two into another.' The reason that *Little Black Sambo* was not included, though she did not go into it, was the controversy over the ownership of the copyright. Her publishers James Nisbet and Co. did not have the copyright of *Little Black Sambo*. Nor did Helen. She ignored that aspect in her letter to Rob and went on to say that she was glad he would not be learning to read from the books: 'That would be "like seething a kid in its mother's milk" to teach you to read out of a book which I made for your amusement, don't you think?'

Without her children, Helen was not working on any more children's books. She was, however, writing bits and pieces for the Bombay Y.W.C.A. magazine – copies of which I have been unable to trace. In December 1910 she sent some of the magazines to Janet: 'It is only the stories I have written so far, in the magazines that I have sent you, and the Editorial in May, because I couldn't get anyone else to write me one. I can't remember how many magazines I've sent. Did you get September? I wrote "Safety" in that but that and "Blind Faith" in October are my only attempts at "poetry" and poor "Blind Faith" has suffered so at the printer's hands that you won't be able to make head or tail of it. But it was not very good anyhow!'

Helen was inclined to put her own vigorous verse into her letters from time to time. Pat played a game called 'hailes' at the Academy – a game unique to this school. It is a kind of hockey or shinty played with a large wooden spoon-shaped stick called a clacken. When he heard that Pat had broken two clackens, she replied:[202]

> There was a young man with a clacken
> Who went about hittin' and whacken'
> Till the poor clacken cried

WILL'S PROMOTION

'I shall have to divide
For I can't stand this smashin' and smackin''

Will was also inclined to include a moral or an appropriate cautionary tale in his letters, particularly in those to Pat, who was most in
need of them. He described[203] the 1910 Bombay St Andrew's Dinner,
with ninety-eight attending, held in the Freemason's Hall with a band
and pipers and very good speeches, 'all about Scotland and the great
men who have gone out of it to help to rule great lands and to do good
in all parts of the world. It is surely a great privilege', he went on, lec-
turing Pat a bit, 'to belong to such a land and we must try to be good
and great men for Auld Scotland's sake.' This is an interesting
example of the way Scots participated in the Empire as Scots. They
did not in any way feel it was England's Empire. While we must
discount a certain amount of Will and Helen's Scottish patriotism as
that of Scots abroad, it is clear that Will thought of himself as Scottish
first and then British. 'Scotland and the Empire', was his rallying call,
as it was, too, for the Scottish liberal peer and British Minister of the
eighteen-nineties, Lord Rosebery. Today's Scots are less clear about
their identity. Their cultural solidity has been considerably weakened
by the impact of the mass media, dominated by London. Will and
Helen, however, had no nationality problems. Nor did they worry
about Scotland's constitutional position, which, as Scotland's cultural integrity has been eroded, has become such an absorbing
concern in recent years.

Will was an acknowledged expert on Burns and on the songs of
Lady Nairne. He was delighted in 1912 to become Chairman of the
Caledonian Society of Madras, set up to help fellow country men in
distress, but also giving an opportunity to exiles to get together. The
motto, for example, on the menu at the St Andrew's Day Dinner in
Madras in 1912 read:

> Here in Madras we freely grant
> We're blest wi' sunny weather
> Frae cauld an' snow we're weel awa'
> But man, we miss the heather.

Will explained that although he did not much fancy making a
speech, 'everyone says I must do it, so like Burns I must try for puir
auld Scotland's sake'.

When it came to the night he found he had to make two speeches,
one proposing the Pious Memory of St Andrew and one on 'The Land
O'Cakes', then, after being carried round on a chair (he was heavily
built and this needed four men) behind a piper, he had to make *another*

speech. 'However, I said I would imitate the brevity of the Sergeant-Major of a Scots Regiment when called upon to make a speech in presenting a silver cup to the Colonel of the regiment who was retiring. He quite forgot the speech he had made up and all he could say was "Cornel, here's the Joog", and the Colonel being equally embarrassed could only reply "Aye man, is that the Joog?" They all laughed very much at that so I did not need to say any more.'

Turning back to December 1910 in Bombay, however, Will's colleague Capt W. Glen Liston and his family arrived back from Scotland and once again shared the Director's house at Parel with Will and Helen. They had left Isabella behind in Edinburgh and had only brought their baby William, a toddler. Helen was delighted to see him again – 'such a contented happy wee boy', she wrote, 'he has been just a little sunbeam in the house.' As well as William, the Listons brought a cheese back with them from Britain – a Stilton. Helen, on her diet of milk and fruit, had a very keen sense of smell. Before she knew it was there, she sniffed it from three rooms away, and followed the scent along the verandah.[204] Although cheese was something she was not allowed to eat she ate some and delightedly reported that it did not do her any harm.

She drew a picture in December[205] 1910 of a tea party in the garden, with relatives who were staying and herself on a chaise longue. She was now an invalid, but her letters remained chatty and cheerful, with references to her illness coming from Will or in reply to queries from the children. 'No, my legs are not sore when they get swollen.' Despite her poor health, her relationship with Will went from strength to strength; when she sent Janet greetings on her seventeenth birthday she expressed the hope that Janet would grow happier each year that passed, as she herself had done.

The time was at hand for decisions about Janet's future – though Will and Helen had to be prompted into thinking about it by one of Janet's teachers. 'You say Miss Farquharson wants to know', Helen replied to Janet[206] 'what you are to do when you leave school. That just shows how accustomed to home Mis Farquharson is. Out here', she added with a hint of tartness, 'we don't make plans two years ahead, we wait and see what we've got to do, and circumstances nearly always decide the question for us. But, (and here Helen showed that even she had some remnants of Scottish prudence left) 'I want you to have at least one year abroad – two if it can be managed, so that you may get up French and German very thoroughly. Failing that, I'd like you to go to the University for a year.' Helen was aware that Janet at seventeen was old enough to have quite clear views on the subject and added, 'But of course I want to know what you want, and I also want to get my big daughter out beside me. But that again depends on when you finish with school and on what you want yourself. What would you *like* to do? You see probably we shall come home in two years and by the time we come out you'll be 20, old enough to come with us, but when will you be done with school? Everything is so uncertain for if Father got an administrative appointment we might not be able to come at the time we plan, and we might come sooner or we might be a year longer.'

Within a few months somebody, possibly Janet's teacher or possibly Ata, must have done some organising. Helen wrote that she was delighted to hear that Janet would be going to school in Geneva and sent her advice on which botany books to take with her from Strathearn Place.

Day, at the age of fourteen, had already made it clear to everybody that she wanted to be a doctor. She had played at doctors since her earliest days; and her family, at a time when women doctors were rare, was not at first inclined to take this ambition seriously. But Day persisted. She wrote regularly about how interesting her hygiene classes were and sent details of the medical exhibitions she went to. She begged her parents for a monkey's skeleton and to their credit they sent her one, even though Will's own attitude to the role of women was a traditional one. In a letter to Janet,[207] for example, written after watching a parade of Boy Scouts, he reported that the General reviewing them had made a fine speech and had told them that he hoped they would grow up good and patriotic men ready to serve their country. Will then got rather carried away: 'I hope so too and that my sons will grow up also good and patriotic men proud of the grand traditions of Scotland and the Empire.' At this point he realised that he was writing to one of his daughters, and he added: 'And a great deal depends on the girls of Scotland too, for without good mothers you cannot expect to have good sons.' Did he then feel that this was perhaps not quite what the recipient wanted to hear? He added a further phrase: 'So we trust our daughters will grow up fit to help in the affairs of the country also.'

Helen's attitude to the position of women is indicated by her horror at the Queens' Tombs which she visited at Ahmedabad. She noted with distaste[208] that the little girls who died were buried outside the burial ground along with the pet monkeys and parrots. She was by no means a campaigning feminist but, as an educated woman she believed in women developing their talents to the full. In the end, with support from both parents, both Janet and Day, after various delays, were to go to university and Day was to achieve her life long ambition and qualify as a doctor.

By Christmas 1910 Helen – despite the care and attention of her own personal doctor – was too ill to go on a planned holiday to Cawnpore with Will and relatives who were staying with them. She stayed in Parel and spent Christmas with the Listons. January was a much more cheerful month, however. Will was sent on a two-month course in Poona and Helen went with him.

Poona was cooler and less humid than Bombay and Helen was soon enjoying herself: 'It is *very* good milk we get from the military farm here and I am getting so fat and strong up here that if I dont take care I shall be knocking Dad down by mistake. All my dresses are getting too tight for me. The only way that I know that I am not *quite* well yet is that when I am tired my feet swell up till they look like the feet of a cloth doll that has eaten too much sawdust.'

Will's course was to train as a P.M.O., and he explained what this was.[209] 'The initials stand for Principal Medical Officer, and it means that the person holding the office is the head doctor of the Brigade or Division to which he may be attached. He has to look after the various officers who have charge of the regiments and hospitals of the Command and to administer the affairs of them all'. He then went on to add that there would be time for various diversions as well: 'As far as I can see the work will not be very hard and we should have lots of time for amusement and making up arrears of work from the laboratory. We have brought up the motor and hope to explore the country all round, and as it is very pretty country and the weather is cool it will be very pleasant I fancy.'

While Will went on manoeuvres setting up mock dressing stations and field ambulances, Helen stayed in the Napier Hotel.[210] 'Our rooms here are really quite nice, only we get rather more of the Western sun than we want, however it is not hot in the meantime so it does not matter. The window beside which I am sitting to write opens into the bedroom, which has a door and another window into this room, so that it is really quite airy, though I don't consider it a very big room. Besides these two Father has a dressing room and bathroom, and I have a wee scrap of a place which has not the courage to call itself a dressing room in the manager's letter, but which contains a basin and a chest of drawers, and two bathrooms, the one of which I use, in the other I keep my milk. We are up a stair and get lots of wind during the day, but it is very still now.'

Sometimes Helen went on trips in a carriage with a friend Mrs Roe, and sent home pictures of what she did and saw. On one occasion she described some Indian children that she visited at an orphanage:[211] 'the compound was full of dear wee bright-faced boys who were racing about in all directions, and playing most merrily, they each had on a bright scarlet coat made of some stuff like a red blanket, and clean white short breeks . . . These boys were famine orphans, and they have been taken by this mission, and are being trained in various trades, so that when they are grown up they will be able to earn their own living.'

Will enjoyed playing at soldiers. As part of his training, he had to be certified as able to ride. After his test the rather ungenerous verdict came that he could ride well enough for a medical officer. In a letter of 3 February 1911, Helen drew a picture for Pat of the army drawn up on a Poona hillside and Will described his role in the mock battle.[212] 'The General told us where the enemy were posted, and then the officers had to write accounts of how they would attack such a position and the orders that should be given. The medical officers had also to say where the hospitals and first dressing stations should be put, and to write out the necessary orders. Then in the evening after dinner we all came to the General's tent and he criticised the different plans and told us what *he* would have done in the circumstances. It was very interesting and instructive and we enjoyed the camp life very much. It was very cold at night in the tents, and one night the water in the basin outside one of the tents had ice on it in the morning. We had to have the tents and baggage sent on by train starting about nine so we had to be up before it was light and breakfasted in the open air so that the tents might be struck and all folded up to go in the vans. So we used to breakfast in our greatcoats and even then shivered with cold.'

In March their interlude in the cooler climate of Poona came to an end. They set off to drive back to Bombay – a considerable undertaking in 1911. Helen describes in a letter to Janet on 10 March how the road was level and shady as far as Lanouli. Then, 'we ran down three miles to Khandala, where we spent Saturday and Sunday night, and on Monday by 7.30 we were off and sliding down the Bhore Ghat as it is called. The road is very steep and very windy.' When they stopped to let the car cool and to picnic, Helen would take out her paints and do a picture from under the mango tree or wherever they were for one of her letters. They both enjoyed such journeys, and in particular looking at the changing vegetation. 'It was lovely and fresh and crisp and cool and we saw such pretty jungly things in flower, but we knew most of them, and as time was rather precious we only stopped once, to get a white flower with beautifully crinkled edges – a Heterophragma I think. When we got down to the plains we passed so many lovely jambul trees (that is our Indian wild plum you know) just covered with huge masses of beautiful tasselly blossom. The flowers look as if they were made of short white stamens, and they are lovely in great feathery bunches.'

After they came back to Bombay, Helen's ill health returned.[213] 'I am in a bad cut this week', as old Nane (her childhood Nanny), 'used to say, and my pictures are all by-ordnar bad'. Then she adds, with a salutary touch, 'However I can't help it, I must e'en send you what I *can* do, not what I should like to do'.

She was able, nevertheless, to go out for drives with Will. One evening in May 1911 after they had been shopping in town, they went for a spin on Malabar Hill because it was too hot to go home and work.[214] 'The Humming Bird just flew over the hill and it was lovely and cool at the top, and the long necklace of lights which stretches from Malabar Point away down to Colaba looked very beautiful in the soft waning evening light.'

They were not to know it, but their days in Bombay were numbered. Within a few weeks they would be leaving at a few days notice in a frenzied scramble. In ignorance of this, however, they laid on an 'At Home' at the Laboratory, to return some of the hospitality they had received. Will made it into a kind of Open Day for those invited, and took the opportunity to offer some public health education. He set out snake exhibitions among the rose bushes, and viewings through microscopes of his most interesting microbes. There was also music and an obstacle golf course running over three badminton courts and a golf course. Over one hundred guests came, and there were 120 dozen strawberries specially ordered from Mahableshwar and 150 pounds of ice to keep the drinks cool.

At the end of May 1911 Will received an unexpected summons from the Surgeon-General of the Indian Medical Service to go to see him in Simla. Could this be promotion to the post of Principle Medical Officer? That would need a three-day journey all the way to Simla and such appointments were usually announced in a brief official note or a telegram. Could it be yet another development in the Mulkowal saga? Or could it be for the most senior medical post in Madras, shortly to be vacant?

They left immediately and had a cheerful journey north, eating mangoes in their sleeper to refresh themselves in the heat and dust.[215] The stone of one of these mangoes slipped from Will's hand and marked his clean white cotton trousers. They were the only pair he had with him, so he washed them in the little basin in the carriage and hung them up on the frame of the electric punkah and then sat enjoying the cool breeze funnelled towards him. They did the last section, from Kalka to Simla in what Will described as 'the twistiest little railway in the world'. The last time he had made the journey in 1903 he had come up in the mail tonga, changing horses every few miles.[216]

When they reached Simla they stayed with Surgeon-General Lukis, head of the I.M.S., at his house, *Craig Dhu*. There on 24 May 1911 Will received the official note he had been expecting or fearing – and, strolling across the lawn to Surgeon-General Lukis' house, he handed it to Helen. She was astonished to read:[217] 'You are appointed Surgeon-General Madras and should report yourself to Madras

Government by 31 inst.' This was an appointmentt which Will had thought he had no hope of getting. It put him in charge of all the medical services for the whole of the Madras presidency.

Helen was delighted.[218] 'I am so pleased that I don't know how to say how pleased I am. And I am sure it is all the D.G. Surgeon-General Lukis's doing, for I think he has seen how well and happily Father ran the laboratory.' The news merited a special cake, called a mikado cake, for tea for the children. She also exorted them to pray for Will 'for we know', she said, 'that there are special difficulties lying ahead of him and even if there were none it is not in man that walketh to direct his steps'. She added that she was specially glad about the appointment because Will had never asked for anything. 'When the question of the next Surgeon General with the Government of Madras began to occupy our minds, it looked as if he had no chance at all, having been so long in Bombay. Some people in Madras had even forgotten that he belonged to Madras at all, and there were three men ahead of him who all seemed to have pretty fair claims. So it really seems like a miracle his having been chosen. I am sure it is thanks to Surgeon General Lukis who went over the army list with the Governor of Madras, discussing each man available till they brought it down to Father and one other man, and then the D.G. said he didn't know the other man but he *did* know Father, and could strongly recommend him, as he had seen how he ran the lab.'

In a later letter, written after she had got there, Helen revealed how unexpected was the appointment in Madras. Will was not the most senior person and he had been chosen over the heads of others. When he sent a telegram to his new office in Madras, telling them when he would arrive, they still had not heard of his appointment. Instead of concluding that he must be their new Surgeon-General, they presumed that he must be passing through on his way to Burma, to relieve the man who would be coming from there to take up the post.

In her recollection of her uncle,[25] his niece Elizabeth Craigie Fitch, who had lived in Madras while he was Surgeon General, was to write that someone from outside was specifically sought at this moment. 'The medical service of the Presidency had fallen on evil days, and needed complete reorganisation. There had been abuses and much underhand dealing and corruption and, above everything, an administrator was needed of absolute justice and honesty, a man of tact and with a knowledge of all types of men, of fearless courage to put an end to abuses; and looking round they found the man whose character answered all these needs.'

If the appointment seemed a miracle, it needed another to get Helen and Will away from Simla, back to Bombay to get packed up and prepare the laboratory for handing over, and arrive in Madras – all within a week. The journey from Simla to Bombay took three days, then it was a further day and a half to Madras. They arrived back in Bombay on the Sunday evening and left for Madras on the evening of Tuesday 30 May 1911. In the middle of all the confusion Helen sat down on the Tuesday to write her four letters home.

You must picture us for yourselves, surrounded by gaping boxes, and groaning under piles of clothes and rubbish some of which must be packed, and some of which must be given away, and all before 10 o'clock tonight. It is rather a dismal sensation raking out all one's almirahs and drawers, especially when it has to be done in a tearing hurry, and at this moment my room seems in a hopeless mess. But as soon as this letter is done I shall turn on and pack some more and then stop and write to Pat and so on, and if anything is not stowed away somehow, it will have to lie where it falls, for by nine tonight Father and I must leave this happy home and we shall only return as visitors some two or three months hence to pack and remove *everything*. At present we are only taking our clothes, and what I may call our toys, because we shall live in a hotel in Ooty but when it comes to setting up in Madras we shall have to take all our linens, silver, glass and china, and furniture. We mean to leave the worst of the furniture to the Listons – "everything that was vile and refuse" – but we shall take all the good things – blackwood almirahs – piano – some chairs – and the best of the beds. However, we haven't time for that now, which is a pity, as two or three months of monsoon will not improve them.

After she had packed a bit more, she stopped and picked up her pen to write to Pat. There were no pictures this week, and the writing was large and scrawly. 'I'm getting into a fearful scurry now, for I seem to have so much to do and so little time to do it in.' Rob came at the end of the line, and he was lucky to get a letter at all. 'You must please write a nice letter to yourself for I haven't time to write you one today, I'm just scurrying to get my packing done, and every half hour or so somebody comes to the door. "Memsahib" "Kya Hai?" "Parcel hai" or "Chittie hai" or "Tar hai" (that's parcel, letter or telegram as the case may be) and I have to clap on my dressing gown and go to the door and see what it is. For it is too hot to pack even in a thin dressing gown, and I am reduced to wishing like Sydney Smith that I could take off my flesh and sit in my bones.'

When they got to the station, nearly the entire staff of the Laboratory, from doctors to manual workers, were there to see them off.[219] They were garlanded and presented with bouquets of flowers. It was both a sadder and happier departure than that in 1903, when Will had left Bombay because of his disagreements with Haffkine in the aftermath of Mulkowal. Now they were leaving after seven happy years in Bombay, during which time Will had strengthened and diversified the work of the Laboratory and guided it through its recovery from the disaster of Mulkowal. With his achievement recognised, they were now delighted to be setting off for 'fresh fields and pastures new'.

The journey to Madras took a night and a day and was so hot that they wore their pyjamas in their sleeper all the time. [220] The water in the cold tap was scalding. They had brought a picnic basket full of food and had tea handed through the window at odd stops. They pulled down the cuscus tatties for shade and drenched them with water for coolness. The tatties only worked on one side, however; on the other side – although it was a first class carriage – they had jammed. In the train, in his pyjamas, Will carried on working. He had to finish a paper he was preparing on the treatment of snake bite with permanganate of potash and he had a large number of congratulatory letters to answer. His writing was rather angular even without the motion of the train; he was, however very good at typing, so he possibly managed to type on the train.

When they reached Madras they went to stay with an I.M.S. friend, Captain Justice, in Mungambankum High Road. For the first time Helen slept in a room with an electric fan. [221] She kept it going nearly all day and resolved to persuade the land-lord of their new house, when they had found one, to put in electricity. She did not care about electric light, she said, but she did fancy an electric fan. Fans in India were not only a luxury; they could save life. Rob remembers his cousin Alec Lorimer, who served under Will in the I.M.S., commenting that next to quinine the things that most prolonged life in the tropics were electric fans and refrigeration. Helen had earlier sent home a sketch of the new paraffin driven fan; but this had the disadvantage of giving off heat. The electric fan, by contrast, was all advantage without disadvantage.

It is salutary to reflect that Helen lived in pre-refrigeration India. Milk was an almost impossible problem. It sometimes went sour as it was boiled, the growth in the bacteria was so great during the heating process. Meat was another problem; it was very hard to keep it fresh and untainted. Before domestic refrigerators there were ice-boxes, supplied by a daily delivery of ice if one lived in a town. But in some of her earliest postings, Helen would have lacked even that.

Helen found that very few houses in Madras, with or without electricity, were available just then. They decided to take one in Harrington Road, Chetput, on the other side of the road from the house they had lived in before and in which Janet and Day had been born. [223] Their new house was called *The Rookery* though there was no sign of any rooks. It had two large rooms for the drawing room and dining room, but the bedrooms opened off each other in what Helen felt was an awkward way. 'However', wrote Helen, prepared to let her fate take its course, to Day, 'By the time you come out we may be in some other house; or perhaps we may be home before either of you can come.'

They stayed only a week in Madras and then set off to the hill station of Ootacummund, where the higher echelons of the Madras Presidency administration conducted their business through the hot weather. Helen described in great detail for Pat and Robin the little rack railway, which took them there.[224] She and Will sat next to a man who pointed out a rubber plantation which the Government had tried to see if Para rubber would grow. Helen thought the rubber trees were not thriving, though clearly plantations of coffee, and, higher up, tea, were enjoying the climate of the Nilghiri hills. 'It was such a pretty line', Helen wrote, 'sometimes running between high walls of rock, sometimes through tunnels, sometimes under half-tunnels, and so green all the way. I think it about the prettiest line I have ever seen, far prettier than the Simla railway – though not so grand as the Highland railways.'

With the cool climate, and the stimulus of all the activity of travelling from Bombay to Simla, then back to Bombay and on to Madras then Ooty within three weeks, Helen's health improved. Will's promotion was obviously just what she had needed. In a quiet moment she picked up all the letters of congratulation and read them through for a second time. Whether it was the influence of India or her Calvinist background with its belief in predestination, her faith that something would turn up had proved fully justified. 'After rain,' she wrote, 'the sky is blue and the sun is shining gloriously, and everything is too good to be true'.

Will's first task at Ooty was to go across to the Stone House, which held the Government offices, and set up a system of improved medical training for Indians and Anglo-Indians who could not afford to go to Britain for training. By a strange quirk of history this was the scheme which his own daughter was to join some years later, when she found herself trapped in India by the war and anxious to start her medical studies. Helen drew pictures of the view from Shoreham Hotel where she and Will were staying, and of the Stone House, and of the Secretariat peons or messengers in their scarlet uniforms.[225] She pointed out that the peons wore long belts over their shoulders; each had a brass badge which told the offices of his master. The belts were of different colours so that the offices of the peons could be identified at once. The Government House peons wore red belts with a gold lace border, the Judges' ones wore yellow with a gold border, and the medical ones wore red and black – appropriate colours, said Will, for blood and death.

They were a good deal further away from blood and death in Ooty than they had been in Bombay. Helen had only been there a week when she got her first taste of the high life. As she had her 'chota hazri' in her bedroom in the Shoreham Hotel on 27 June 1911, a battery of six guns on a platform opposite fired a salute to celebrate the coronation of King George V in London. The guns were only 150 yards away, and the crash, said Will, was, 'enough to split your ear drums'. Then he and Helen went to a church service, where they sat in the seats allotted to them, in the row behind the Governor. Also there were the members of the Council, in Civil uniforms, (black with gold collars, cuffs and pocket flaps) and many officers in uniform and a Chaplain and a Bishop with a grand silver crozier carried before him.[226] 'The service was beautifully read', reported Helen, used to something far simpler, 'and the stained glass windows and the scarlet and white dahlias and annunciation lilies and the lighted candles and the music all made a very impressive setting'. She sent one copy of the service sheet home to her mother and one to Ata and they were doubtless impressed too. Lest anyone should think she was getting carried away, however, she felt she had to add: 'But I would not like such pomp and circumstance every day, my eyes and mind kept straying from the prayers to the people.'

It is difficult to realise how seriously people then took the British Empire, and how they, in their phrase, dedicated their lives to its service. In the *Handy Atlas of the British Empire* published by John Bartholemew and Co. of Edinburgh in 1904, the preface describes it as the greatest empire the world had ever seen, not only in area and population but in wealth and power. It covered more than a fifth of the land surface of the globe. The British navy was the most powerful in the world and the United Kingdom was then the world's leading trading nation with a volume of imports and exports over twice that, for example, of the U.S.A.

However, not even the World's Greatest Empire could get everything in India to run as it wished. The Bannermans, after giving praise to God's goodness towards His Majesty's Dominions, ran into a series of difficulties caused by the collapse of the road bridge connecting Ooty with Madras.[227] They had to have their car sent from Bombay to Nanjengud near Mysore, instead of to Matapolliyam as they had first arranged. Their driver had to drive it the last eighty-five miles instead of thirty-one. The car arrived safely but then began to give nothing but trouble. Though the Bannermans could get back to Madras by rail, the car was then marooned, through the bridge collapse, at Ooty.

Leaving the car and the driver in Ooty, Helen and Will went back to Madras, though only for a week. Then they got on that hot train across India again and set off for Bombay, to complete Will's hand-over at the laboratory and to pack up their furniture. Will's successor at the Laboratory was his friend Major W.G. Liston, who served as Director from 1911 to 1923. Helen was delighted to report that the Listons had, 'a dear wee tiny, tiny baby, who was born last Wednesday, and she is so small and tender that she needs to be kept very warm. She hasn't even been washed and properly dressed yet, just oiled and wrapped in cotton wool and shawls.'[228]

The bustle of packing was muted so as not to disturb her, but even so, a great wind sprang up as their furniture lay on the drive, waiting for the carts to take it to Dadar station.[229] It blew a table top over, and this crashed against a cupboard with glass doors and this fell onto the sideboard with a smashing noise that brought everybody out to see what had happened. 'And lo!' wrote Will, 'when the cupboard was lifted up the panes of glass were quite whole! The cornice of the cupboard had fallen on the edge of a big flower pot and sheared its way through it and it was the breaking of the pot that we had heard.'

As well as packing, Helen was invited to a special gathering of the Y.W.C.A. and presented with a silver chain purse in recognition of her work for them over the years.[230] From that moment on she had no magazine to edit. She must have missed this; she certainly was sad when she left Bombay for the last time in July 1911. She drew a picture of the railway station at night, seen as they looked back as the train pulled away:[231] 'This represents goodbye to Bombay,' she wrote 'but how can you represent a mist of tears and an ache of heart? Very sad were we as the lighted sheds of the station, and all the signal lights gradually receded and receded till they vanished from our sight, with all the kindly faces and friendly waving handkerchiefs which were there to see us off.'

It must have been some consolation, though, that when they got to their house in Harrington Road, at least one old friend was waiting for them. They found a large gathering of men and women on the varandah steps.[232] These were a variety of servants who wanted to work for them, 'and foremost among them was old Muregesam (pronounced Mooroo*gay*sam) with the chit we had given him so long ago'. This was the Mali who had worked for them when Janet and Day were small, 14 years previous. He had another job by this time, with a Mr Jones at the Observatory. 'We did not like to take him away without asking, but Mr Jones was very kind and said that if he wished to go he might, and he actually did wish it, so we have got him now and he is working away as if for dear life.'

Helen and Will rebuilt the Fern House which had become delapidated and arranged for two horses and two gharries while their car was in Ooty. They soon settled into a comfortable life with more travelling for Will than he had had to do in Bombay, and more of a duty to attend functions for Helen. However, she had no small children to keep her at home, and was reasonably fit, so this was something she adapted to. Attending functions meant entertaining in return, and Helen was soon worrying about a dinner she was due to give for the Director-General of the I.M.S. when he visited Madras. She ordered a new table, large enough to seat eighteen, and new chairs. When the table arrived she was horrified.[233] It would certainly seat eighteen – but it was the size, she said, of a railway platform. She had to make arrangements for it to be cut into sections so that it could be reduced for herself and Will.

If Helen thought dinner for eighteen was grand, it was nothing compared to what she experienced when she went with Will to the Delhi Durbar. This was the celebration in 1911 to mark the visit of King George V and Queen Mary, attended by the select from all over India. It was the peak of British self confidence in their rule over India. *The Times* of 13 December 1911 described it as, 'this day of days in which princes and people gathered, after more than fifty years of tranquility, to do glad homage to a British Emperor who came as a guarantor of peace and upholder of justice and freedom.' Many of those attending were probably quite unaware that the growth of the Indian nationalist movement had already begun. The Indian National Congress had held its first meeting in Bombay as early as 1885, and the All-India Muslim League had been founded in 1906. But to the ruling elite of the day they were not a serious political threat. Almost everyone attending the Durbar thought of these future rulers of India as 'agitators' and concentrated on enjoying the celebrations.

Helen and Will were no exception. They described in detail for the children the encampment with all the distinguished guests living for ten days in furnished tents.[234] There were strips of grass in front of the tents, gravel avenues and flowers in pots down the sides of the roads. Helen drew a sketch of the inside of their tent, showing the beds, the wicker chairs upholstered in chintz, the toilet table with mirrors, the writing tables with chairs, the almirahs, the portable stove and the tub. She picked out the gossip which would amuse the children: 'It is very funny to hear all the speculations. "Has the Chief Justice got to wear his wig only – won't be allowed a topi on top of it?" "May we turn opera-glasses on the royal carriage or will that be a sort of lèse-majesté?"' But she did not entirely neglect the serious political side. As she wrote to Pat on 14 December:

This is our first tamasha (ceremony) after the State Entry of which we wrote last week – the laying of the foundation stone of the All-India Memorial to King Edward. I thought it was going to be a hospital or an institute or something of that sort but it is only an equestrian statue. I think it will be very like the statue of him as Prince of Wales that stands in front of the Esplanade in Bombay. I rather wondered at their choosing Delhi as the place it was to stand but the reason is plain now, for as you have doubtless heard through the papers, the King-Emperor announced at the Dubar that in future Delhi was to be the capital of all India, and Bengal is to come down to a Governor, like Madras and Bombay. It is a very great change, for it means that the partition of Bengal into two Lt-Governorships, about which there has been a great deal of agitation among a certain section of the Bengalis, is to be done away with, but also that Bengal is to lose the advantage they had by having the capital and the Imperial Government in their Presidency. I think these same agitators will be very angry, but they can't make much of a grievance about it.'

This was a reference to the decision to end the partition of Bengal which had been masterminded by Lord Curzon when he was Viceroy in 1905.[235] To Curzon's surprise this partition, which he had planned for administrative convenience, was bitterly opposed. Curzon had resigned shortly afterwards, and now in 1911 the current Viceroy Lord Hardinge re-unified Bengal and transferred the capital to Delhi.

Processions, dinners, ceremonies, and a decoration for Will – all these are described in detail. Then comes a sentence which indicates a shadow in their lives for many months to come:[236] 'We have seen such a grand review this morning. They say there were over 50,000 troops, and they stretched away in long lines along the horizon, but father is so ill it spoils everything.' Will's illness was serious. It came to a head the day he was presented with his medal by the King. 'He was a very miserable looking old Dad, with a very grey face, and a very swollen jaw, who walked up, making three solemn bows, and received his decoration. But the king's touch seems to have its ancient virtue, for the night after he kissed the King's hand, something seems to have burst, and the next day he was able to eat food again.'

Back in Madras, Will was X-rayed. To get a good picture, the rays were switched on for thirteen and a half minutes. He described the plate which was obtained:[237] 'You can see the outlines of the lower jaw and teeth, and the hyoid bone and cartileges of the larynx beneath, and above the hyoid the shadow of the stone in the centre of the gland. This stone must have been forming for some fourteen years, for I had the first attack in the house just across the road, in 1897 I think. And every now and then I have had slight attacks when I got cold, so now I am tired of the horrid thing and must have it cut out.'

The operation was done in his own bedroom, and Helen described it at length and painted a number of pictures of Will on the operating table and in the various ensuing stages. 'This is what I saw', she wrote on 11 January 1912, under her watercolour of the operating table, 'when I peeped through the curtains of my dressing room on Sunday morning. They had put a long operating table in the bedroom, some blankets and sheets and pillows on it, and then Dad. The shadowy shape at his head is supposed to be Major Niblock who performed the operation, the man on his left is Major Kirkpatrick, who is considered just particularly good at giving chloroform. He held a sort of black extinguisher sort of thing (I didn't see it close) over Dad's face, and Major Niblock told me if he had not been so skilful they would have had to do artificial respiration several times, for Dad was very lazy and wouldn't breathe properly, and twice he bothered them by falling asleep.' Since he was already unconscious from the chloroform this presumably was a euphemism for stopping breathing. The treatment was a couple of hard thumps on the back.

It turned out that the stone was not in the gland but behind it.[238] 'When Major Niblock had ligatured the duct and dissected out the gland and taken it away, there was the stone "lying grinning at them", as he said. So it was a good thing the operation was done when it was, for no one can say where the stone would have wandered to next.' 'It is quite a pretty stone', added Will, 'and I offered to get it set in gold as a locket for Mother to wear, but she would not have it on any account so the stone will go to the Museum and live there in a bottle with a label to say what it is. The operation was done last Sunday forenoon and it is now Thursday, and though the wound is nearly healed up, there is one corner where the drainage tube was which is oozing a little still. So I must endure for a few days longer being bullied by Mother until the stitches are taken out next Sunday. Then we will go to Bangalore for few days to recoup and after that return to work.'

Will indicated that the operation had proved considerably more complicated than they had expected: 'The wretched old gland got stuck to its surroundings on account of old inflammation, so instead of shelling out of its bed like a pea out of its pod, it had to be dissected away, and there was a great deal of bleeding and the surgeons got all covered in blood which spouted out of the cut arteries in all directions. And when it was all done Major Niblock told the nurse to let mother know the operation was all finished, thinking she would be anxious. But naughty mother had been peeking through a curtain all the time, and when the nurse came and told her she came forward and saw all the horrid bloody men standing round the table. And when they saw her they shouted to her to go back, for they were afraid she would faint at the sight of blood, when all the time she'd been keeking through the purdah! What a NAUGHTY MUM!!!' Will's colleagues had apparently failed to take into account the fact that they were dealing with the author of a number of conspicuously gory children's books. What was mere blood after the explosion in *Little Black Mingo* with dismembered limbs flying everywhere, followed by tea off the Mugger's severed head?

Apart from the operation, Helen looked back on 1911 with considerable satisfaction:[239] 'Dont you think Father has had a very eventful year? At the beginning of 1911 he was just a Lieutenant-Colonel, and at the end, after being a Brevet-Colonel for a bit, he is a Surgeon General and a C.S.I. (Commander of the Star of India)' But the operation took a lot out of Will. A month later the wound had still not quite healed; and after two months it had healed but he was still tired.

At the end of February the visit to Madras of the Director General of the Indian Medical Service, Sir Pardey Lukis, came round. There is no mention in Helen's letters of the eighteen-guest dinner party which she had planned to give, so it was presumably not held because of Will's condition. Helen was probably relieved. According to an Edinburgh relation[240] who visited her at that time in Madras, shining in company was not Helen's strong point – she was too shy. She could be amusing within her family circle but outside it she was nervous and anxious. When the Lukises arrived, Helen and Will gave up their bedroom for them and moved into a tent in the garden. This was quite common practice in India at that time when extra accommodation was needed. By day the tent was so hot that Helen came into the house for her rest, and stretched out on her dressing room floor. At night, however, she added, the tent was so cool that they needed two blankets.

After a further few months, with Will working hard at his medical administration and Helen busy running the household, the time came round for their long leave. They must have been more than ready for the break and left at the end of May 1912 to spend four months with their children in Edinburgh.

Chapter Nine

The Last Years in India

For Helen the leave of 1912 was a sad one. Her mother died while on holiday with them at Benderloch in the West of Scotland. Mrs Watson was eighty-one and had been looked after for some years by Helen's youngest sister Elspeth, known in the family as Apy. In the way of youngest daughters of those days who looked after elderly parents, Elspeth was now forty and unmarried. It was decided that she would go out to India and stay with Helen and Will. As she set sail she was not to know that, once war had broken out, in 1914, she would be unable to get a passage back to Britain and would have to stay in India till 1918. Also travelling back to India in 1912 was Janet. She was now nineteen and had completed her year's further schooling in Geneva.

This was for Will and Helen the beginning of their last spell in India. With the outbreak of war they were to get no more home leaves and were to stay in India for six years continuously till Will retired in 1918. These years were to prove very demanding ones for Will. The burdens of administration are always more harassing than those of research, and the shortages of men and materials, brought about by the war, were to put great strains on those doctors who remained at their posts.

Will was at the top of his profession, and his work was absorbing and fulfilling. His neice Craigie described how he appeared to her at this time. [25]

Six feet high and broad of shoulder, with a fine erect carriage; his hair latterly was grizzled and he had a heavy grey moustache. But the most noticeable feature of his face were his eyes – large and dark and very searching, so that one felt that little escaped his notice. ... One of the most charming things about him was the boyish spirit he retained all through life, and he was an incorrigible tease to the last. His laugh, loud and hearty, with his head thrown back, was the most infectious thing to hear, and I fancy that his great sense of humour was one of the most valuable assets he had in his career.

Craigie added that Will's marriage to Helen was one of the happiest she had ever known. Their home in India, she said, was a refuge for 'every kind of lame dog. At meals one used to meet the strangest assortment of guests, who had just dropped in, typical of their large-hearted kindness and breadth of interest.' Brides would arrive to be married from their house, and mothers to have their babies. Helen also gave work such as mending and darning to social casualties, as, for example, a former teacher who had lost her post through drinking too much. 'Sometimes she disappears for long intervals and we think she is dead', wrote Janet, 'but in the end she always turns up, usually smelling of drink and in need of money.'

The Bannermans received a warm welcome back to Madras in October 1912. They needed a larger house and moved into one called *The Cloisters* in Cathedral Road which, from Helen's pictures, looked large and impressive, with four pillars at the front and curving verandahs round the sides.[241] It was just as well it was bigger than their previous house; as soon as they arrived they had five guests to stay – their friends the Listons from Bombay and three I.M.S. doctors who were attending a conference in Madras. To give decent accommodation to the guests, Helen and Janet and Elspeth shared a room with three camp beds, with one mosquito net draped over all three.[242]

As soon as they had settled in, Helen wrote home to describe their new house. She drew pictures of it from the outside, from the dining room looking through to the drawing room and from the inside looking out. So that the children really understood how it was laid out, she also sent them an architectural-type plan of it, and wrote:[243] 'The chief feature of the house is a large circular hall, round which runs a long stair. Just behind you is a wee square room whose sides are doors, leading into the dining room, drawing room and a small, flattened hexagonal room which we hope to furnish with a billiard table. Alongside the dining room' – with its railway platform table – 'is the matey room, a sort of large pantry, and opening off it a kind of rough store room. On the opposite side, next to the drawing room, but not communicating with it, is Apy's room, with her bathroom off it. Upstairs, Dad's office room is over the billiard room, my bedroom over the dining room, and Janet's over the drawing room. Above the matey room and Apy's bathroom are the dressing rooms and the bathrooms.' Round all the curving reception rooms were verandahs for shade.

This was a house of a scale and grandeur greater than Helen had enjoyed before. In keeping with the house, there were large grounds, and substantial accommodation for the servants. Their go-downs, as they were called, were also drawn for the children by Helen,[244] and made up three sides of a square with white ornate pillars at the entrance. 'There are three [dwellings] on either side and two at the end, only the two at the left-hand corner are run into one great L-shaped kitchen. Next to it is a box room, and next to that is Bagwan's room, such a nice clean tidy well-arranged room.' (This Bagwan was different from the man of the same name who had run away in Bombay because of his debts; this Bagwan had begun as a syce for Pat and Rob's pony, and was now Will's chauffeur.) 'On the other side of the kitchen is a small dark go-down, where they heat the bathwater, next to that, round the corner, is Joseph's go-down, next to that the matey's and next to that the old boy's, which has been occupied of late by Col Wilkinson's clerk. 'There were wives and children too, and Helen sent details of the children as well: 'The old boy has three girls, and Joseph has a wee girl and an orphan nephew of about two. The cook has two or three (one of them is an orphan niece or nephew too) but they don't live here. Besides this there are several rather vanishing imps who I think are responsible for the cows that graze in the compound.'

Now that Will was Surgeon-General, they not only had a larger house, but also moved in the higher reaches of society. Their first social engagement after their return was a small dinner party with the Pentlands, the Governor of Madras, and his wife. Will wrote about Janet,[245] who went with them. She was dark-haired, tall and slim; he thought she looked lovely. 'Jan was a little nervous, I think, but did not show it and she looked very nice in her white dress with white bead fringes. She and her A.D.C. (her partner at dinner) Capt Butchart, seemed to get on very well together and had lots to talk about apparently.'

The transition to India was not easy for Janet, however. She was full of laughter, with a bubbling personality; she was also a person of serious interests and intentions. Her years with Ata in Edinburgh had left their mark and distanced her from Helen. The influences from Helen over the years had been to make her more sociable and less studious. Janet arrived in India after a year in Geneva – that home of Calvin – to find that she was expected to enjoy a life of pleasure. 'I didn't like India much at first', she told me, 'No, having been brought up in a studious sort of atmosphere, I did not like the continual going out to parties and things like that'. Her letters to Day contained wistful queries about their friends and the school hockey team. 'In fact my mother nearly reached the point of sending me back to Edinburgh.'

Day, meanwhile, persisted in writing to her parents about her intention to become a doctor, and about whether she was in or out of the hockey team. Her father posted her a human skeleton – very useful for a medical student, he said, and then added: 'Or do you want to become a suffragette?' Helen was worried about playing hockey. 'They don't play much hockey here, you know'. Tennis, she said was much more useful, and she suggested to Day that she also ought to learn to ride. In later years Helen was to tell her daughter-in-law Cecilia, Rob's wife, that she found it surprising that both her daughters turned out to be quite so unworldly.

Helen was quite a well-known figure in Madras society in her own right. At one dinner,[245] the chairman introduced Will, who was the main speaker and said he did not know whether Will had written any books, but at least he was the husband of, 'the lady who had written the best books for children which he knew', and recommended everyone to read *Little Black Sambo*. It was widely read in India, where there was a dearth of appropriate books. Not every child, however, appreciated its special qualities. Helen described the son of a friend of theirs, who had just learn to read, reading it aloud to his baby brother, then two weeks old. Before long he shut the book up and walked off. 'It's no good spoiling the child', he said. 'He's not attending one bit'.

Helen still had her eye on a wider literary world. While at Ooty in 1913 she and Janet and Elspeth went to tea with some friends who were given to seeing ghosts. They heard some first-hand accounts, which sparked Helen's interest. So much so that Janet reported: 'Mother is going to write a book to prove that the human race is developing a sixth sense, by which it can discern things which have been in a place but are no longer there, just as you can sometimes smell things which have disappeared.' It could have made an interesting study though some might feel that the sixth sense in humans was diminishing rather than developing. Whatever its merits, however, the idea came to nothing.

Helen's interest, and Will's, in Church affairs[246] continued and in 1913 she sent home an assessment of the state of the churches in India. It was sparked off by hearing a sermon from a new Indian Bishop, Bishop Azariah, at the Episcopal Church of St Stephen's at Ooty. He addressed a large and fashionable audience and Helen commented: 'It seems to me a very important point in the history of churches in India, and if the Church of England is to become the national Church of India they must have Indian Bishops. But I don't myself believe that the Church of England will become the National Church of India. They are evolving a Church for themselves along the lines of the panchayets, which manage the affairs of all the villages, and that is a sort of spontaneous indigenous growth, which is more likely to spread all over India than either Episcopacy or Presbyterianism. Meantime this Bishop Azariah seems a very good man and he gave us an excellent sermon on union in Christ. 'Through him we both have access by one spirit, unto the father', shewing that only in Christ can Indians and English be truly united.' The folly of disunity within Christendom became more and more widely recognised as the years passed, but it was not until 1947 that the Episcopal, Methodist and South Indian United Church (which by an earlier union included the Presbyterian and Congregational Churches) united to form the Church of South India.[247]

Helen's comments are also interesting for what they reveal about her thinking on India's development. She thought it right that Indians ought to move into positions of power and authority – by no means a common view among British people in India before the First World War. It is revealing that she quotes: 'Only in Christ can Indians and English be truly united.' Non-Christians might feel this indicates an arrogant assumption of the superiority of the Christian faith over all others. Indeed it does; but such assumptions are common in adherents of any particular faith, including, for example, Islam. What is significant, though, is that she saw the unity of English and Indians as the goal to aim for, at a time when this was unthinkable to many of her contemporaries.

Helen and Will were free to develop such thoughts – clearly influenced by their missionary connections – because Will, as a doctor, was not responsible for governing India. Missionaries tended to have what were branded as 'unrealistic' attitudes to the advancement of Indians and were thought of by many Mandarins of the I.C.S. as a 'confounded nuisance'. It was with the thinking of the missionaries rather than the I.C.S. that Helen and Will identified themselves.

Helen's commitment to the Church involved her in charitable work which took her to parts of Madras which were in a different world from tea parties and Government House dinners. She served on the committee of a group called *The Friend-in-Need*, which organised sewing work for Indian women.[248] 'I had to go down to the work room where about eighty poor women of all ages sit and work. Some do the coarsest of hand quilting, sewing together squares of red cloth and unbleached cotton and counterpanes for the general hospital, others do the most beautiful embroidery and drawn-thread work. But I had forgotten my specs so it was more or less of an empty form for me, and I tried chiefly to say a few kind works to as many as possible. And I felt very silly and awkward all the time. Then I went back at five, and saw them all paid – oh such poor wee wages some of them got, 6d and 7d for a week's work, some not even that and the most highly paid did not get much more than about 5/-.'

The poverty of India always shocked the newly-arrived; Helen had now been living there for twenty-four years. Through her charitable work and visits to hospitals, leper asylums and other places which tried to help the poor, Helen was aware of the conditions in which so many lived, and never became inured to it. Nor was poverty the only enemy; ignorance could sometimes be a greater one. For example, Helen drew a picture one week of their water man, showing his huge deformed 'elephant leg'. She explained that this condition was common in Madras. It was thought to be caused by a parasite, she said, which got into people's groins and bred and 'gradually fills the whole leg with horrible little descendants, and when they are as bad as this old man's there is no cure possible, so far as they know at present. If only people would go into hospital at once they might be cured, but they won't. I once offered a sweeper woman to give her her pay for two months, and keep another woman to do her work and give her the place again, if she'd go into hospital, but no, she said she was an old woman, and she would soon die, and so it was better to stay where she was.'

The aspect of Will's work which made the greatest difference to the lives of ordinary people was Public Health. This was known then as the Sanitary Department, and Will, as a former Sanitary Commissioner, took a particular interest in it. He was keen that money should be spent on improving the purity of water supplies, seeing to the removal of sewage and refuse, and trying to eliminate mosquitoes, flies, rats and other disease-carrying pests. There was also the question of the purity of water in which pilgrims immersed themselves. Sometimes this was heavily polluted and a real hazard to the pilgrim. In January 1914 he went[249] to Hardwar in the Saharanpur district of the United Provinces where the Ganges emerges from the Himalayas into the plains, Thousands of Hindu pilgrims, he explained, visited the holy river at Hardwar at the time of their new year. 'We went with about sixty other members of the Sanitary Conference to inspect the arrangements for the proper sanitary convenience of the pilgrims. The first place we saw was a holy pool called Bhimgoda or Bhimgora, where the pilgrim begins his purification bathing. It is said to have been made by the kick of the horse Bhim, one of the five Pandavas, when he came here to wash away his sins after the Mahabharat, or, as some say, to show the sacred Ganges which way to flow through the plains. Anyhow, it was a dirty mud hole till the Government took it in hand and paved it with bricks and put nice tidy brick steps all round. They also made an underground drain to bring nice clean fresh water from the river, so now water flows in at one side and out at the other and no one is a bit the worse, but in fact much better for cholera has been banished by this means.'

At this same Sanitary conference, Helen records, the medical experts were shown a cheap and simple way of preventing mosquitoes from breeding – a method which later came to be widely adopted with considerable success. Tanks were set up at the conference, with glass sides, and full of mosquito larvae. A few drops of oil were added, and this formed a film on the surface. Before long the larvae stopped wriggling and died.

Will's interest in science dominated his home life as well as his working life. Sometimes he was in danger of going too far. Janet complained in one letter to her sister that his study stank – it smelt as badly as a beast's cage, she reported. This was because he had a collection in it of the skins of rats and mice, assembled to send off to the Bombay Natural History Society, of which he was an enthusiastic member. After dinner,[250] when they were in Ooty in 1913, he would clear a table in the drawing room, and, helped by his nephew Alec and his sister-in-law Elspeth, he would set about skinning the various species he had managed to collect. The Natural History society was trying to make a collection of all the rats and mice from all over India. He had to skin his examples at once, he explained, before they became feechan. By now he was one of the world's greatest experts on rats and their role in the spread of plague, and he clearly thought Day ought to know how to tell one species of rat from another as well.

> There are three or four different kinds of rat here. One kind lives in or near the bazaar; this is the *mus rattus* which is found all over India. It is a nice rather pretty rat with delicate paws and leaf-like ears and a very long tail, in fact much longer than the length of the head and body put together. It very often has a white waistcoat underneath and then it is called *alexandrinus*, because the first one of that variety was caught in Alexandria. These rats are the same that used to be so common in England long ago, and were known as the Old English Black Rat. Then the brown Norwegian Rat was brought in in shipping and being a fierce and truculent beast, it fought with and chased away the poor feeble black rat and the result is that there are now very few black rats left in either England or Scotland. . . . You can always tell it by its long tail. For the brown rat has a short tail, not so long as the length of the head and body together. The other kinds of rat here are the Bandicoot, a big bristly pig-like animal which burrows in stables and outhouses, and a field rat of the same family only smaller.

Neither Helen nor Janet helped to skin the rats – Helen sat and sketched Will and Alec and Elspeth at their work. Despite evenings spent in this way, Janet enjoyed Ooty. She and Elspeth each had a horse, and she learnt to ride and even, on one occasion, went hunting. Elspeth's horse was splendid animal, but Janet's was a rather aged mare which had cost much less than Elspeth's even with a trap for it thrown in as well. Janet also took up golf at Ooty, and had lessons from a professional, and attended various fêtes, races, garden parties and other social diversions. She began to enjoy India, despite her doubts about the frivolity of the life, and told Day to hurry up and pass her exams so that she could come out to India too.

By June 1914 Day had finished with her exams. She was not interested in going to Switzerland to improve her languages; she only wanted to join the small group of pioneer women studying medicine at the University of Edinburgh. But her parents thought it would be good for her to come to India first, for a year or two, like Janet. Like Janet too, she was to become trapped in India for the entire duration of the war. While Day was waiting for a suitable escort for the journey out, war was declared.

In a letter dated 13 August 1914, Helen describes how she and Will heard the news. 'Dad and I have been travelling all night, and now at skreigh of day we have stopped at Basin Bridge. Dad's eagle eye has at once discovered a fellow-passenger who has somehow got hold of a paper, and the poor man hardly dares to call it any longer his. Dad is eagerly reading out the latest references to the war – you can't call it war *news* for we are getting none – and the ticket collector and sundry other people are gradually gathering round and listening with all their ears. "Rumoured engagement in the North Sea. Belgium invaded. Germans attack Liege' that's what he's reading" (Here Helen was describing her drawing of the scene at the railway station, with Will and the other passengers all trying to read the one newspaper.) 'Can you imagine our excitement when we got back after three days at Humpi to the station at Hospet, and met a man who told us of the dec-laration of war between Germany and France, and then when we got to Kurnool we heard of Britain's having declared war with Germany and when we got to Madras we heard that four I.M.S. men had got orders to be ready to start and before we had been six hours in Madras the orders had come.'

The immediate problem for Helen was whether Day could come out. She wrote to her daughter the following week to say she was not sure that she would be able to travel, and then added, with that opti-mism which was so universally shared, 'but if the war finishes and a good escort offers I think Dad would like to get you out in time to see Ooty'. This meant that she hoped the war would be over and Day in India by mid–October.

In another way, too, Helen shared the attitude of her generation. Pat was fourteen and in the class at school which prepared boys for entry into the army. He hoped to become a Royal Engineer and was a keen Boy Scout. In writing to him on 13 August 1914 she showed no sense of foreboding about what the war would do to Pat's generation.

Almost a whole year of school leavers from Edinburgh Academy was to be wiped out, but Helen wrote: 'I wonder if you'll ever get a chance of doing any service? Anyway I hope you'll see to it that yours is not the sin of the unlit lamp and the ungirt loin, but that you will make ready for every emergency by asking Jesus to make and keep you ready.'

Because of the war, it was arranged that Day would stay on longer at school and come out to India in the spring. Day was pleased. Her school, St George's, had just moved from its premises in Melville Street, in the centre of Edinburgh, to a new site farther out, and the new building had sports fields all round it. 'You'll be able to keep the windows open' wrote Janet, 'which will be a great advantage. Has each class its own room?'

As well as following Day's activities, Janet, along with many others in Britain and the Empire, put up a map that showed the changes in the position of the Allied and German armies by means of little flags.[251] Helen and Elspeth and Janet also joined working parties and knitted and sewed for the troops. They went to first aid classes and filled three large crates with comforts for wounded soldiers.

For Will the war meant extra effort with fewer staff. Many of his officers disappeared to go to the war with their regiments. Will's personal staff of forty-five was reduced to eleven. Despite this, he was in demand to advise on how the voluntary effort could be most effectively organised. On 3 September, the question of how to use the money collected in the Madras War Fund had become so urgent that the Governor of Madras, Lord Pentland, called on Will early in the morning. Will received a message that the Governor was waiting outside on horseback:

So there was nothing for it but to rush out in my Arab coat dressing gown and without a topi, and see what the great man wanted. He was very much amused at my appearance, but he got off his horse and we walked up and down in the sunshine – for it is cold now in the mornings – and discussed various plans and alternatives which he wished to place before the Military Authorities at Simla for their decision. One plan is to hire and equip a hospital ship which would go back and forward between India and the base hospitals, so as to bring back sick and wounded men who belong to India.

Another plan is to apply some of the money to the purchase of warm socks and balaklava caps and flannel suits and quilted resais and coats for the sick men in hospital. For the Indian troops will feel the cold of Europe very much, and will want warm things to make them feel comfortable and happy.

A third plan is to buy up a lot of horses and send them to the front to replace those that are shot or die.

The people of Simla have not yet said which plan they prefer but anyhow we know that all sorts of comforts will be wanted for the hospitals, so the ladies all over the country are knitting socks and comforters and vests and such like, and also making operating gowns and swabs and bandages and so forth, which will be sent after the men to be ready for them when they are sick or have to go to hospital.

Simla – the hot-weather seat of the Government of India – made a quick choice between the alternatives. Two months later a fully equipped hospital ship, the *Madras*, set sail for East Africa and then the front.[252] Her role was to pick up wounded Indian soldiers and bring them back to India. She contained three hundred beds, with room for an additional hundred if necessary. A saloon had been converted into an operating room, with two operating tables and special electric lights. Next door was an X-ray room, and a bacteriological laboratory. The former pantry had been converted into a sterilising room. Outside, the ship was painted white, with a large red cross on the side. 'I only hope', Will added darkly, 'that the Simla people will not play the fool and will employ her properly.'

The people of Madras had had their first experience of being fired at.[253] In the last week of September the German cruiser *Emden* had arrived off the city at about nine o'clock at night. She fired some twenty-five shells at harbour installations, and hit a steamer called the *Chupra*, killing a cadet and one or two sailors. Then she fired at the Burmah Oil Company tanks and set two of them on fire. These burned for a couple of days. 'Some people', Will reported, 'think the *Emden* was trying to destroy the wireless station which is on the glacis of the Fort. I think this is quite likely, as we have destroyed a good many of the German wireless stations in various parts of the world. Anyhow, one shell flew over the General Hospital and burst somewhere near, for in the morning the base of a shell was found in the compound, and the point in the Penitentiary which is a short distance behind the hospital. No one was hurt I am glad to say, but it must have been quite exciting for the nurses, who were on the roof of the hospital at the time.'

Two months later he was delighted to give the news that the *Emden*, 'had at last been snaffled down at the Cocoa Keeling Islands where it had gone to try to cut the telegraph cables which are landed there. However one of our ships the *Sydney*, one of the Australian squadron, came up in time and she (the *Emden*) was destroyed, losing some two hundred of her crew. She was forced ashore and is burning, and we in Madras are not sorry to hear the end of her. In her last raid on British shipping she sunk a ship which had all the Christmas stores for Madras aboard, and also the tinned milk supply for the hospital ship *Madras*.

By January 1915 Helen and Will were in mourning for the son of a friend, killed in an attack with the London Scottish. He was the first of many they were to mourn for, and the list was soon to include Hal, the son of Helen's sister Isabella.

The hospital ship the *Madras* was not, however, scuppered by the bureaucrats in Simla; she reached Bombay with three hundred sick and wounded from East Africa just before Christmas. She was then sent up the Persian Gulf and in April 1915 she arrived in Madras and unloaded a cargo of wounded. They were transferred on stretchers on to a train which took them to Bangalore.

Meanwhile, despite the dangers to British shipping from enemy action, Day had set off from Edinburgh. Elspeth, who was increasingly used as a useful maiden aunt, went to Bombay to meet her. They then came together by train to Madras. It was due in the station at five thirty in the morning. The train was an hour late, Helen reported,[254] but the morning was cool and she and Will and Janet watched the dawn break. Then Day and Elspeth arrived, with Day, her father thought, looking unchanged from when he had seen her last, two and a half years previously. 'Her cheeks', he noted with pleasure, 'were as red as though she had just come across Bruntsfield Links in an East wind gale'. (Bruntsfield Links is a little park between Strathearn Place, and the centre of Edinburgh; it is open and exposed, and familiar as a cold and draughty spot.) Day, nearly nineteen, was shorter and plumper than Janet. She was pretty but less sophisticated than Janet. She was inclined to be boisterous, and, like Janet, had a laugh that constantly bubbled up and showed that she found almost everything amusing.

Day settled down, without any homesickness for Edinburgh, to the serious business of being a lady of leisure. She and Janet attended classes in cookery and dressmaking, and took outdoor sketching lessons and golf lessons. They went riding, played billiards at home, and also croquet and badminton. They attended sewing afternoons to help the war effort, and sales of work and sports days and garden parties. There were constant picnics and amateur theatricals. In the evenings they were asked to dinner parties and dances.

Helen, though she very much enjoyed her daughters' company, found the hurry-scurry of such a busy household a little tiring. Her letters at this time are full of references to 'rushing to catch the post' and 'I haven't had a minute to look at your photos'. She continued to travel with Will on his tours whenever she could. In the heat, and the conditions of travelling in those days, this was very wearing. By 1916

Will was fifty-eight and due to retire, but with the shortage of men during the war, they had to stay on. As she explained to Pat on 20 July 1916:

> In six days Dad will become, not a dug-out, for that means a man recalled to work from his retirement at home, but a *dug-in*, at least that seems to me the natural name for a man whose service is at an end, yet is not allowed to retire. I had meant to send you a picture of an agitated peon, coming to my window and explaining to me in my dressing gown, in fluent – too fluent – Hindustani that this (5th July) was a great day, a burra burra din, because something about service and one year. I thought he was referring to Dad's birthday and could not make out what he meant at all, till he pulled himself up and spoke more slowly, and then I gathered that a letter had come to the office saying that Dad's service was to be extended by one year, and that as we were his father and mother he was rejoicing that he was to have his beloved Chargin-Gin'ral over him for another year. When I asked Dad, I found the order was that his services were to be retained for another year, unless the war came to an end sooner, in which case reference was to be made to the Government of India. But I had done my pictures for that week, and the incidents of travel have occupied me ever since, so the agitated peon never reached paper.

A similar message was to arrive the following year; the extended stay in India did not suit Janet or Day. They both wanted to go to university. Neither showed any sign of getting married. There were, of course, few young men in Madras or Ooty who would have been thought appropriate; the young men of their generation were either fighting in France or already lying in graves there. Day, anxious to begin her medical studies, enrolled in Madras Medical College, and completed her first year there. Janet was more patient – or was unable to find a suitable course. She had to contend herself with running a troop of Girl Guides.

Will, meanwhile, was making do despite a shortage of men and materials. He was also active in trying to move Madras General Hospital away from its cramped central site.[17] Government approval was obtained for a new building at Spur Tank, and the first stage was completed – a reception centre with a domed roof. In the end, however, the new hospital was never completed on this site. After Will had left it was renovated on its original site, spreading over some of the few open spaces left in the crowded city area. Will also at this time gave substantial support to the Madras Medical College and to what became the Christian Medical College at Vellore.

With work on those projects, as well as more than the usual amount of administrative work – at one point he carried out the duties of Sanitary Commissioner as well as Surgeon-General because the post could not be filled – Will's health deteriorated. He suffered from black-outs and severe headaches.

Despite this, he still kept travelling, carrying out the inspections which were an essential part of his work. The letters for July 1915 show that he started a tour from Ooty, then he travelled over one hundred and fifty miles to Salem, then another hundred and fifty to Madras, then fifty miles to Vellore, then two hundred and fifty back to Ooty, then three hundred miles north to Kurnool, and finally all the way back to Ooty again – all within a month. Near the beginning of this trip, Helen reported that he was ill with a bad chill and fever, and had to cut out a visit to a little town that had asked for his advice:

The Collector wanted Dad to inspect a cemetery which lies just above the new water supply for Yercaud, and which some old-fashioned people there are most anxious should not be shut up, but it is fortunate that we can cut Yercaud out of the programme, as the cold, and probably damp, would not have been good for your Daddy. If it had been a bigger place with a large hospital and gaol I suppose we'd have had to go up. Today I am glad to say Dad seems all right, only he is still rather tired and fushionless. I hope he will be all right tomorrow, for we have to start at 7.5 for Vellore, and our host and hostess here go out into camp next day.

There were almost no hotels for anyone travelling in India. Will and Helen either stayed with friends, or at the Government Dak bungalows which were for hire along most routes. For the sick, the problem of staying with friends was that the hosts might well have arranged, from good-will, a dinner or reception. The problem with Dak bungalows was that they varied in quality. Occasionally they were so unhygenic that even Will got angry. On 13 August 1915, Helen sent home from Kurnool Dak bungalow a picture of Will, in a cloud of flies, scowling, and writing in a book with a dirty-looking servant reading over his shoulder. 'I couldn't help laughing yesterday when a very irate Dad called for the complaint book at Nandyal refreshment room, and the defaulting boy stood just behind him in an attitude of polite attention and read "I have never been in such a fly-infested refreshment room, and I see that the gauze doors of the cook house are carefully jammed open, giving free entrance to dogs and children". Dad then went on to say that there was no bread, that the milk was so suspicious we had to open a tin of preserved milk – really we had a poor breakfast, and as we had dined in the train overnight on three wee tinned tongues and half a loaf of bread we rather wanted our breakfast. However, lest the boys should be unduly blamed for what they couldn't help, Dad took care to add that the glass and china were clean and the silver bright.'

On this same trip, they had called at Vellore and had found Miss Hesterlow, the doctor looking after women and children, managing to see a hundred patients in a morning. The demand for her services was so great that she had put a rope across her room and only let one patient past at a time. Life was less exhausting at Ooty. There was the constant burden of paper work and administration – some evenings, Helen reported, Will would be typing away till midnight – but there was also the opportunity to get away from the office for a picnic or a game of golf. Will played when he could with Mr Sivaswamy, the Indian member of the Madras Council. They got to know each other well, and attended functions at each other's homes, with Mr Sivaswamy, for example, inviting them to an At Home at Ooty, complete with obstacle golf in his garden.

In her study of *Little Black Sambo* Marjorie McDonald mentions that Helen lived in, 'racially segregated India'. There were, however, no laws forbidding the races to inter-marry or to mix with each other. The social intercourse between the Indians and the British was indeed limited; but it did take place. Helen's letters show that she went out of her way to entertain Indian women in her home. On 8 April, 1916, for example, Janet wrote about an 'At Home' they gave in Madras for Indian ladies. The guests had been invited for five o'clock, but the first ones arrived at twenty past four before their hostesses were ready. There was some hurried dressing, and the party began. They were offered oranges, bananas and lemonade for, being Hindus, Janet explained, they could not eat food prepared by pariah servants. The Indian Christians took tea or coffee and cakes. After tea they played badminton in the garden. On another occasion, Indian guests – again women – tried their hands at billiards.

In 1916 Helen was asked to judge the flowers at the Madras Flower Show, jointly with the Hon Sir P.S. Sivaswamy Tyer; when it came to the final choice between phloxes, it turned out that neither he nor she could tell a rare one from a common one – though Helen's knowledge of flowers was otherwise almost encyclopaedic. Will and Helen attended weddings and other functions given by Indians, and Will was visited regularly by a Subadar-Major of the 64th Pioneers who had served with him in his very early posting, before he was married, in Baluchistan. They had known each other well, 'so when he is in Madras', wrote Will, 'he comes to see me and we talk over old days together. He is a nice old man, and takes a great interest in the war, as is but natural'. He was called Subadar-Major Sholapori; Will, in his letter to Pat, exhorted him to remember the name and be good to his father's friend should they ever meet.

Will also worked alongside Indian colleagues in the Indian Medical Service. Entry was by competitive examination. Anyone who had sufficient funds to reach the necessary standard was eligible. There were also some Indians in the Indian Civil Service, where entry, again, was by competitive examination. To pass the exams, a candidate would almost certainly need to have been educated at one of the better universities of Britain – a severely limiting factor. The area in which discrimination was open and based on colour was in the clubs of India; the rules of entry in these were drawn up by club committees and were often blatantly discriminatory. The thinking behind leaving such practices alone was that it was an aspect of individual freedom to allow people to set up a club for the one-legged if they wanted to, or for any other group; but it had the unfortunate consequence that distinguished Indians, such as those on the Viceroy's Legislative Assembly, could be barred from membership. There were voices in the British community raised against this practice – though not many. For the Bannermans, however, 'the Club' was never the social centre of their lives; that place was held by their Church.

Churches in India tried hard to be open to all races, though naturally most of their adherenents – apart from the Mission Churches – were European. Helen noted, however, a Japanese couple who converted to Christianity in Bombay and joined their congregation and an Englishman married to a woman from Madras in their congregation in Madras. Helen did not know them well, but she presumed that this was the wife's second marriage and that her children, who also came to Church, were from a first marriage.

As Helen's time in India draws to a close, the answer should already be evident to the question: was she a racist? Criticisms of her books were to be made, mostly after her death and in the United States, that the use of the name Sambo was derogatory to black people and that the pictures with which her books were illustrated were stereotyped and demeaning in their representation of black people. These charges are examined in the last chapter; the concern here is with her character and her attitude to racial questions.

A racist is someone who dislikes people of other races and is convinced of the superiority of his or her own. Two things about Helen's approach are clear: she approached other races with a very Christian approach: 'in God we are all one', and she had a deep sympathy and warmth towards the people of India. The Christian ideal is that the individual should approach all others, whatever their race or background, in a spirit of love. It is ironic that she, accused of being a racist, came nearer to the Christian ideal in her behaviour than some of those who make the accusation. Rob recalls that it was impressed upon him, when he was a child, that no one had any superiority *ab initio*: fundamentally they were all the same. What counted, he was taught, was effort.

It was because Helen was interested in other races, and could identify with their feelings, which she knew were much the same as hers, that she chose a black child as her hero. With the hindsight of history it is a pity she did not choose a brown child. Had she set *Little Black Sambo* in India the detail could have been authentic and the spurious connection with cotton plantations in the U.S.A. would never have developed. But she chose to set her book in a land of which she knew little. She had never visited Africa, and probably never knew any Africans. Her books were set in a vaguely African world of her imagination; it is not surprising if the detail is mixed. The reader can be assured, however, that the motive in setting her stories there was not to ridicule or demean black people in any way. She simply regarded them as part of the human race.

Someone with a similar approach today is Richard Scarry, author and illustrator of many children's books, including *Busy Busy World*.[256] He offers caricatures or stereotypes of the races round the world, often unflattering. Russians are shown as bears, Indians as tigers and elephants, African as lions, and the Poles and Scots and Irish as pigs. So far as I know, there have been no complaints about this; nor should there be – though he does come under fire for alleged sexism[285] The animals are drawn with sympathy and humour; if a few stereotypes are reinforced, such as a peasant way of life in the case of the Irish or bagpipes that make an appalling noise in the case of the Scots, no matter. Richard Scarry is a story teller, and children delight in his stories and his funny pictures.

That is all that Helen would have claimed for herself. In her books, and her letters, she had an eye for a good story. Had she wanted to make a serious contribution to our understanding of a particular area of human knowledge, she would have embarked on a massive tome, as her father had done with his study of the scaphopoda and gasteropoda from the *Challenger*. Her ambition was much more modest: to amuse. It is as true of her letters as of her books, though her letters are pitched at rather older children than her books. For example, writing to Pat, when he was sixteen, on 23 May 1916, from Ootacumund, she did not write to tell him to clean his teeth or do his school work or be kind to his sisters and his brother; she picked out a story which she had heard and knew he would enjoy:

Capt and Mrs Russell, who are staying with us for two nights, have been in Kotagiri for nearly a month and there is a young missionary lady – I think her name is Miss Grierson – staying in the same house. She was out sketching all by herself the other day, some two or three miles out, when a tiger walked out of the bushes and stood in the road gazing at her. She suddenly became aware of his presence, and stood one instance gazing paralysed at him then she turned and fled, leaving her easel and her paint box, her stool and her coat, and ran, and ran, and ran, never stopping till she reached Kotagari. Then she went and reported her adventure – to the Police! She has been much chaffed about that, and reminded of the Station-Master's telegram "Tiger in possession of platform, please wire instructions" but of course the real reason was that she did not want to lose her coat and her sketchables. The men in the house where she stays went out and measured the distance of the pugs from her easel, they say it was only about six yards, so it's no wonder she was scared.

By the beginning of 1918, Helen's opportunities to go for walks in the jungle, on which she might, just *might*, meet a tiger, were drawing to a close. Will was almost sixty, and his retirement was overdue. His health was poor, and at last, in July 1918, his retirement began. It was preceeded by three months leave, and it became effective from April of that year.

Chapter Ten

The Treasure House

Although Will's retirement had been agreed, they still had to get their passages home. This proved very difficult. They disposed of their house, and split up to stay with different friends, so that they could go at short notice. Eventually, Will, Helen and Elspeth were all classed as invalids, with Janet and Day as their attendants, and they were able to book berths on a ship going from Ceylon.

As they finally packed up the last of their goods, Helen noticed a package sewn up in hessian. She had no idea what it was but it was addressed to 'General Bannerman' and she presumed it had been ordered. It travelled with them, and when they unpacked their baggage in Edinburgh, Helen undid this bundle and found it was a Persian rug. It was a gift to Will, the origin of which went back more than thirty years. In his early days in India, Will had operated on the son of a Rajah and saved the boy's life. The Rajah, in his gratitude, had wanted to pay Will or give him a present. Will had declined. He was paid an adequate salary, he said, and there were rules against accepting gifts other than perishables such as fruit. The Rajah had then asked whether he would be able to accept a gift when he was no longer in Government service. 'Yes', Will had said, 'There would seem to be no ethical objection, though I should not expect to receive anything at all. I, too, am glad of your son's recovery.' This then, was the gift that had arrived as they left India for the last time.

Helen's son Rob, who tells the story,[257] admits that he is not sure whether the gift was from a Rajah or from some other wealthy Indian. 'Never mind', he says, quoting his mother on a different topic, 'A false anecdote may be true history.'

It is impossible to know Helen's thoughts as she left Colombo and sailed past the tip of India. The last of the letters which have been preserved are dated a year before their departure – January 1917. There is one single one from August 1917 and then silence. It is possible that one, or two, volumes covering January 1917 to April 1918 are missing; one other volume in the series, presumably cleared out in error, found its way to an Edinburgh book shop. It was bought and treasured by an Edinburgh family, who donated it back to the Banner-

144

man family when they were approached about it in 1971 after a BBC Radio Four broadcast. This missing volume or volumes may yet turn up; the letters are so attractively illustrated that no one would be likely to throw them away. Another explanation of the gap, however, could be that Helen's health was so poor that she stopped doing pictures. This is far less likely; even through the worst of her sprue she had carried on, and Janet and Day were also sending picture letters, later bound into the volumes as well.

Because their departure had been so delayed, and because they were in poor health, it is likely that she and Will felt considerable relief at leaving India. But sorrow too. Leaving Bombay in 1911 she had spoken of 'a mist of tears and an ache of heart'. She had spent almost thirty years in India. She was fifty-five years old, and was leaving behind the people and places of her early married life, of her middle years when she wrote most of her books, and of her later years when Will and she had had their place among the leading administrators of India.

As her ship sailed back to Britain, the voyage had its excitements. One boat in the convoy was hit by enemy action. A destroyer stayed with her and escorted her into a Spanish port. The Bannerman's ship sailed on and reached London during the last air raid of the war. Their problems were still not over: they had no ration cards and they had difficulty getting any food in their London hotel.[258]

When they got back to Edinburgh, however, they were welcomed into a warm circle of loving friends and relatives and difficulties were smoothed away. Pat and Rob were now young men of eighteen and sixteen. Pat had already been through Woolwich to train for the Royal Engineers. In early 1918 he was gazetted in the Artillery, but his luck was with him – or his mother's prayers were answered – and by the time the war ended he had still not been sent abroad. Helen and Will settled into 11 Strathearn Place. On her parents' death this had been left to Helen's sister Elspeth; she in turn sold it to Helen and Will. The family was united again, with Will occupying himself with the affairs of the Royal Society of Edinburgh, of which he was a Fellow, and with the United Free Church of St George's West in Shandwick Place, of which he was an elder and Secretary of the Foreign Missions Committee.

The Bannermans are remembered in Edinburgh as being rather exceptional. As Miss Bridie Reegan, later Mrs Tweedie, who looked after Helen in her later years, put it to me: 'They were an extraordinary family. They were so kind and loving. They would never say a bad word about anyone, but always find an excuse to explain why someone had behaved as they did.' There were prayers in the household every day and always the expectation that others would be put before oneself. Characters of this kind, moulded by generations of Christian example and influence, are less and less common today. Like rare species, they only linger on in remote parts.

The other side to the coin was a certain unworldliness. Helen was no housewife. From a large establishment of servants in India, she managed in Edinburgh with one housekeeper. The housekeepers, her grandson Paddy Bannerman recalls, 'always ate with us and held their full part in the conversation. They were always treated as part of the family.' The house, with six people in it, was always untidy and books were scattered everywhere. There were so many books in the bookshelves that the bound volumes of manuscript illustrated letters from India were stored for many years in the laundry.[259]

Pat was an enchanting young man – full of charm, without an enemy in the world, an accomplished artist and an agreeable singer. He was also unpunctual, untidy, lackadaisical and completely uninterested in money.[260] He remained in the army for four years after the war ended, then resigned his commission. The Plague Laboratory at Parel, with its flasks in its darkened ballroom, and its cages full of snakes and guinea pigs, and its cricket on the lawns in the evenings, still had a grip on him. He decided to become a doctor and enrolled at the University of Edinburgh. According to his sister Janet, he was rather wild as a student, but, as with his lack of attention to Helen's early attempts to teach him to read, he must have discovered the use of study in the end, and he qualified in due course.

Rob was quieter – a very agreeable and kindly person. He left school in 1921 when he was nineteen and took a degree course in engineering. After an apprenticeship in Edinburgh he worked in the Sudan, searching unconsciously perhaps, for the kind of life he half remembered from India. He managed to find a vast adult equivalent of the Mali's pool, in which he had spent so many happy hours in Bombay. This was the Sudan Plantation syndicate, a very large, successful and complex irrigation scheme, built to irrigate the cotton crop. He was for many years one of the engineers working on this scheme.

Janet and Day enrolled in the University of Edinburgh as soon as they could, Janet taking a B.Sc. in zoology and Day, after her year's study of medicine in Madras, moving into the second year of medicine at Edinburgh. After graduating, Janet did a year's teacher's training course, and then, with the pull of her upbringing on her as it was on her brothers and her sister, she went – and by then she was twenty-nine – to the Church of Scotland missionary training centre in Edinburgh, St Colm's Missionary College.

Helen was later to tell Janet how glad she was that all the children, and especially the boys, had some years of their father's influence. But they turned out to be very few. His spells of unconsciousness returned, and crippling headaches, as he had had from time to time in India.[261] He was a heavy smoker; he developed a growth on his jaw, and this was the area, it will be remembered, that had been X-rayed with early X-ray equipment for thirteen minutes in 1911. His palate and upper jaw on one side of his face were removed in an operation and he seemed to improve. Not long after that, however, his elder sister Ata died. She had been a mother to him from the time his mother died when he was ten, and then mothered all his children in turn, while he and Helen were away. A month later, Will, at the age of sixty-five, lost consciousness and died within a few hours on 3 February 1924, at his home. His death certificate records the cause of death as epileptic seizure and heart failure.

Helen's daughter-in-law Cecilia quoted her as saying at the time: 'I knew he was dying, but when he died I just went cold.' The evidence is that she never entirely got over his death. As Jean Hyslop who looked after her in her last years, told me: 'Her heart died when he died. She lost interest in everything.' Her faith in a future re-union with Will never faltered, however. She did not withdraw into herself but remained the centre of her family, and, as her son Rob puts it, 'continued to shed light and laughter wherever she was'. Her interest in the world around her was as keen as ever. She won a crossword competition and learnt to drive. She even talked – though Rob feels this was to please him because he was keen on aeroplanes – of learning to fly. Friends and relatives continued to visit her frequently and her home was busy and active. In her later years in India she had entertained and lived a sociable life; this met the needs of her family at the time, with two daughters to bring into society and her husband in a responsible public position. In her widowhood there were fewer demands of this kind upon her; she was able to be herself. For her it meant being the centre of the family, there if needed, and always available for advice or diversion.

Her children, however, were finishing their studies and leaving home. Janet, her missionary training at St Colm's completed, returned to Madras as a teacher and a missionary – that Madras which she had at first found too frivolous when she had returned to India as a young woman. She took up a post in Madras, teaching science at Northwick School for Girls. While on holiday at Kotagiri she met Fred Kibble, Professor of Mathematics at Madras Christian College. In 1930, when she was thirty-seven, they were married, and two years later she had a son, Tom. She and Fred lived on in Madras, well known for their missionary work, until they retired in 1961.

Day had left Edinburgh before her father died, and took up a hospital appointment in Bolton. After his death she came back to Edinburgh, to a post in the Royal Infirmary and then the Elsie Inglis Hospital. She next became a general practitioner in the Davidson Mains suburb of Edinburgh, and moved there to live.

Nor did Pat stay in Edinburgh, though he, too, was to come back to it. After qualifying, he married a nurse he had known at Edinburgh Royal Infirmary, Margaret Robertson, whose background had some echoes of his own: her parents had been missionaries in India. He became a general practitioner in Cupar in Fife where three sons were born, Burney, Francis and Patrick. After some years he moved to Haddington, in East Lothian, and there Kenneth and Douglas were born.

Rob, with his wife Cecilia Lawlor, and in due course their children Paddy and Anne, spent many years in the Sudan. He moved into Government service during the depression to carry on with irrigation work. For his children there was the same pattern of separation as Rob had been through, though their parents came to Scotland on annual leaves.

Helen, now a grandmother, still had, surprisingly enough, one more book to write. This was *The Story of Sambo and The Twins*. The initiative for this came not from her but from an energetic New York publisher, Horace Stokes, of Frederick A. Stokes Company. After the book had appeared in 1936 in the U.S.A. – it was published in Britain by James Nisbet and Co. in 1937 – he revealed how he came to persuade her to write it, and part of the story still remains in a letter he sent to her on 28 May 1936:[262]

'I have been requested to write an article for a magazine on how I happened to persuade you to do this book. Would you have any objection to my doing this and perhaps including some of your very amusing comments in correspondence, such as "Remember that Little Black Sambo is middle-aged now"? I should like to tell how you refused to do the book by telegraph, how I came to see you, give a brief (and wholly complimentary) description of you and your home, and how, a few days before leaving London, much to my delight and somewhat to my astonishment, the complete hand-written manuscript of the book arrived.'

Rob recalls that Stokes first called to see his mother on a Sunday. She declined to talk business but offered him a cup of tea. He had to stay an extra day in Edinburgh, and it was only when he called again on the Monday that they got down to a discussion about a further book.

In this, Sambo was not quite portrayed as middle-aged, but he had matured a little and acquired twin baby brothers. If it were published

Parel, BOMBAY,

19th. March, 1910.

My dear Day,

Is'nt this a gay tamasha :

This is what our front lawn looked like last

Saturday, when the Laboratory gave a big

"At Home" to all our friends in Bombay.

33. In India, Helen lived a life of privilege — as she did in Edinburgh too.

The Cloisters
Cathedral Road
Madras

34.　Helen's home in Madras (see page 23).

Abernyte
Kodaikanal
16 - 4 - 13

my dear Pat,
I wonder if you
will recognise Abernyte at
Kodaikanal where you were

35.　Her holiday house
in Kodaikanal, named
Abernyte after the Perth-
shire home of her husband's
family (see page 23).

Parel, Bombay
Friday Aug 27. 1909

My own dear Janet
        Can you guess wh...
this little visitor is, wh...
came in to see me the S...

36.   Helen took a great interest in those she lived amongst, as is shown by this picture she sent to her children of their servant Poonoosawmy's wife and daughter.

The Cloisters
Cathedral P.
Madra
3ʳᵈ Novᵇ
1916

My dear Pat,

This is the
picture of a retired
Indian officer,
a Sudedar-Major of the
64ᵗʰ Pioneers, who came
to see me a few days ago

37. Helen drew this sympathetic picture of a friend of her husband; contrast it with the degraded representations of people of another race offered by a variety of artists in the U.S. editions of her books (see page 140).

38. and 39.   Some of the pictures — not by Helen Bannerman — which gave the book a bad name. This 1908 edition by Reilly and Britton, illustrated by John R. Neill, was the first to take Sambo away from his imaginary land and set the story in the south of the U.S.A.

40.   The Cupples and Leon edition of 1917, with pictures by John B. Gruelle, continued the unjustified link with the humiliations of slavery.

made a huge big plate of m
And she fried them in th
the Tigers had made, and

41.   It was distasteful pictures such as this by Nana French Bickford (Stoll & Edwards, 1921) which provoked the charge that the book made black people look greedy. A child eating by himself off bare wood is not a happy sight; Helen's original picture showed Sambo and his parents at a table with a white tablecloth.

42. Some editions have been criticised for their excessively primitive setting. This is the McLoughlin edition of 1931, illustrated by Hildegard Lupprian.

43. Golden Press, 1948, pictures by Gustaf Tenggren.

44. Platt and Munk 1972 edition, illustrated by Eulalie. In an attempt to defuse criticism, the locale has been shifted to India. Black Mumbo has been changed to Mama Sari — but Sambo and his father stay as they were in previous Platt and Munk editions.

45. The transition to India is complete — Golden Press 1961, pictures by Bennie and Bill Rutherford.

46. Color and Fun Book, by Bill Woggon for Sambo's Restaurants Inc., 1976.

47. The final humiliation of a once-proud child — Sambo loses his racial heritage and is turned white. Peter Pan Records 1958.

today, children's book experts would welcome it as 'a constructive book for children troubled by sibling jealousy'. At the time she wrote it Helen had seven grandchildren under five; it would be surprising if some of the thinking behind the book had not come out of her experience as a grandmother. Her grandson Tom, Day recalled, was hammering pieces of wood, just as Sambo did in the book, at around this time. But the book also has echoes from her days in India as a mother. The little twins wear sashes round their waists just as Pat and Rob had worn in Bombay. Helen had her drawing of 29 October 1904, done at the time for a home letter, to remind her how they looked. She also had a book called *The Home Life of a Golden Eagle*, given to Will by Ata for his birthday in 1911; this would have helped with detail for the drawing of the eagle who rescued the twins from the monkeys who had carried them away. Also in her letters were innumerable drawings of monkeys from her days in India. The material was there for her to take: it was a comparatively simple matter for her to organise it into a book.

Marjorie McDonald,[4] has an interesting theory about Helen's motivation in writing *Sambo and the Twins*. She feels that the trigger for the book was the separation of a parent from a child or children, and that Helen wrote this sequel in response to the pleas of Mr Horace Stokes for a book for his two small daughters in the U.S.A. As Marjorie McDonald puts it:

'The American publisher of *Sambo*, Frederick A. Stokes Company, had tried for many years to persuade the author to write more *Sambo* stories, but she had always refused. A speculation is that circumstances surrounding the requests had always failed to call forth the unconscious reinforcement she sensed to be so necessary to her creativity. Without this pressure from within she could not duplicate her own "effortless perfection". Rather than compromise her standards for *Sambo* she wrote nothing, and no promise of financial reward could change her mind. Not until the visit of her publisher Horace W. Stokes, in 1936, was she able to write more about Sambo. Stokes describes this eventful visit:
"Mrs Bannerman wrote other books . . . successfully published . . . but the child of her heart and of her public was *Little Black Sambo*. She refused to write more about him. The writer of this article has, like Mrs Bannerman, two little girls. Time and again he begged to get Mrs Bannerman to write another Sambo story. Letters were written to her but remained unanswered. Finally, in March of the present year, he begged for an interview from London.
'I'll be glad to see you,' replied Mrs Bannerman 'but I cannot

write another story of Little Black Sambo. You must remember that nearly forty years have passed. . . .'

Mrs Bannerman is a sweet-faced elderly Scotchwoman, but she has a firm chin.

'I won't – I can't – I tell you it's impossible. I couldn't possibly write anything more', she reiterated.

'My own little girls have been giving me no peace. . . . They *must* have the new book!' said the publisher." '

As we know, Helen completed the manuscript within three weeks and sent it to him. 'You must remember' she wrote to the publisher, 'that this is your own children's book. If it had not been for them I should never have written it at all.'

It is quite clear that without Mr Stokes' visit, Helen would not have written another book. It is interesting that, as Marjorie McDonald points out, the theme of this book is also separation – the kidnapping of the twins by the monkeys. Perhaps this preoccupation with the pain of separation, Marjorie McDonald speculates, may have arisen from some incident in her childhood. Yet she experienced no separation from her parents on the scale that her own children suffered. She had travelled with her parents to Madeira, and had returned with them. She came, however, from a very loving home and loved both parents deeply. It is likely that when she was apart from her own children she could imagine what she would have felt had she been separated from her beloved parents at a young age. And indeed, although by then an adult, she was in fact separated from her own parents when she wrote *Little Black Sambo*. Adults, especially in another continent, can miss loving parents too.

In the summer of 1939 Helen spent a holiday at Lochinver with Pat and Day. The weather was good, and they had an enjoyable time. But then, Day explained, came the journey home: 'We were coming home, Mother, Pat and I, and in the evening we went for a drive along the sides of Loch Ness and looked for the monster. It was a lovely day which we spent in the sun. In the night Mother got up and couldn't get back. I had to get Pat to help me. She was paralysed all down her right side.' Helen had had a stroke. She was unable to speak, though this improved as time passed. She had always hoped that when her time came she would go quickly; but in the event it took seven years.

Helen was taken to Pat's house in Haddington and looked after there. When the war broke out Pat's wife Margaret took advantage of a scheme run by the American Medical Association and took her five sons across to the U.S.A. for safety for the duration of the war. Pat, doing the work of three doctors in Haddington, had Polish refugees billeted on him. It became impossible to look after Helen there and she was moved to a nursing home in Edinburgh.

The nursing home was in Chester Place; Helen made it clear that she was unhappy there.[263] Day was a busy G.P., but she could not bear seeing her mother so miserable. Against all advice, she reopened the house at Strathearn Place, which had been closed since Helen had been ill, and employed a nurse and a housekeeper, and moved in herself to look after her mother.

Back at Strathearn Place, Helen waa much more content. She was never able to walk again, but a book support was rigged up for her and she was able to read a little. A mirror device was arranged through which she played patience. For many older people their homes matter deeply. This is especially true of women, who have been used to being in charge of their domain, whatever its scale. In Helen's case, her home was a treasure-house, a museum of her life. Her grand-daughter Anne[264] describes it at this time as, 'a 15-room Victorian house, bulging with books. You only had to open a drawer and out would fall carvings and sketches from India or a minute pair of date-stones carved into faces many years previously by my grandmother. After her stroke she lay in a great brass bed in the room downstairs on the right as you went in. The grandchildren used to drift in and out; the room was always warm and friendly, comfortable and interest-ing. My grandmother was then a frail old lady with a tiny face and very white hair. I can understand why she was unhappy in the nursing home; her home was her life. She was the centre of the household; she could not be uprooted from it and live.'

Pat used to come every week on his half day and take a glass of madeira with her and play cards. Because of anxiety about fire and bombs a wheeled trolley was bought for her; it was never needed but in the summer it was very useful to wheel her out under the pear tree in the garden. Pat came to call this tree his 'hat tree' because this was where he would hang his hat in the summer.

It was a garden which must have held many happy memories. Her bedroom on the ground floor looked out over it, and in the many long hours of her disablement she watched the flowers and the birds and the changing seasons just as she had done in Parel during her long illness in 1909.

Despite being bedridden, she was alert and cheerful. Day would read Dickens and Shakespeare to her, and the Bible at night. 'She took a great interest' Day explained to me, 'in all the young relations, and wanted to hear everybody's news. I never had trouble getting people to visit her – they gained from her as much as they gave.' According to her nurse Bridie Reegan, now Mrs Tweedie, she talked of things that were joyful or happy; though on rare occasions when she thought she could not be heard she would ask God to take her away to her husband.

She died at 2.30 a.m. on 13 October 1946, aged eighty-four years, with a fractured femur and cerebral thrombosis. Will had been buried in Grange Road Cemetery, very near their home; Helen was cremated and her ashes placed by his grave.

There was still, after her death, one more book to appear in her name. This was *The Story of Little White Squibba*, published in 1966 by Chatto & Windus in London, but not published in the U.S.A. On the cover the publishers explain, under a claim that this was a new story by the author of *Little Black Sambo*:

> *Little White Squibba* was written many years ago, but was not published until 1966. The text and pictures were left among Helen Bannerman's papers: the story complete but some of the illustrations in an unfinished state. With the help of Dr Davie Bannerman (her daughter) the publishers have prepared the book for the press, confident that lovers of *Little Black Sambo* and the other famous Sambo stories will find Little White Squibba's adventures with the Tiger, the Elephant and other fierce and friendly Jungle beasts just as irresistible as their old favourites.

This explanation goes some way to explain why *Little White Squibba* is such a poor book. The text and pictures do not fit, in contrast to Helen's other books where the match is exact and satisfying. In page 32 of the text, for example, Squibba is thrown off a precipice by an elephant, 'but her big hat was just like a kite so she sailed down beautifully and landed lightly'. The picture, however, shows that it was not her hat (which fails to look like a kite) which acted like a parachute, but her umbrella. Later, on page 36, there is an entirely unconvincing picture of Squibba and the Mongoose, falling through the air in an upturned umbrella, while the text reads 'now we can sail down in the Parasol together'.

Day threw more light on the origins of this book when she told me:

> The bones of it were written by my mother before Sambo and the Twins, but none of the pictures were finished. They were sort of scribbly pictures and I took some of the pictures from her other books, for example the pictures of elephants. The pictures petered out towards the end and I had to invent them. The publishers altered the pictures a little and made the mother's dress shorter and more modern. The text also petered out before the end but it was clear what was going to come.

Chatto & Windus would have done Helen a service had they

declined to publish this unsatisfactory goulash of Day's efforts on top of scribbles of her mother's. Day thought that her mother had done it as a parody of her other books. This is very likely; she enjoyed laughing at herself. But it is not a book that particularly appeals to the childish mind. Helen was careful in her other books not to write them to appeal to adults. She resisted the temptation to put in jokes which adults would see but children could not understand. It is highly unlikely that she would ever have completed *Little White Squibba* as a book for children. It *is* quite amusing, however, as a parody. When Squibba comes to a snake and an elephant, expecting them to try to eat her up, like the tiger and the mugger before them, they pay no attention. 'Don't you want to eat me up?' she asks. 'No, I don't,' said the snake. Then she said to the elephant, 'Don't you want to throw me over the Precipice?'. 'No', said the elephant. 'Why should I?'

Day completed the book and offered it to Chatto & Windus from the best of motives. She was aware by 1966 of the criticisms of *Little Black Sambo* as racist in the U.S.A. She may have wanted to show that her mother wrote in a similar way about a white child – a white child, incidentally, who was a lot less clever than Sambo. It may be that motives of this kind influenced Chatto & Windus to include 'Squibba' in the set of boxed Bannerman books. If this was indeed the reason, then *Pat and the Spider* or *Degchiehead* would have met these requirements, and are far better books.

After Helen's death, Day continued to live on at Strathearn Place. It was divided into flats, with Day on the ground floor, and, when they came back to Edinburgh from being abroad, Rob and family in the middle and Janet and family on the top. It was only a few years after Helen's death that Pat suffered a coronary thrombosis. He recovered, and tried to work again, but had a further attack. He described this to Day as being like climbing a long flight of stairs, only to plunge all the way to the bottom again. He gave up his practice in Haddington and came to Glencairn Crescent in Edinburgh where his wife opened a small private hotel. But on February 12 1955, he suffered another heart attack and died. It was an unexpectedly early death for the vital personality who had matured from 'naughty Pat' into a respected and well-loved family doctor.

Rob returned to Edinburgh from the Sudan in 1954. Then in 1956 he moved to Kent and was one of the team of hydrologists who completed the Surface Water Survey of England and Wales. Sadly, while she was on holiday with him in France in 1976, his wife Cecilia was killed in a road accident.

Day worked on as a widely respected G.P. in Edinburgh, but, by the end, perhaps a little eccentric. She became a familiar sight, in a windjammer, with bare legs and gym shoes, taking her collie and her mongrel out in all weathers for walks on the hills of the city.

Janet and Fred returned from India and retired to Coventry, where Fred had come from. As they grew increasingly infirm, they moved to Edinburgh, back to the familiar nest of Strathearn Place, to join Day for their mutual support. In her eightieth year Day died in an Edinburgh nursing home on 16 April 1976 and at the end of the same year Janet died too.

None of Helen's descendants now live in Edinburgh, though her eldest great-grand-daughter, Helen Kibble, went to the University in Edinburgh in 1979 to study physics. Pat's widow and two of his sons settled in New Zealand with their families; the second eldest of these sons, Francis, died there in 1979. One other son is in Australia and the remaining two are in England.

In 1979, Rob married again, a widow, Alison Brackenridge, who had known his family from the time she had been a medical student in Edinburgh along with Pat. They settled, for part of the year at least, in Hayling Island. The Mali's Pool was not forgotten: within a few months Rob, aged seventy-eight, had explored every creek and never tired of watching the sea.

Chapter Eleven

Sambo Blacked

Towards the end of her life, Helen was aware of criticisms of *Little Black Sambo* as racist. These originated in the United States and grew into such a chorus that by the early 1970's the book was excluded from many public libraries and many lists of recommended reading. In Britain the reaction suddenly erupted in 1972. It is worth looking at the growth of hostility to the book, first in the U.S.A. and then in Britain, and examining how the book holds up against codes on racism in children's books, such as that prepared by the World Council of Churches.

As her son Robert was to say in answer to critics of his mother who attacked the book as racist in the columns of *The Times* in 1972:[265] 'My mother would not have published the book had she dreamt for a moment that even one small boy would have been made unhappy thereby.' Nevertheless, a variety of charges were made against the book. Among the less substantial were accusations that eating so many pancakes made black people look greedy and that the garish colours for their clothes symbolised the artist's view of their childish minds. Among the more substantial complaints were charges that the pictures showed stereotypes or caricatures of black people, that the book showed black people in primitive jungle settings, or in demeaning slave plantation settings, and that the name Sambo had derogatory overtones for black people because it had come to be used in a generic way for any negro.

To understand the strength of feeling behind these charges we have to understand that when people in the U.S.A. speak of *Little Black Sambo* they are probably not thinking of the book with illustrations by Helen Bannerman. Though no figures are available, sales of the edition with her pictures were vastly outnumbered by sales of other editions with other illustrators. Phyllis Yuill in *Little Black Sambo: A Closer Look*[2] lists 29 editions with other illustrators, and I can add another two editions to her list – *The Story of Little Black Sambo* published by Stoll and Edwards (New York 1921) illustrated by Nana French Bickford and *Little Brave Sambo*, Peter Pan Book and Record, (published by the Ambassador Record Corporation, Newark, New

Jersey 1971, with no illustrator credited.) There were also the versions of *Little Black Sambo* appearing in anthologies (at least eight), in plays and records (at least seven) and in additional stories written about little Black Sambo by other authors (at least six).[2] This means that over fifty illustrators had offered their image of Little Black Sambo to the American public.

Some of the pictures are horrifying. No wonder people took offence. Seeing the pictures by some of the other illustrators, the surprising thing is that the reaction took so long to find expression. The 1908 edition by Reilly and Britton, for example, shows the mother as a grotesquely fat plantation Mammy wearing a spotted apron. The Cupples and Leon edition of 1917 has Sambo as a primitive grass-skirted savage. Between then and 1935 there were at least sixteen editions, with the Stoll and Edwards edition of 1921 showing Sambo in trousers that are too short for him, the Saalfield Publishing Company version of 1932 offering Sambo as a piccaninny with spiky hair, and the 1931 edition from the McLoughlin Brothers showing Sambo almost as a golliwog.

If Helen Bannerman's friend Mrs Alice Bond had not sold the copyright of the book on her behalf in 1899, none of this would have been possible. The variety of versions, some with acknowledgement to Helen Bannerman and some without, were only possible because her claim to the copyright was very weak and she therefore could not pursue anyone who infringed it. She clearly knew of the existence of one such version – the Stoll and Edwards version with pictures by Nana French Bickford. A copy of this was among her books after her death. This used her story virtually word for word but gave no credit to her whatever. Apart from the weakness of her claim to the copyright, she was not a litigious person and she took no action.

All her best pictures were caricatures. She admitted it herself. She had had no instruction in drawing and she had developed the technique of 'heightening' the important aspects of a picture. When Sambo weeps, for example, his tears are as big as his hands, and when he is frightened his eyes open excessively wide. But this was how nearly all her pictures turned out. She caricatured her husband, her children, her friends, anyone within range – and herself. There are pictures of her stepping out of a carriage and falling flat on her face, brushing the dust off a hat with extreme distaste,[266] and drinking sour milk through a straw as though it was cyanide.[199] In February 1914 she drew a picture of herself taking off her husband's shoes that was such a caricature that he complained about it. As she explained in her letter to Rob:[267]

This needs a lot of finishing but it won't get it, because my paper takes so long to dry that life is not long enough, at least that portion of life which comes in before the post goes out. So you must take it as it is, and finish it for yourself if you are particular. And any way the finishing does not much matter, for the grand central idea – that which makes all the difference between a work of talent and a work of genius – is there. And the grand central idea of my picture – though of course you may not be able to see it – is

AGONY.

Mark the drawn brow, the clenched hands, the rigid posture of my great central figure, note the long-drawn anguish of my arms which are at least three inches beyond what nature made them, and shed a filial tear of sympathy. Poor Dad does not approve of this picture, but I tell him nothing could more fully show you the misery of his condition than the fact that he cannot get down to take off his own boots and has to get me to do it for him. He ricked his back last Saturday and has been very wretched ever since.

Helen used to paint pictures for Will's letters, as well as her own. One of them showed the guests at a picnic in Ooty in June 1914. Will described how it had been held near the ruins of the house Lord Roberts had lived in when he was Commander-in-Chief in the Madras Army. By 1914 it was a pleasant ruin and Will went on to explain who the various people were whom Helen had drawn. 'Miss Bemester is the stout lady [and indeed Helen had drawn her *very* stout] facing me sitting on some stones. She is very nice but much troubled with her over-fatness.' Being a kindly man, he then thought it necessary to add: 'If ever she should call at Ann Street do not show her this picture for she might be mortified you know!'

On another occasion, in March 1911, Helen drew a picture of herself and Will fighting over a book. 'Don't you think it must be a very verrrry bad set of children who set their parents on to fight?', she asked Rob, 'yet that is what you four have done. Oh, I am shocked at you! ! By last week's mail you sent me out that delightful Scottish Fairy Book, and now Father and I have the most fearful fights as to who is to have it. He is much stronger than I, so he can take it away from me, but then he has to go to office, and then comes my chance, and I just steal it back. He pretends he wants to take it away, because I waste my time reading it, when I ought to be doing other things, but I know it is not really that, it is because he wants to read it himself! ! ! ! So I scream and fight and tear out his hair by handfuls and if anybody could see us they would say "Oh! What awful people!!" but nobody has seen us yet. And now as I have read it all through once, I am going to be very kind and let him have it when I do not want it myself, so that he won't lose all his hair.'

Helen would have been an excellent cartoonist, given the opportunity – a better cartoonist than an artist. The way she could caricature people was, however, simply an aspect of her style. There was nothing racist about it.

Were her pictures stereotypes? A stereotype is something constantly repeated without change, a character without humanity. Helen Bannerman's *Little Black Sambo*, however, is an appealing child with individualistic parents. The same is true of the characters in her other books, with the exception of *The Story of Little White Squibba* in which Squibba significantly lacks personality. It was her daughter Day who was responsible for the major part of the Squibba drawings. So while I would accept the charge that there is an element of the caricature in her drawings, the charge that they are stereotypes cannot be sustained. It should be clear by now that I accept fully the charge that many of the pictures by other artists are blatant stereotypes.

Does Helen Bannerman make black people look greedy by showing them eating so many pancakes? Not all black people take themselves so seriously that they accept this charge. Most, like Helen Bannerman, have a sense of humour – as Helen showed, for example, in writing to one of her sons to warn him against a certain kind of conduct: 'That was a fearful kind of race between those two boys in your class who tried which of them could eat the most lead pencils. I hope when you try races it's not in eating lead pencils, for that's far too rich a diet for little boys and besides, it's very extravagant to eat your pencils instead of using them to write with. When you want to try an eaaing race, try with paving stones or lamp posts or something large and satisfying. There's something too epicurean about lead pencils.'

In Helen's picture of eating the pancakes, mother, father and son are sitting politely at the table, set with a clean white cloth and plates and forks. In the Stoll and Edwards edition, however, Little Black Sambo, who is almost gross, is seen sitting by himself shovelling the food into his mouth off a plate on the plain wood. Like someone drinking alone, a child eating alone is not a happy sight.

Does Helen Bannerman's use of primary colours for the clothes of Little Black Sambo and his parents indicate that she thought they liked these bright colours because they had childish minds? Helen used primary colours because she wanted to appeal to the genuinely childish minds of her readers. The appeal of her pictures was that they were simple, direct and brightly coloured. Although this was revolutionary in its day, this is now a standard approach to pictures for young children. There is nothing derogatory in the clothes Helen Bannerman gives her characters – though the same cannot be said about the clothes shown in, for example, the Reilly and Britton edition. Helen Bannerman's characters are nicely dressed, with a pride in their appearance; the opposite is true in the Cupples and Leon edition of 1917.

We come now to the question of the name 'Sambo'. Phyllis Yuill, using the *Etymological Dictionary of Modern English*,[2] points out that a tribe called the Samboses were frequently mentioned in the accounts of the English sea Captain John Hawkins, who made slaving trips to West Africa in the sixteenth century. In Senegalese Foulah there is a word 'sambo' meaning uncle, and in the Hausa language in Northern Nigeria the name 'Sambo' was often given to a second son. It seems therefore that this is an African name which found its way to the United States with the slaves. In this it was unusual; most names used for slaves had no connection with Africa. It was used as a name for an individual slave in *Uncle Tom's Cabin*, first published as a serial in 1851–52[42] As the years passed, this name, which must have been in very common use, became applied more and more to any black male. Jock or Mick are two common names used for the Scots and the Irish; they too have come to be used for the type, not the person. This is derogatory, because it takes away the individuality of a person, and indicates that the person using the name is thinking of a category not a unique person. The name 'Sambo' was used in this way in Hollywood films in the nineteen-twenties and thirties for any black shoeshine boy or bartender.[41] It appeared in comic strips and in black and white minstrel shows and was frequently used for a black person in a subservient position. It is no wonder that this label – for it had lost its original function as a name – came to be bitterly resented by black people. It typified the depersonalisation of slavery and the shame of the subsequent years of exploitation.

The question arises whether the use of the name would have developed in the way it did without the book. Certainly the book, in all its versions, had a very powerful impact on people's instinctive images. It was one of the very few books then available which even acknowledged the existence of black people. For generations it gave black Americans an image of themselves, and white Americans an image of black Americans. This is what gives the book an importance out of all proportion to its original significance. There is an interesting passage, for example, in the *Autobiography of Malcolm X*, as told to Alex Haley.[268] After explaining that he used the symbol X as his surname because his original African name had been stripped from his slave forefathers and the name of his American master imposed instead, Malcolm X, the militant black leader, went on to describe his early image of Africa as one of 'naked savages, cannibals monkeys and tigers and steaming jungles'. This probably came from a mixture of the popular writing of the day, including comics and Tarzan films, but the inclusion of tigers (found only in Asia and in Helen Bannerman's imaginary jungle world) indicates that her book or books, possibly illustrated by other artists, had a hand in forming his image too.

Selma Lanes in *Down the Rabbit Hole*,[41] though she feels that the book has had its day, has a sympathetic passage about the impact of the book on white consciousness in America.

> For the first time, a story had caught American parents and children off their guard, allowing them to recognise freely the humanity of black people. Sambo's mother sews him a beautiful coat and pair of trousers. His father buys him "a lovely pair of Purple Shoes with Crimson Soles and Crimson Linings." (I can still recall taking stock of the slippers in our local shoe store as a child, hoping to find a pair exactly like them). We could all approve of Sambo and his family without feeling either guilty or anxious. Quick wit and intelligence were no threat in a black boy from the primitive and faraway land of tigers, as they might have been in someone black walking down an American city street. Just as nature abhors a vacuum, so the human soul rebels against evasion and dishonesty. By the time Sambo arrived on these shores, the slaves had been free for some forty years. Thousands of blacks had left the plantations of the rural South to form an observable element in most cities' populations. Yet they might have been invisible for all the recognition they received as fellow human beings in white America. Sambo was taken to everyone's heart precisely because he allowed us to acknowledge what we knew inside but avoided confronting: that black people were human beings just like us. In loving Sambo unreservedly, in some way every white had the feeling that he was also accepting the black man as a fellow human being.

This aspect of the book may help to account for its popularity in the U.S.A. in the first half of this century. After the appearance of at least thirty editions before 1935 there were a further twenty editions between then and 1980. There were also at least twelve editions for countries outside the U.S.A. or Britain. It was translated into French, Spanish, Arabic, Dutch, Hebrew, German and Danish. Another measure of its popularity was the way it was featured on lists of recommended reading. Phyllis Yuill shows how it was included, often with a star rating, in at least twenty-one lists of recommended books.

The first stirrings against the book began in the early nineteen-thirties. Barbara Bader in *Picturebooks*[269] quotes a line from the American Library Association's *Yearbook* of 1932 which referred to A.V. Weaver's *Frawg* and *Little Black Sambo*. These, it said, 'are both popular with young children but may awaken self-consciousness in older ones because of the illustrations'. In 1938 the author of a novel in integration, Marjorie Hill Allee,[270] called it a caricature, and in 1941 Charlemae Rollins[271] drew attention to the whole problem of the portrayal of black people in children's books in an influential work called *We Build Together; A Reader's Guide to Negro Life and Literature for Elementary and High School Use*. She argued that plantation stories, dialect and the portrayal of black people in subservient roles strengthened the stereotype presented on stage and screen. She omitted *Little Black Sambo* from her list of recommended books.

Nevertheless, *Little Black Sambo* continued to be included in many other reading lists, including lists of books for black children. In 1935 and 1941 the School Libraries Division of the Tennessee State Department produced a list called *The Negro: A Selected List for School Libraries by or about the Negro in Africa or America*. Charlemae Rollins was one of the eminent advisers from the black community who helped over this list, and *Little Black Sambo* was included. In New York, meanwhile, Augusta Baker was assembling the James Weldon Johnson Memorial Collection of books for Negro children. She at first included the book, then changed her mind. As Phyllis Yuill reported:[2] 'she indicated in a recent interview that she had had reservations about the Bannerman books early in her career, but she had felt pressured by her superiors in the New York Public Library system.'

The Association for Childhood Education included the book in their lists in the nineteen-forties and fifties and in 1942 Frederick A Stokes Company published *The Jumbo Sambo* with six of Helen's stories including *The Story of Little Black Sambo*. It received a warm reception from the press and public.

The continuing controversy, however, began to affect the illustrations in the editions produced from this time onwards. Most publishers commissioning new pictures altered the setting to India, to remove offensive connections with Southern plantations. The most striking example of this occurred with the Platt and Munk edition. This had been illustrated by Eulalie for the 1925 edition, and showed a plantation locale. Two pictures were altered for the 1972 edition, changing the mother into Mama Sari and the father into Papa Simbu; but while the mother unquestionably becomes Indian, Sambo and Papa Simbu retain more than a trace of their original African appearance.

In an even more determined attempt to avoid the charge of prejudice, Peter Pan Records produced a book with a record in 1971 called *Little Brave Sambo*. Without any credit to Helen Bannerman or to any illustrator, the book shows a simpering, naked white two year old, swinging on a branch in a jungle alongside a parrot and a monkey. It is notable for its cheapening of the text – for example:

> Sambo saw the melted butter
> Jumbo put it in a pot
> Mumbo took the melted butter
> Look at what she's got.

All that remains for Sambo in the years ahead is a sex-change.

Meanwhile the movement to change people's attitudes to the portrayal of black people in children's books was gaining strength and becoming more influential. In 1965 Nancy Larrick published a widely-regarded study *The All-White World of Children's Books*[272] which singled out *Little Black Sambo* as objectionable. But probably the most authoritative influence was that of May Hill Arbuthnot who published *Children and Books* in 1964.[273] She clearly admired *Little Black Sambo* and spoke of how, 'American children took it to their hearts with a fervour and unanimity that have necessitated reprint after reprint ever since its first appearance in the United States. The story, which might almost have come out of some folklore collection, has about it an effortless simplicity which baffles analysis. Its extreme simplicity is deceiving. Just try to duplicate it!' Her final conclusion, however, was that if 'black' applied to people was a cause of grief to any children then the book should be omitted from school lists.

By the early nineteen-seventies the consensus of published opinion, according to Phyllis Yuill, herself a children's librarian in the U.S.A., was that it could no longer be defended as a suitable story for children and it was dropped from most professional lists of recommended books. Not from all, however. In 1973 it was commended in Jean Spealman Kujoth's *Best Selling Children's Books*[274] as, 'a book that speaks the common language of all nations and has added more to the joy of little children than perhaps any other story'.

The book still has fans and defenders today and can be bought widely in the U.S.A.. In early 1980 Selma Lanes reported that it was in stock in some of the larger children's book departments in New York, such as Scribner's, Brentano's and B. Dalton, where it is in stock, though not on display. Brentano's, curiously, carry a Platt and Munk and a Golden Book edition but not the original edition with pictures by Helen Bannerman. It is also available, particularly in editions with illustrators other than Helen Bannerman, from supermarkets and other mass outlets.

Controversy, however, still surrounds the name 'Sambo' not only in the book but in a chain of restaurants, based in Santa Barbara, California. *Sambo's* – 'pleasant family dining from coast to coast' – takes its name from joining together parts of the name of its founder *Sam* Battistone with his partner Newell *Bohnett*. The chain developed a connection with the book in their original publicity, with pictures of pancakes and tigers and 'Little Sambo' in a turban. On their postcards Sambo went up to the tigers fighting over his clothes, 'and told them that if they stopped fighting and gave his pretty clothes back he would treat them to a plate of the finest, lightest pancakes they ever ate. So they gave him back his beautiful red coat, his green umbrella and his pretty purple shoes. Then they all went to a *Sambo's* restaurant where each tiger ate 75 pancakes but Sambo ate a hundred and sixty nine because he was so-o-o-o-o hungry'.

The restaurant chain *Sambo's* has come in for much the same criticism for its use of the name as the book. In 1977 some residents of Reston, Virginia, protested when the group planned to open one of their restaurants there. There were no claims that the chain discriminated in any way; it was simply the name that was objectionable. William Raspberry, columnist of the *Washington Post*, picked up the controversy on 14 November 1977. As he put it: 'If Alan *Ki*ng and Gene *Kel*ly opened a restaurant, they wouldn't call it Kike's Kitchen. If *Da*niel Inouye and Henry *Go*nzales went into the fast food business, they wouldn't call it Dago's Diner. If Bruce *Ni*gel, *Ge*rmaine Greer and *Jim*my Stewart started a franchise, they wouldn't call it Nigger Jim's.' He argued that the name Sambo was taken as an insult by black Americans across the country and that it was hard to imagine that the owner of the chain did not know this.

Following this article, a number of white observers claimed that the controversy demonstrated that blacks had become supersensitive and were looking for insults where none were intended. On this basis, they would soon be taking offence at *Aunt Jemima's Pancake Mix*. William Raspberry took up this point in a further article two days later. If the pancake mix, or *Uncle Ben's Rice*, were to be launched today, he said, they would have different names. If such titles were introduced now they would be offensive. But, he went on, 'there are a couple of reasons why those two brand names, both featuring black caricatures, are not offensive to blacks now. First , they have been around a long time, giving them the innocuousness that comes with familiarity. Second, they were never particularly obnoxious to begin with. (Hardly any black youngster today will know that "uncle" and "aunt" were devices used by Old South whites to give a modicum of respect to older blacks without going to the unthinkable extreme of actually calling them "Mr" or "Mrs"). Even so, the companies that package *Uncle Ben* and *Aunt Jemima* have been sensitive to changing times. Look at the face on the pancake box and, if you're over thirty, try to remember what *Aunt Jemima* used to look like. She always did wear a big smile, but in the earlier days she was a big coarse-featured woman in, say, the Hattie McDaniels mode – a black nanny. Today she is younger, slimmer, prettier, and her bandana is closer to the headwraps you're likely to see at cocktail parties.'

With this sleeker and more modern image, these two products have distanced themselves from the days of slavery from which the brand names sprang, and have remained acceptable. Not so – for many people – *Sambo's* restaurants; the negative charge carried by the name is too strong for cosmetic improvements to make any difference.

In September 1978 the restaurant chain were taken to court in Massachusetts by the state attorney general's office.[275] The charge was that the name Sambo was 'understood by numerous residents of the Commonwealth of Massachusetts as offensive and demeaning to black people. It is understood as a badge of slavery and as a racial epithet'. Lawyers for the firm argued that to ban the use of the name 'deprives the company of property without due process, abridges its right to free speech and conflicts with federal trademark status'; they succeeded in getting the case transferred to a federal court. At Reading, Massachusetts, Judge James L. Vallely ruled[276] in April 1979 that to ban the use of the name would violate the company's 'First Amendment rights'. A similar ruling was made a few weeks earlier in Toledo,[277] Ohio, where the judge ruled that to deny the company the use of its name (on which it had spent substantial sums of advertising) would be to 'strike a mortal blow at the advertising business'.

Trade names – even, it seems, controversial ones – are valuable to a business. The *Sambo* group also runs restaurants under the name *The Jolly Tiger*; this name, though more acceptable, was doing less well commercially, and in the early part of 1979 the company decided to convert nine of its restaurants from the *Jolly Tiger* name to *Sambo's*. The firm also hired a public relations company who put out releases such as, '*Sambo's* Attracts Black Customers', claiming that the idea that black Americans did not eat there was pure fantasy.[278] Handling the public relations on such a project – selling Sambo to the blacks – must have been a demanding assignment. Whether it was the efforts to improve their image – the emphasis is now, in their newer restaurants, simply on tigers – or the support for their right to their trade mark in law, the chain is still trading under the name of *Sambo's*.

In Britain, protest against the use of the name Sambo in Helen Bannerman's book developed much later than in the U.S.A.. This was because the only edition available in Britain has been the Chatto and Windus edition with the original pictures. Britain has been spared the plantation images – and also the more recent Indian ones. The book is not available in bastardised versions in supermarkets; it can be bought in bookshops in the original edition or not at all. Nevertheless, in 1972, a protest against the book erupted with a virulence which made the British establishment sit up in astonishment.

Before the nineteen–fifties, Britain's black population was very small. But as immigration from the West Indies got under way, with West Indians being encouraged to come to Britain to work on London Transport and in the National Health Service, it increased substantially and quickly. On 31 March 1972 *Teachers Against Racism* triggered off by an advertisement for a new boxed edition of Helen Bannerman's books, sent this letter to the then Chairman of the book's publishers, Chatto and Windus:[279]

We wish to register a strong protest against (a) the continued publication and distribution of the Helen Bannerman books and (b) your recent issue of the boxed set of these books. In the multi-racial society which exists in Britain today, these books are both damaging and dangerous.

Teachers Against Racism is strongly opposed to the continued distribution of these books particularly *Little Black Sambo*, *Sambo and the Twins*, *Little Black Quibba*, *Little Black Quasha*, and *Little White Squibba*.

In all of these books the underlying racist message is made all the more sinister by their appearance of innocence and charm. Along with the whimsical stories the reader swallows wholesale a totally patronising attitude towards black people who are shown as greedy (Black Sambo eats 169 pancakes), stereotyped happy, clownish, irresponsible plantation "niggers" – they are shown giving their children away, and jumping for joy at the slightest provocation throughout all the books.

All black adults are portrayed as having the minds of children, and the clear insinuation is that all blacks live in jungles with tigers etc.

The drawings in all the 'Little Black . . .' books are racist caricatures; although they are supposed to take place in India (Ghee and Tigers) the people are shown as Kentucky Pancake House Niggers with rolling eyes, watermelon smiles, and comically fuzzy hair. Contrast this with *Little White Squibba* clearly written as a conciliatory sop, but failing utterly in so far as the illustrations are pictures and not caricatured cartoons.

The names of the characters throughout the series reinforce patronising and racist attitudes towards black people, viz: Sambo, Mumbo, Jumbo, Little Black Rag, Little Black Tag, Moof and Woof, etc.

We feel most strongly that these books which foster basic racist attitudes in children should be withdrawn at once from circulation and removed from children's libraries and schools.

We should be interested to hear your views on the subject.

This attack put Chatto and Windus in something of a dilemma. On the one hand they were, as publishers, proud of a liberal list; on the other hand, *Little Black Sambo* was a valuable commercial property. Nor was the matter just as simple as that. As Ian Parsons, the Chairman of the firm, pointed out in his reply, wider issues were involved:[280]

At first, your letter filled me with amazement, mingled with despair. Can it really be true, I asked myself, that responsible people could be so utterly devoid of humour, so totally without imagination, as to put forward the views that you express. So my initial reaction was to send you a one-line reply in the form of a quotation – Honi soit qui mal y pense. But on reflection it seemed to me that, however intemperate and misguided your letter might be, it had been written with deeply held conviction and for a cause which I have supported all my life. (If you doubt this, just ring up Jim Rose of the Race Relations Board, or Laurens van der Post, the distinguished anti-apartheid author). I therefore felt that it merited a considered reply.

First, then, your letter proceeds with a series of categorical statements, as if they were acknowledged matters of fact, when most of them are wide open to argument, if not highly tendentious, and some of them simply untrue. I refer in the first place to phrases like 'the underlying racist message', 'a totally patronising attitude to black people', 'the clear insinuation is that all blacks live in jungles with tigers etc.'; and in the second place the statement that *Little White Squibba* was clearly written as a conciliatory sop. It wasn't. It was written, like all Mrs. Bannerman's books were written, for the enjoyment of her own children, and far from thinking of it as a 'conciliatory sop' (in which case she would naturally have published it) she put it on one side and it was only discovered among her papers long after her death.

Secondly, there is the inescapable fact that generations of children have loved *Little Black Sambo*. After close on three-quarters of a century it is still as popular today as it was when it was first published: indeed much more so. All these thousands of children, have, I am sure, accepted it as an enchanting story, an enthralling fantasy. Little Black Sambo and his parents are no more like real people than the tiger is like a real tiger.

Could a tiger turn into butter with which to make pancakes, and could any child, black or white, eat 169 of them? It is all a flight of fancy. The sad thing is that in the deplorable climate of our times it can be twisted to seem, or so you would have me believe, an attack on coloured people. More's the pity. But that's no reason why countless children of this and future generations should be denied the pleasure which time has proved that these books provide.

There is another thing, too. Once you start operating a censorship (for that's what it amounts to) of the kind you and your colleagues advocate, there is no knowing where it will stop. I imagine that you will have written similarly to Frederick Warne protesting against the continuing publication of several Beatrix Potter titles – you'll recall that *Pigling Bland* runs away with a *black* pig, who is not very clever, and that in *The Tale of Mr Tod* one of old Benjamin Bouncer's daughters had committed the unpardonable sin of marrying a *black* rabbit. Terribly racist, I fear. And equally you would have to ban yet another children's masterpiece – Joel Chandler Harris's *Nights with Uncle Remus*. And this, before one could say Brer Rabbit, would lead the R.S.P.C.A. to demand the suppression of *Alice in Wonderland* and *Alice Through the Looking Glass*. For what could be more sadistically cruel than to make animals race each other round a pool, and a pool of tears at that; or to force a live dormouse head first into a pot of tea? The R.S.P.C.A. would then feel obliged to ban Kingsley's *Water Babies*, as unfair to chimney sweeps and fostering class distinction. One could go on indefinitely, but I hope I've made my point.

Seriously, though, I think you and your colleagues should stand back and take a long, slow look at yourselves and your attitude, and ask yourselves whether in fact it is not *you* who are the racists. You who, with the very best intentions but a crippling blindness to reality, import into the innocent and unsophisticated minds of little children the idea that there is something derogatory in having a coloured skin. Frankly, it appals me that people entrusted with the upbringing of children should think this way. For all you will succeed in doing, in the end, is to add fuel to Mr Enoch Powell's fire. Do you really wish to that?'

There the matter might have rested had not *TAR* at the same time sent a copy of their letter to the Children's Books Editor of *The Times*, Brian Alderson. He brooded about it for a few days then on 12 April came out with a powerful article 'Banning Bannerman'. He was kind to the authors of the letter in that he left out all reference to their claim that the book shows black people to be greedy, because of the 169 pancakes, but he vigorously refuted the racialist label . . .

Once external considerations are allowed to affect our criteria for judging texts, critical anarchy supervenes. Billy Bunter is banned because there are fat boys in Ipswich, the Bastables are frowned on for their deplorable view of Woman's Place in Society, and, for all I know, Helen Bannerman is also condemned by conservationist associations for allowing such dreadful things to happen to her tigers, polar-bears, snakes and crocodiles.

The issue which T.A.R. have raised is not really to be resolved by the banning of Bannerman, but by acknowledging the qualities that have given her books their popularity and by encouraging people to see the complete context in which they stand. For these unpretentious little stories do not take themselves seriously enough to warrant the use of such forcefully emotive accusations as 'racist' and the pleasure which children (black as well as white) gain from them is a pleasure (pace the tigers) of friendliness.

Had the protagonists been white, and caricatured as whites are caricatured by such illustrators as Edward Lear and Tomi Ungerer, everyone would be delighted. But because there are so few books of any real character about black children, those which offer anything more than a safe, pallid domesticity are exposed to our social critics – who, like the old lady obsessed with obscenity, are not above standing on the dresser with a powerful pair of binoculars.

This was too much for the secretary of *TAR,* Briget Harris, to let pass, and her reply appeared in the correspondence columns of *The Times* on 24 April, 1972.

Brian Alderson, who we understand to be an expert on children's books, cannot by the same token be unaware of the 20-year-old campaign waged by the National Association for the Advancement of Coloured People and progressive teachers' groups in the United States of America against *Little Black Sambo*, which they hold to be "the epitome of white racism in children's literature". (United States Council on Interracial Books for Children).

Helen Bannerman's books have become both dangerous and obsolete in the multi-racial Britain of 1972 where people of good will are trying to foster respect for black people amongst white children, in order to avoid the kind of terrible race tension and separatism which has occurred in the United States. The so-called "friendliness" which Alderson says *Little Black Sambo* generates is in fact the friendliness of paternalism towards a "child race".

From this point on, the story became world news. Chivalry was abandoned. Brian Alderson hit back with a revelation of the claim by *TAR* that Helen Bannerman made blacks look greedy. Other newspapers followed up with feature treatment of the story, including the *Daily Mail*, which did a quick sample of the views of black children and found they loved it. There was a programme in Russian on 9 May in the BBC's World Service about it – fifteen minute programme on this one controversy. And above all, the letters to *The Times* kept flooding in. Some, like that from Michael Flanders, the composer and variety artist, picked up the point about the pancakes and shed tears for the tiger:[281]

All lovers of the tiger and conservationists in general must deplore a work (*Lttle Black Sambo*) in which a great number of man's noblest and rarest eaters is wantonly oleaginated without rebuke. Nor, as parents, should we tolerate the encouragement it gives our children, at an age when eating patterns are established for a life time, to over-indulge in pancakes (obesity forming carbohydrate), cooked in saturated fat (cholesterol – prime suspect in the fight against heart disease).

Others took the racial argument further, like Mr. J. Khalique of London Hospital Medical College:[282]

The book depicts the Negro as an almost unclothed, illiterate and inferior savage from whose antics great humour can be derived. That, contrary to B. Alderson's article, seems to be racist.

Thirteen years ago in primary school, this book was read to the class I was in and being a coloured child from Pakistan, I suddenly became a *Little Black Sambo* to my class mates. Only the development of extraordinary defensive mechanisms prevented me from going home crying or getting regularly into fights over this. Consequently the book lost its innocence quite early for me. Nor did I gain much pleasure from reading it.

I am sure that even now thousands of immigrant children will unconsciously be building psychosocial defences to racialistic remarks like *Little Black Sambo*.

The removal of such books would make words like Sambo, golliwog and darkie obsolete to small children.

That in itself would be a blessing, as to coloured children such words give deep offence, and to their parents such words are obscene. Any harmonious multiracial society of the near future will find books like *Little Black Sambo* intolerable.

The three remaining children of Helen Bannerman, by then in their seventies, let all the letters pass without comment until the one by Mr Khalique appeared. Temperamentally disinclined to enter the public arena, this letter seemed to Robert Bannerman to demand a reply:

> I have been following the correspondence with interest and for the most part with pleasure, discounting the charge of racialism as mere prejudice against which it is idle to argue – so I thought until I read Mr Khalique's letter (April 28th). May I offer him my sincere sympathy? I do believe that his life could have been made quite intolerable by the little savages with whom he was forced to associate at the time and who cruelly nicknamed him 'Sambo'. Three of my school fellows were severally nicknamed Fatty, Sparrow Legs and Nigger. I'm sure they suffered almost as acutely as Mr Khalique (with the exception of Nigger who was a first-class rugger player and much too big and strong for the rest of us).
>
> I would like to assure Mr Khalique that it is my firm belief that my mother would not have published the book had she dreamt for a moment that even one small boy would have been made unhappy thereby. She would never allow us to "do evil that good might follow", however small the evil and however great the good. And I think good has followed, for more children like Sambo than hate him.
>
> Nevertheless, I do not accept the charge that the book is racialist. Sambo is not held up to ridicule; he wore as many clothes as I did at his age; his parents were kind and good to him, just as mine were to me; he dealt adquately not only with a bunch of tigers but also with a heap of pancakes and returned home with his clothes intact. In fact he exhibited degrees of prowess and skills far in advance of my modest achievements at the same date.

The correspondence in *The Times*, and the publicity surrounding it, changed the views of a number of figures in the children's books field. Janet Hill, for example, Children's Librarian in the London Borough of Lambeth, and influential as a champion of good books for black children, had up to this point supported *Little Black Sambo*. She had banned Enid Blyton's *Little Black Doll* from her shelves, and some of the Biggles books, but had always kept a place for Sambo. Now she changed her mind and explained her views in an article in *The Times Literary Supplement* of 3 November 1972, reprinted in 1980 in *Racism & Sexism in Children's Books*,[285] edited by Judith Stinton:

> Helen Bannerman's books have had a long life, and the time has come to consign them to oblivion. They should have no place in a multi-racial society.

Talk of banning the books, however, drew the scorn of the white establishment. Banning was a very blunt instrument, arousing a lot of resentment and ridicule; but the controversy did draw attention to the very real need for more books with a black character as hero. Meanwhile in Britain *TAR* received the full force of the derision of figures such as Michael Howard of All Soul's College, writing to *The Times*:[284]

> Like many of your readers I have followed with fascinated interest the correspondence in your columns about *Little Black Sambo*. I do not, however, understand why your correspondents have focused exclusively on the problems of our coloured population. Why has no-one yet sprung to arms on behalf of, for example, the unfortunates whose mutilation is so vilely exploited in the character of Long John Silver in *Treasure Island*? Wht about those in our midst of less than average height, or with other deformations, who are caricatured in the dwarfs and hunchbacks of *Grimm's Fairy Tales*? And should not all those thrillers which depict Chinamen, Frenchmen, Germans and Jews in a less than amiable light be also removed from the shelves of public libraries?
>
> It is clear that what we need is a commission to survey the whole field of English literature and entirely eliminate all those works which might in any way exacerbate the existing tensions in our society. The impoverishment, or even the total disappearance, of our literary heritage would surely be a small price to pay for the more peaceful community which might be expected to result. If an adequately staffed and properly qualified team set to work now, it might complete its work by, perhaps, 1984.

Since 1972, understanding of the dearth of good books for racial minorities and of the need to make sure that text books do not portray an outdated concept of the world, has increased substantially. In 1980 Britain's National Union of Teachers produced *In Black and White: Guidelines for Teachers on Racial Stereotyping in Textbooks and Teaching Material*. This followed the guidelines produced in 1978 by the World Council of Churches, reprinted in the *Children's Book Bulletin*,[286] published in London in June 1979 by the Children's Rights Workshop. According to this, the following are the kind of criteria which should be applied:

> Does the book present events from a Eurocentric perspective?
> Do other continents come into the picture only when 'discovered' by Europeans?
> Is the contact with Europeans described as being beneficial to the other country?

Is the other country regarded as problem country?

Does it endorse European lifestyles exclusively?

Is power and leadership regarded as an attribute of the Europeans only?

Is the European lifestyle presented as superior?

Is a non European language regarded as a dialect?

Is the non–European country regarded as a 'tribe' and their homes as 'huts'?

Are the characters of the dominated group glorified for the interest of the dominant people?

Is the dominated group associated systematically with hypersexuality and the occult?

Are derogatory adjectives usually used to describe non-Europeans e.g. lazy or teacherous?

Is 'black' always symbolic of inferority?

Are Europeans regarded as the problem solvers?

There are many more such criteria. I can only say that *Little Black Sambo* does not stumble at a single one of the W.C.C. hurdles – though he has round his neck the unique impediment of the name he was born with, and the handicap of the portrayals by a variety of artists.

There remains one further accusation of racism in the book, not so far explored. This is made by Dr Marjorie Mcdonald, who feels there is a hidden sexual dimension to the book through which a subliminal racist message is offered. Dr McDonald beings by conceding that the story is not overtly racist. 'Even when it is subjected to a psychoanalytic interpretation, there still appears to be no obvious evidence of racism. All that psychoanalysis reveals is a fascinating glimpse of childhood sexuality. *Sambo* is just a story of growing up, of separation, of a primal scene and conception, and of childhood excitement and castration anxiety. It is a story of childhood sexuality in disguise. But it is just this unconscious childhood sexuality that underlines Sambo's racism.'

Dr McDonald interprets the tale as springing from Helen Bannerman's anxiety about her daughters as she journeyed away from them. (Dr McDonald bases her understanding of Helen's life on the only previous source, that of the publisher's foreword to *The Jumbo Sambo*. In this it was claimed that Helen wrote the book while returning to her husband's post in India after leaving her two daughters in Edinburgh to be educated. We now know that the journey involved was from Kodaicanal to Madras; but this does not invalidate Dr McDonald's line of reasoning.) Dr McDonald sees Sambo as a child bedecked by his parents in clothing and gifts to help him endure his separation from them. As he goes on his way he meets various dangers and copes with them by using his parents' gifts.

The scene in which the tigers turn to fighting each other is based, according to Dr McDonald's analysis, on a child's attempt to rationalise a visual experience of intercourse. The tigers, representing the parents, take off their clothes and chase each other round, 'wrangling and scrambling' and catching hold of each others' tails in their mouths. Sambo asks why they have taken off their clothes, but the tigers only answer 'Gr-r-r-rrrr!' While the tigers are absorbed in each other, Sambo picks up his clothes and walks away. As for the tigers, 'they still ran faster and faster and faster, till they all just melted away, and there was nothing left but a great pool of melted butter (or "ghi" as it is called in India) round the foot of the tree'. After this climax, Dr McDonald argues that the parents reappear in their normal guise and are loving and kind to their son and give him a large plate of pancakes.

Dr McDonald speculates that the 'effortless perfection' of the story, to use the phrase of May Hill Arbuthnot, arises from a visual experience in childhood. It is this, she feels, which gives the book its power and fascination and makes it comparable in strength to a classic fairy story. She then goes on to try to explain that the book's hidden sexuality is at the root of the distaste which many black people feel for it: 'The book is the story of a little *black* boy's sexuality. That the author has woven the word "black" into her repetitive cadence of colours is not mere chance. The black skin colour is an essential element in the story and the cadence of brightly coloured clothing helps to under line that the story is about *colour*. The racial message of *Sambo* is that forbidden sexuality belongs to little black boys and their families. The white reader uses this story to deny his own childhood sexuality. *Sambo* reassures him that the sexual thought and feelings of childhood belong just to primitive black people from the jungle, not to civilised white Americans. However, underneath the skin black people are no different from white, and they too would like to deny children sexuality. The story of *Sambo* is for blacks a blatant contradiction of that denial because it assigns the forbidden sexuality specifically to people with their own skin colour. Thus the black reader's rejection of Sambo resembles the impassioned rejection which greeted Freud's discovery of infantile sexuality.'

Dr McDonald is right to pinpoint Helen's separation from her children as the trigger or inspiration for *Little Black Sambo*. That the separation was a source of great anxiety to her is borne out by the poem she wrote when she left Janet in Edinburgh and sailed back to India, 'Far Away, Far Away Over The Sea. This is a poem full of the imagery of loving motherhood: 'Slumber my pretty one, precious to me . . . Though no mother's lips have kissed thee, slumber soft my little bird

... may a fond lip breathe a blessing o'er thy little sleeping head.'
Janet was only two when Helen left her in Edinburgh, and from the
evidence of the poem it was for Helen a very painful experience. It has
to be remembered that Janet was at this time Helen's only child
(though when she sailed for India she was expecting another). She had
been born, following an earlier miscarriage, after four years of marriage. By the time Helen wrote the poem she was thirty four.

I find Dr McDonald's interpretation of the symbolism of the gifts
to Sambo very convincing. It is one of the most pleasing aspects of the
book that Sambo, wearing the clothes his parents have given him, and
carrying his umbrella, should go out into the wide world with perfect
confidence in himself. This is indeed how we would all wish our children to behave when they go off on their own. That part of the analysis, however, can stand quite separately from Dr McDonald's interpretation of the tigers chasing each other as a child's eye view of
intercourse. If there were an unconscious sexual parallel to the story,
however, this could explain why people are inclined to describe *Little
Black Sambo* as a *satisfying* book. But even if one accepts this, why
should Helen Bannerman transfer imaginings from her deepest sub-
conscious onto the form of a small child who was black?

There are many simple and quite possible explanations. She may
have wanted a story for her children which took them away from the
everyday routine of their life. Most fairy stories happen somewhere
far away. Very few are set on the doorstep. She may have known they
liked stories with tigers in them; certainly her sons did later on and she
herself had enjoyed tiger stories from her own childhood. She may
have been reading to her daughters from her copy of Heinrich Hoff-
mann's *Struwwelpeter*. This gory book of cautionary tales features a
picture of a black boy striding out with an umbrella which could well
have been the inspiration for Little Black Sambo. (*Struwwelpeter* is a
book which Robert Bannerman confirms that he had as a child, and
particularly disliked.)

Racism, however, is not about drawing pictures of black people. It
is about denying people of another race their humanity. If Helen Bannerman chose Sambo as the vehicle for some of her most intimate feelings, what more could she do to acknowledge the common humanity
of Sambo and of herself? We have come a long way since Freud first
published *Creative Writers and Day-Dreaming* in 1907. We are not
shocked by unconscious sexuality now. Just as the associations of the
word 'black' have altered in recent years, so that it now has a positive
image, so for many people sexual fulfillment, and even hidden sexual
interests in children, are now understood as a matter for pride not
shame. It may be that in the years ahead people will become less concerned with racial riddles and see the story for what it is, that of a child

going out into the world and triumphantly overcoming its dangers.

Helen, too, in her day, had gone confidently into the world. She had met her first tiger at Mulkowal. After her death more tigers reared up accusing her of racism. Her letters are the gifts she casts towards them. Those who accept the message of her letters will have understood that the racial controversy has been chasing itself round a tree. Helen Bannerman was – as Will had said of her father – a good person, who deserves, at the end of the day, to be honoured by all.

Helen Bannerman's Books

The Story of Little Black Sambo   Grant Richards (London 1899), Frederick A. Stokes Co. (New York 1900)

The Story of Little Black Mingo   James Nisbet and Co. Ltd. (London 1901), Frederick A. Stokes Co. (New York 1902)

The Story of Little Black Quibba   James Nisbet and Co. Ltd. (London 1902), Frederick A. Stokes Co. (New York 1903)

The Story of Little Degchiehead   James Nisbet and Co. Ltd. (London 1903) Published in the U.S.A. as: *The Story of Little Kettlehead* Frederick A. Stokes Co. (New York 1904)

Pat and the Spider   James Nisbet and Co. Ltd. (London 1904), Frederick A. Stokes Co. (New York 1905)

The Story of the Teasing Monkey   James Nisbet and Co. Ltd. (London 1906), Frederick A. Stokes Co. (New York 1907)

The Story of Little Black Quasha   James Nisbet and Co. Ltd. (London 1908), Frederick A. Stokes Co. (New York 1908)

The Story of Little Black Bobtail   James Nisbet and Co. Ltd. (London 1909), Frederick A. Stokes Co. (New York 1909)

The Story of Sambo and the Twins   Frederick A. Stokes Co. (New York 1936), James Nisbet and Co. Ltd. (London 1937)

The Story of Little White Squibba   Chatto and Windus (London 1966)

Notes on Sources

1. Schiller, Justin G. 'The Story of Little Black Sambo', *The Book Collector* Vol. 23, No. 3. (London, Autumn 1974).
2. Yuill, Phyllis J. *Little Black Sambo: A Closer Look.* (New York 1976).
3. Yuill, Phyllis J. 'Little Black Sambo: The Continuing Controversy', in *The School Library Journal* (New York, March 1976).
4. McDonald, Marjorie 'Little Black Sambo', in *Psycho-Analytic Study of the Child* Vol. 29, 1973 Conference of the American Academy of Child Psychiatry.
5. Fish, H.D. 'Book Visits in England and Scotland', *Horn Book Magazine* 13 (U.S.A. 1937).
6. Stokes, H.W. 'Sambo and the Twins', *Horn Book Magazine* 12 (U.S.A. 1936).
7. Smith, Elizabeth J. *Far Away, Far Away, Over The Sea*, Documentary on BBC Radio 4. (London 6 April 1971).
8. Watson, Charles B.C. *Alexander Cowan of Moray House and Valleyfield, His Kinsfolk and Connections*, (Perth 1915).
9. Quayle, Eric *Ballantyne The Brave* (London 1967).
10. Bannerman, Helen Ms letter to Janet 19 June 1903. One of 17 volumes of unpublished letters from India to her children in Edinburgh, written between 1902 and 1917, and in the possession of the Bannerman family.
11. Watson, Charles B.C. *Traditions and Genealogies of Some Members of the Families of Boog, Heron, Leishman, Ross, Watson.* (Perth 1908).
12. Scott-Moncrieff, George *Edinburgh.* (London 1947).
13. Kibble, Janet In interview.
14. Bannerman, Helen MS notebook in possession of the Bannerman family, inscribed, 'Miss Nellie Watson, 20 Merchiston Terrace, Edinburgh, 1880', and elsewhere 'Miss Helen Watson, F.C. Manse, Cardross, Dumbarton'.
15. Hill, Ninian *Story of the Scottish Church* (Glasgow 1919).
16. Bruce, David *Sun Pictures: The Hill Adamson Calotypes*

(London 1973).

17. J.C.W.K. Note on Will Bannerman, in possession of the family, identified by the initials J.C.W.K. and the date 1969.

18. *British Medical Journal* Obituary in the edition of 23 February 1924, and in the *Proceedings of the Royal Society of Edinburgh* Vol. 44 1924.

19. Bannerman, William B. 'A Scots Sabbath in Perthshire', in the *Dundee Advertiser* 15 February 1906.

20. Turner, A. Logan *Story of a Great Hospital, The Royal Infirmary of Edinburgh*.

21. Watson, Robert Boog *Report of the Scaphopoda and Gasteropoda Collected by H.M.S. Challenger during 1873–6* Vol. XV (London 1886).

22. Cant, R.G. *The University of St Andrews: A Short History* (Edinburgh 1946).

23. Turner, A. Logan *History of the University of Edinburgh* (Edinburgh 1933).

24. Churchill, Winston S. *The Malakand Field Force* (London 1898).

25. Fitch, Elizabeth Craigie *Uncle Will and his Work: To the Nephews and Nieces from Aunt Cragie*. MS in possession of the Bannerman family.

26. MS certificate in possession of the Bannerman family.

27. Indian Medical Service *Record of Service* of the Hon Surg.-Genl. William Burney Bannerman, M.D., D.Sc., C.S.I., held in the India Office Library in London.

28. Crawford, Dirom Grey *History of the Indian Medical Service* (London 1914) see also: McDonald, Donald '*Surgeons Two and A Barber*, being some account of the life and work of the Indian Medical Service 1600–1947'. (London 1950).

29. Bannerman, Cecilia In interview.

30. Bannerman, Mary (Ata) MS diary in possession of the Bannerman family.

31. Bannerman, William B. *Plague in India* published by the Research Defence Society (London 1908).

32. Popovsky, Mark *The Story of Dr Haffkine* (Moscow 1967).

33. Kibble, Janet In interviews.
    Bannerman, Day
    Bannerman, Robert

34. Kibble, Janet Letter to Elizabeth Hay, dated 30 January 1972.

35. Bannerman, Dr Day In interview.

36. Richards, Grant *Author Hunting* (London 1934).

37. Bond, Alice M.E. MS letter to Grant Richards 20 June 1899, in possession of Chatto and Windus.

38. Bond, Alice M.E.   MS letter to Grant Richards 22 June 1899 in possession of Chatto and Windus.

39. Bond, Alice M.E.   MS letter to Grant Richards 9 August 1899 in possession of Chatto and Windus.

40. *Spectator, The*   'Modern Nursery Books' 2 December 1899 (London).

41. Lanes, Selma G.   *Down the Rabbit Hole* (New York 1972).

42. Stowe, Harriet Beecher   *Uncle Tom's Cabin* (U.S.A. 1851–2).

43. Dickens, Charles   *Nicholas Nickleby* (London 1838–9).

44. Richards, Grant   Letter to Helen Bannerman, March 1900, a copy of which is at the University of Illinois at Urbana-Champaign, U.S.A. The library dates their copy March 1899; it is faint and almost indecipherable. With the reference to the 'plain cover' – a notable feature of the first edition of *The Story of Little Black Sambo* – and the absence of any indication that Helen Bannerman published any book before this one, it is reasonable to assume that the correct date for this letter is March 1900.

45. Richards, Grant   Letter to Helen Bannerman, 21 July 1898, a copy of which is held at the University of Illinois at Urbana-Champaign, U.S.A.

46. *Times of India, The*   Inoculation Against Plague in India 11 August 1905.

47. Dalal, P.A.   Article in *The Indian Practitioner* September 1959.

48. Sheppard, Samuel T.   *Bombay* (Bombay 1932).

49. Barr, Pat   *The Memsahibs* (London 1979).

50. Pandit, Vijaya Lakshmi   *The Scope of Happiness* (London 1979).

51. Richards, Grant   Letter to Helen Bannerman dated 26 June 1900, a copy of which is held at the University of Illinois, Urbana-Champaign.

52. Richards, Grant   Letter to Helen Bannerman dated 29 November 1900, a copy of which is held at the University of Illinois, Urbana-Champaign.

53. *Manchester Guardian, The*   Manchester, 20 November 1901.

54. *Bookman, The*   Review of *The Story of Little Black Mingo* November 1901.

55. *Scotsman, The*   Review of *The Story of Little Black Mingo* (Edinburgh 14 October 1901).

56. *Spectator, The*   Review of *The Story of Little Black Mingo* (London 2 November 1901).

57. Bannerman, William B.   MS letter to Day 25 March 1905.

58. Bannerman, Helen   MS letter to Day 21 January 1904.

59. Bannerman, Helen   MS letter to Day 1 May 1903.

60. Bannerman, Helen   MS letter to Day 18 December 1903.

61. *Times of India, The*   Review of *The Story of Little Black Quibba* 10 December 1902.
62. Kipling, Rudyard   *Kipling's Stories for Children* (New York 1940).
63. Kibble, Janet and Bannerman, Day   Interviews.
64. Bannerman, Robert   Interview.
65. Bannerman, Helen   MS letter to Day 2 January 1903.
66. Bannerman, Helen   MS letter to Day 26 December 1902.
67. Bannerman, Helen   MS letter to Janet 26 December 1902.
68. Bannerman, Helen   MS letter to Day 9 January 1903.
69. Bannerman, Helen   MS letter to Day 22 January 1903.
70. *Bombay Plague Proceedings*   Parliamentary Papers 106, 1907, Vol. S 8. India Office Library, London.
71. Bannerman, Helen   MS letter to Janet 20 March 1903.
72. Bannerman, Helen   MS letter to Day 20 February 1903.
73. Bannerman, Helen   MS letter to Janet 22 January 1903.
74. Bannerman, Helen   MS letter to Janet 10 April 1903.
75. Bannerman, Helen   MS letter to Janet 27 February 1903.
76. Bannerman, Helen   MS letter to Day 14 November 1903.
77. *Report of the Commission of Enquiry into the Mulkowal Disaster*. Parliamentary Papers 106, 1907, Vol. S 8.
78. *Evidence to the Commission of Enquiry into the Mulkowal Disaster*, as above.
79. Bannerman, Helen   MS letter to Janet 23 December 1904.
80. Kibble, Janet   Interview.
81. *Report by Mr E.L. Cappel*   Parliamentary Papers as above.
82. Bannerman, Helen   MS letter to Janet 28 August 1903.
83. Bannerman, William B.   MS letter to Janet 4 September 1903.
84. Bannerman, William B.   MS letter to Janet Undated, but likely to be 1 August 1903.
85. Bannerman, Helen   MS letter to Janet and Day 1 August 1903.
86. Bannerman, Helen   MS letter to Day 4 July 1903.
87. Bannerman, Helen   MS letter to Janet 21 August 1903.
88. Bannerman, Helen   MS letter to Janet 15 August 1903.
89. Bannerman, Helen   MS letter to Janet 18 September 1903.
90. Bannerman, Helen   MS letter to Janet 3 October 1903.
91. Bannerman, Helen   MS letter to Day 9 October 1903.
92. Bannerman, Helen   MS letter to Day 6 November 1903.
93. Hoffman, Heinrich   Struwwelpeter (English edition: London 1848).
94. Bannerman, Helen   MS letter to Day 10 December 1903.
95. Bannerman, Helen   MS letter to Day 17 December 1903.
96. Bannerman, Helen   MS letter to Janet 17 December 1903.
97. Bannerman, William B.   MS letter to Day 17 December 1903.

98. Bannerman, Helen   MS letter to Day 14 January 1904.
99. Bannerman, Helen   MS letter to Janet 28 December 1903.
100. Bannerman, Helen   MS letter to Janet 28 January 1904.
101. Bannerman, Helen   MS letter to Janet 7 January 1904.
102. Bannerman, Helen   MS letter to Day 7 January 1904.
103. Bannerman, Helen   MS letter to Day 17 March 1904.
104. Bannerman, Helen   MS letter to Janet 14 January 1904.
105. Bannerman, Helen   MS letter to Day 4 February 1904.
106. Bannerman, Helen   MS letter to Janet 7 April 1904.
107. Bannerman, Helen   MS letter to Day 11 February 1904.
108. Bannerman, Helen   MS letter to Day 3 March 1904.
109. Bannerman, Helen   MS letter to Day 21 April 1904.
110. Bannerman, Helen   MS letter to Day 4 May 1904.
111. Bannerman, William B.   Letter to the General Dept (Plague) 13 July 1904 *Bombay Plague Proceedings* 6943 India Office Library.
112. *Report on Plague in the Punjab 1902–3*   India Office Records, included in Parliamentary Papers 106 1907 Vol. S 8.
113. Communiqué, published in Parliamentary Papers, as above.
114. Report of the Lister Institute, published in Parliamentary Papers, as above.
115. Bannerman, William B.   MS letter to Day 31 December 1904.
116. Bannerman, Helen   MS letter to Janet 7 April 1905.
117. Bannerman, Helen   MS letter to Janet 4 May 1904.
118. Bannerman, Helen   MS letter to Day 13 June 1904.
119. Bannerman, Helen   MS letter to Janet 13 June 1904.
120. Bannerman, Helen   MS letter to Day 18 July 1904.
121. Bannerman, Helen   MS letter to Janet 17 September 1904.
122. Bannerman, Helen   MS letter to Janet 2 September 1904.
123. Bannerman, Helen   MS letter to Day 4 November 1904.
124. Bannerman, Helen   MS letter to Day 9 September 1904.
125. Bannerman, Helen   MS letter to Janet 14 October 1904.
126. Bannerman, Helen   MS letter to Janet 29 October 1904.
127. Bannerman, Helen   Unaddressed MS letter, dated 9 September 1904.
128. Bannerman, Helen   MS letter to Day 25 November 1904.
129. Bannerman, Helen   MS letter to Day 9 December 1904.
130. Bannerman, Helen   MS letter to Day 18 November 1904.
131. Bannerman, Helen   MS letter to Janet 9 December 1904.
132. Bannerman, Helen   MS letter to Day 2 December 1904.
133. Bannerman, Helen   MS letter to Janet 10 February 1905.
134. Bannerman, Helen   MS letter to Janet 10 March 1905.
135. Bannerman, Helen   MS letter to Day 5 March 1905.
136. Bannerman, Helen   MS letter to Janet 31 March 1905.

137. Lane, Margaret *The Tale of Beatrix Potter* (London 1946).
138. Bannerman, Helen MS letter to Day 30 September 1904.
139. Bannerman, Helen MS letter to Janet 5 January 1905.
140. Bannerman, Helen MS letter to Janet 17 Feb 1905.
141. Bannerman, Helen MS letter to Day 13 May 1905.
142. Bannerman, Helen MS letter to Day 10 March 1906.
143. Bannerman, William B. *Journal of Hygiene* 1906 and 1907.
144. Lamb, Major *Summary of the Work of the Plague Commission* 1908 (India Office Library).
145. Bannerman, Helen MS letter to Rob 6 January 1910.
146. Bannerman, Helen MS letter to Day 31 March 1906.
147. Bannerman, Helen MS letter to Rob 13 November 1909.
148. Bannerman, Helen MS letter to Janet 12 May 1906.
149. Bannerman, Helen MS letter to Day 26 May 1906.
150. Bannerman, Helen MS letter to Day 7 April 1906.
151. Bannerman, Helen MS letter to Janet 12 April 1906.
152. Bannerman, Helen MS letter to Day 5 October 1906.
153. Bannerman, Robert Interview.
154. Bannerman, Helen MS letter to Day 21 April 1905.
155. Bannerman, Helen MS letter to Janet 3 March 1906.
156. Bannerman, Helen MS letter to Janet 2 March 1907.
157. Bannerman, Helen MS letter to Day 5 May 1906.
158. Bannerman, Helen MS letter to Day 19 April 1906.
159. Bannerman, Helen MS letter to Janet 28 April 1906.
160. Bannerman, William B. MS letter to Day 27 October 1906.
161. Bannerman, Helen MS letter to Day 26 November 1906.
162. Bannerman, Helen MS letter to Day 9 February 1907.
163. Bannerman, William B. MS letter to Day 13 July 1906.
164. Bannerman, Helen MS letter to Janet 16 February 1907.
165. Bannerman, Helen MS letter to Janet 29 September 1906.
166. Bannerman, Helen MS letter to Janet 27 April 1907.
167. *Indian Gazette* 'Report on the Mulkowal Accident.' 1 December 1906, reprinted in 1907, Vol. S 8.
168. Parliamentary Papers 106.
169. Simpson, W.J. 'The Evidence and Conclusions Relating to the Mulkowal Tetanus Case', *The Practitioner* June 1907.
170. Ross, Ronald Letter to *The Times* 1 June 1907. See also *The Times* 29 July 1907.
171. Naidhu, B.M. Obituary of Haffkine, Bombay Bacteriological Institute. See also *Haffkine Institute Platinum Jubilee Commemoration Volume, Haffkine Institute 1899–74, edited by Dr Francis Saldanha.*
172. Lutzker, Edythe *The Jewish Standard*, New Jersey U.S.A., 21 December 1973 '75-Year Salute for Haffkine'.

173. Bannerman, Robert   Interview.
174. Buchan, John   *Lord Minto: A Memoir* (London 1924).
175. Bannerman, Helen   MS letter to Pat 18 June 1910.
176. Bannerman, Helen   MS letter to Janet 29 July 1910.
177. Brecher, Michael   *Jawaharlal Nehru: A Political Biography* (Oxford 1959).
178. Bannerman, Helen   MS letter to Day 24 July 1909.
179. Bannerman, Helen   MS letter to Janet 27 August 1909.
180. Bannerman, Helen   MS letter to Pat 31 July 1909.
181. Bannerman, Helen   MS letter to Day 24 July 1909.
182. Bannerman, Helen   MS letter to Pat 23 July 1909.
183. Bannerman, Helen   MS letter to Pat 3 September 1909.
184. Bannerman, Helen   MS letter to Rob 2 October 1909.
185. Bannerman, Helen   MS letter to Pat 15 October 1909.
186. Bannerman, Helen   'My Friend Framji', in *Flowers from the Manse Garden* (Ajmer 1906).
187. Bannerman, Helen   MS letter to Day 1 October 1909.
188. Bannerman, Helen   MS letter to Pat 27 August 1909.
189. Bannerman, Helen   MS letter to Rob 4 August 1909.
190. Bannerman, Helen   MS letter to Rob 3 September 1909.
191. Bannerman, Helen   MS letter to Janet 10 September 1909.
192. Bannerman, Helen   MS letter to Janet 18 September 1909.
193. Bannerman, Helen   MS letter to Rob 24 December 1909.
194. Bannerman, Helen   MS letter to Day 12 January 1910.
195. Bannerman, William B.   MS letter to Janet 13 January 1910.
196. Bannerman, William B.   MS letter to Day 19 January 1910.
197. Bannerman, Helen   MS letter to Pat 19 January 1910.
198. Bannerman, Helen   MS letter to Rob 23 September 1910.
199. Bannerman, Helen   MS letter to Day 3 December 1910.
200. Bannerman, Helen   MS letter to Pat 2 September 1910.
201. Bannerman, Helen   MS letter to Rob 21 October 1910.
202. Bannerman, Helen   MS letter to Rob 16 December 1910.
203. Bannerman, Helen   MS letter to Pat 2 December 1910.
204. Bannerman, Helen   MS letter to Day 3 December 1910.
205. Bannerman, Helen   MS letter to Rob 24 December 1910.
206. Bannerman, Helen   MS letter to Janet 29 October 1910.
207. Bannerman, Helen   MS letter to Janet 11 February 1911.
208. Bannerman, Helen   MS letter to Day 31 December 1909.
209. Bannerman, William B.   MS letter to Pat 6 January 1911.
210. Bannerman, Helen   MS letter to Janet 6 January 1911.
211. Bannerman, Helen   MS letter to Rob 3 February 1911.
212. Bannerman, William B.   MS letter to Pat 3 February 1911.
213. Bannerman, Helen   MS letter to Rob 13 June 1911.
214. Bannerman, Helen   MS letter to Rob 12 May 1911.

215. Bannerman, Helen MS letter to Day 14 May 1911.
216. Bannerman, Helen MS letter to Day 24 May 1911.
217. Bannerman, Helen MS letter to Janet 24 May 1911.
218. Bannerman, Helen MS letter to Janet 30 May 1911.
219. Bannerman, Helen MS letter to Janet 8 June 1911.
220. Bannerman, Helen MS letter to Rob, dated 8 May 1911. (This and the following letter are misdated, and should be dated 8 June 1911).
221. Bannerman, Helen MS letter to Pat dated 8 May 1911.
222. Bannerman, Robert Interview.
223. Bannerman, Helen MS letter to Day 13 July 1911.
224. Bannerman, Helen MS letter to Rob 13 June 1911.
225. Bannerman, Helen MS letter to Rob 21 June 1911.
226. Bannerman, Helen MS letter to Day 28 June 1911.
227. Bannerman, Helen MS letter to Pat 13 July 1911.
228. Bannerman, Helen MS letter to Rob, undated, likely to be 22 July 1911.
229. Bannerman, William B. MS letter to Rob 26 July 1911.
230. Bannerman, Helen MS letter to Janet 26 July 1911.
231. Bannerman, Helen MS letter to Day 26 July 1911.
232. Bannerman, Helen MS letter to Janet 10 August 1911.
233. Bannerman, Helen MS letter to Rob 23 November 1911.
234. Bannerman, Helen MS letter to Day 7 December 1911.
235. Lovat, Fraser *India Under Lord Curzon and After* (London 1911).
236. Bannerman, Helen MS letter to Rob 21 December 1911.
237. Bannerman, Helen MS letter to Pat 28 December 1911.
238. Bannerman, William MS letter to Rob 11 January 1912.
239. Bannerman, Helen MS letter to Rob 11 January 1912.
240. Muriel Crummelin Brown Interview.
241. Bannerman, Helen MS letter to Rob 31 October 1912.
242. Bannerman, William B. MS letter to Pat 22 November 1912.
243. Bannerman, Helen MS letter to Rob 31 October 1912.
244. Bannerman, Helen MS letter to Rob 21 November 1912.
245. Bannerman, William B. MS letter to Day 5 December 1912.
246. Bannerman, Helen MS letter to Pat 22 May 1913.
247. Hewat, Elizabeth K. *Vision and Achievement: A History of the Foreign Missions of the Churches United in the Church of Scotland* (Edinburgh 1960).
248. Bannerman, Helen MS letter to Rob 12 December 1912.
249. Bannerman, Helen MS letter to Day 30 January 1914.
250. Bannerman, Helen MS letter to Day 14 August 1913.
251. Bannerman, Janet MS letter to Day 24 September 1914.
252. Bannerman, Helen MS letter to Day 19 November

1914.

253. Bannerman, Helen   MS letter to Rob 1 October 1914.

254. Bannerman, Helen   MS letter to Pat 25 March 1915.

255. Bannerman, William B.   MS letter to Pat 3 November 1916.

256. Scarry, Richard   *Busy Busy World* (London 1966).

257. Bannerman, Robert   Interview.

258. Bannerman, Day   Interview.

259. Bannerman, Cecilia   Interview.

260. Stewart, John P.   Interview.

261. Bannerman, Day   Interview.

262. Stokes, Horace   Letter to Helen Bannerman 28 May 1936 in possession of the Bannerman family.

263. Bannerman, Day   Interview.

264. Fisher, Anne   Interview.

265. Bannerman, Robert   letter to *The Times* 4 May 1972.

266. Bannerman, Helen   MS letter to Day 3 February 1911.

267. Bannerman, Helen   MS letter to Rob 6 February 1914.

268. X, Malcolm   *Autobiography*, as told to Alex Haley (London 1966).

269. Bader, Barbara   Picture books (1976) 'Negro Identification, Black Identity'.

270. Allee, Marjorie Hill   *The Great Tradition* (U.S.A. 1938).

271. Rollins, Charlemae   *We Build Together: A Readers' Guide to Negro Life and Literature for Elementary and High School Use* (Chicago 1941).

272. Larrick, Nancy   'The All-White World of Children's Books' in *Saturday Review* (U.S.A. 11 September 1965).

273. Arbuthnot, May Hill   *Children and Books* (Illinois 1964).

274. Kujoth, Jean S.   *Best Selling Children's Books* (New Jersey 1973).

275. New York Times News Service   28 September 1978.

276. New York Times   26 April 1979.

277. New York Times   2 February 1979.

278. New York Times   18 November 1978.

279. Harris, Bridget   Letter to Ian Parsons 12 April 1972.

280. Parsons, Ian   Letter to Bridget Harris 12 April 1972.

281. Flanders, Michael   Letter to *The Times* 2 May 1972.

282. Khalique, J.   Letter to *The Times* 28 April 1972.

283. Bannerman, Robert   Letter to *The Times* 1 May 1972.

284. Howard, Michael   Letter to *The Times* 4 May 1972.

285. Stinton, Judith (ed.)   Racism and Sexism in Children's Books (London 1979).

286. World Council of Churches   *Guidelines on Racism in Children's*

and School Textbooks 1978 (Arnoldshain) reprinted in The Children's Book Bulletin June 1979.

Index

INDEX

INDEX

INDEX

INDEX

INDEX

INDEX